Digital Drawing for Designers

A Visual Guide to AutoCAD 2012

ALSO BY THE AUTHOR:

Hand Drawing for Designers:
Communicating Ideas through
Architectural Graphics

(with Amy Korté)

Digital Drawing for Designers

A Visual Guide to AutoCAD 2012

Douglas R. Seidler

LEED AP, NCIDQ, Associate AIA, IDEC
Marymount University

FAIRCHILD BOOKS | NEW YORK

Executive President & General Manager: Michael Schluter

Executive Editor: Olga T. Kontzias

Assistant Acquisitions Editor: Amanda Breccia

Senior Development Editor: Joseph Miranda

Assistant Art Director: Sarah Silberg

Production Director: Ginger Hillman

Associate Production Editor: Linda Feldman

Ancillaries Editor: Amy Butler

Associate Director of Sales: Melanie Sankel

Cover Design: Carolyn Eckert

Cover Art: Douglas R. Seidler and Lori Anderson Weir

Text Design: Ron Reeves

Library of Congress Catalog Card Number: 2011943824

ISBN-13: 978-1-60901-411-7

GST R 133004424

Printed in the United States of America

TP09

for my father

CONTENTS AT A GLANCE

EXTENDED CONTENTS

PREFACE

Objective

The original edition of this book was one of very few AutoCAD books that focused on instruction for architecture and interior design students. This was critical to the book's current success as most AutoCAD books are thick with technical language and excessively complex discussions about the software to teach relatively simple tasks. The original edition solved this challenge by teaching through clear illustrations, by limiting instruction to architectural drawings, and by creating strong connections between AutoCAD and manual drafting.

The second edition built on this success with updates to over 20 command and interface changes released with AutoCAD 2011. The revised edition also included a completely rewritten chapter on printing and updates for associative text and dimensions.

Now in its third edition, *Digital Drawing for Designers* continues to provide a visual, clear, and concise guide for interior design and architecture students to better understand digital drawing in AutoCAD. Revised for AutoCAD 2012, the book includes improvements and updates to 15 commands, including the new path array and blend tools. Also new to this edition is a chapter dedicated to AutoCAD WS, also known as AutoCAD mobile. AutoCAD WS is Autodesk's free mobile version of AutoCAD that runs on the iPhone, iPad, Android phones, and Android tablets.

Audience and Prerequisite Knowledge

AutoCAD continues to dominate the two-dimensional drafting marketplace for architects and interior designers. This book aims to help the design community by visually teaching for understanding. You can broadly sort the numerous AutoCAD books into two categories—"guides for dummies" and "exhaustive references"—neither of which specifically addresses how professional designers use AutoCAD. *Digital Drawing for Designers* sits between these two categories, providing both a thorough primer for new learners and expanded conceptual discussion for design professionals. The progressive introduction of concepts (chapters build on previous chapters), digital exercises, and visual examples make this book easy to follow for learners new to AutoCAD. The only prerequisite for the book is a fundamental knowledge of manual drafting techniques.

AutoCAD Version Compatibility

The instruction in this book is compatible with AutoCAD version 14 through version 2012. While most universities teach and use the latest version of AutoCAD, many professional offices do not update their AutoCAD software annually due to hardware requirements and professional education costs. I have written this book to help students switch between versions of AutoCAD as they transition from the classroom to the office.

Content Overview

We learn best when we can create connections between the new information we are learning and information that we already know. Chapters 1–4, therefore, introduce AutoCAD and digital drawing through the language and concepts of manual or hand drawing. Lines, circles, and arcs are the fundamental building blocks of all architectural drawings. Understanding how to use these building blocks in AutoCAD will allow you to create any type of drawing.

Chapters 5–8 introduce you to graphic standards that will help you use AutoCAD to create drawings that communicate your design ideas. Understanding these standards keeps you in control of your drawing and allows you to "ask of the computer" rather than let the computer dictate how your drawings will look. You will learn organizational strategies to efficiently draw plans, sections, and elevations. Each chapter introduces these new skills using AutoCAD standards that can be adapted to any office environment.

Chapter 9–14 introduce many advanced AutoCAD concepts like dimensioning drawings, creating your own drawing stencils (blocks), and linking drawings (XREFs). Learners who have a basic understanding of AutoCAD will appreciate the in-depth visual discussion about XREFs, editable blocks, dimension styles, and text leaders. By combining these advanced concepts with a strong foundation for drawing in AutoCAD, you will be prepared to work on or create any digital drawing.

The final chapter introduces AutoCAD WS, Autodesk's mobile AutoCAD application. The chapter includes instructions on using AutoCAD on the iPhone, iPad, Andriod phones, and Andriod tablets.

The step-by-step guides in this book will help you master digital drawing while building your confidence and understanding of AutoCAD 2012. I hope that through the visual guides and pedagogical approach of this book you will become a better designer as you strengthen your visual communication skills through digital drawing.

ACKNOWLEDGMENTS

This book began several years ago as a reader for a series of design drawing and AutoCAD courses offered by the Department of Interior Design at the New England School of Art and Design at Suffolk University. The strategies for teaching and learning used in this book are largely influenced by my experience teaching AutoCAD and by *Teaching for Understanding*, a course for design educators taught by Tina Blythe at the Boston Architectural College.

I would like to thank my students and colleagues in design education whose discussions and critical feedback helped shape and test the pedagogical approach in this book. Special thanks are due to Cheri Kotsiopoulos, Kristine Mortensen, and Lori Anderson Wier for contributing their drawings to this book.

I am very grateful for the time Molly Hayes gave to this edition. Molly's enthusiasm for the sometimes mundane tasks and her attention to detail were incredibly helpful in juggling the multiple updates and revisions for this edition.

I also greatly appreciate the enthusiasm, guidance, and collaboration of the team at Fairchild Books. The efforts and talents of Olga Kontzias, Joseph Miranda, Linda Feldman, Sarah Silberg, Amy Butler and Vanessa Han are more than I could have asked for in an editorial team.

Finally, I would like to thank my mother for allowing me to take things apart, my father for teachning me to put things back together, and my sister for unwillingly donating her toys to this noble cause. To my wife and daughter, thank you for you continued love, support, and enthusiasm for my writing.

Hand Drawing
and Digital Drawing

CHAPTER 1
Digital Drawing Tools

This chapter introduces you to AutoCAD's digital drawing techniques and tools using a visual vocabulary that you are already familiar with from your experience with manual drafting. One of the best ways to learn something new is to refer to something you already know.

By the end of this chapter, you will be familiar with the AutoCAD equivalents to many of the drawing tools you use daily in manual drafting.

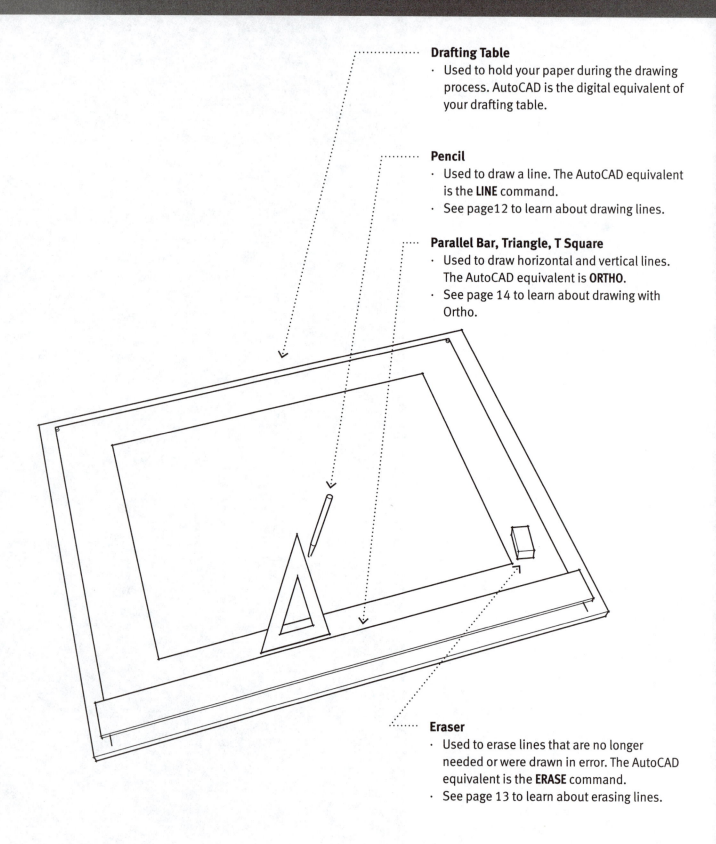

Drafting Table

· Used to hold your paper during the drawing process. AutoCAD is the digital equivalent of your drafting table.

Pencil

· Used to draw a line. The AutoCAD equivalent is the **LINE** command.
· See page 12 to learn about drawing lines.

Parallel Bar, Triangle, T Square

· Used to draw horizontal and vertical lines. The AutoCAD equivalent is **ORTHO**.
· See page 14 to learn about drawing with Ortho.

Eraser

· Used to erase lines that are no longer needed or were drawn in error. The AutoCAD equivalent is the **ERASE** command.
· See page 13 to learn about erasing lines.

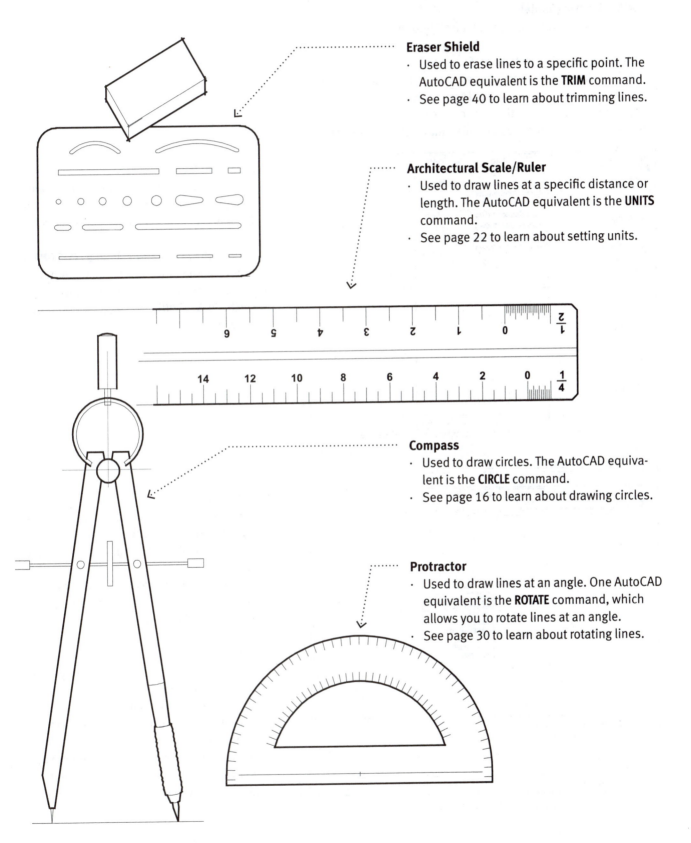

Eraser Shield

- Used to erase lines to a specific point. The AutoCAD equivalent is the **TRIM** command.
- See page 40 to learn about trimming lines.

Architectural Scale/Ruler

- Used to draw lines at a specific distance or length. The AutoCAD equivalent is the **UNITS** command.
- See page 22 to learn about setting units.

Compass

- Used to draw circles. The AutoCAD equivalent is the **CIRCLE** command.
- See page 16 to learn about drawing circles.

Protractor

- Used to draw lines at an angle. One AutoCAD equivalent is the **ROTATE** command, which allows you to rotate lines at an angle.
- See page 30 to learn about rotating lines.

AutoCAD (Drafting Table)

The window below represents the typical AutoCAD interface.

- Many of AutoCAD's menus and buttons are similar to those of other programs (e.g., Microsoft Word, Excel, and PowerPoint).
- This book introduces AutoCAD's gizmos, buttons, and menus as it introduces drawing concepts and techniques.
- You can use the index at the back of this book to quickly find additional information about a particular AutoCAD command or concept.

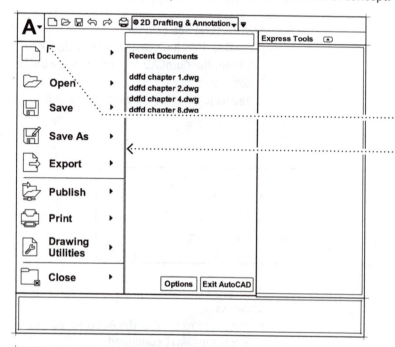

Application Menu

- The Application Menu in AutoCAD contains many of the items you would find under the file menu of typical computer programs.

- Launch the Application Menu by **CLICKING** the letter **A** in the top left corner of the AutoCAD.
- Items in the Application Menu allow you to **OPEN, CLOSE, PRINT,** and **SAVE** your AutoCAD drawings.

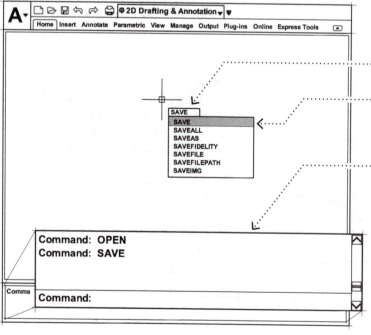

Dynamic Input

- Most commands in AutoCAD are started by typing on the keyboard.
- **Dynamic Input** displays this text input next to the AutoCAD cursor.
- The **AutoComplete** selection box lists all AutoCAD commands that match the letters you type on the keyboard.

Command Prompt

- AutoCAD commands are also displayed in the command prompt.
- The command prompt area in AutoCAD also provides feedback about options during a command.
- Keep one eye on the command prompt as you work and you will improve your AutoCAD learning experience.

RIBBON INTERFACE

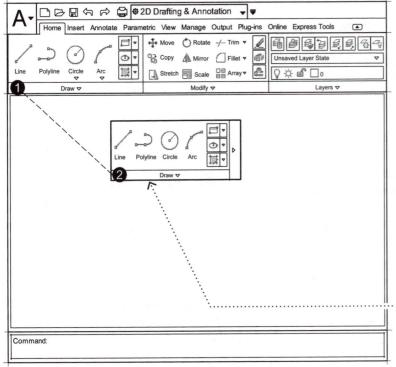

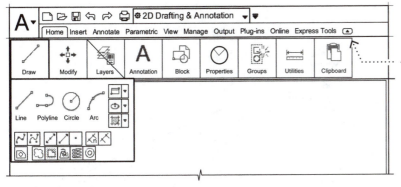

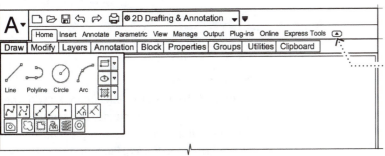

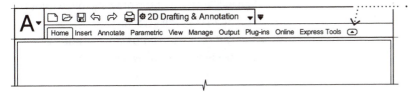

AutoCAD Ribbon

The Ribbon interface in AutoCAD contains many of the commands and tools previously located in toolbars, drop-down menus, and dialog boxes. Because buttons in the ribbon interface change their appearance and location from one version of AutoCAD to the next, this book encourages you to use keyboard commands rather than buttons when drawing in AutoCAD.

· The ribbon is organized by tabs. Each tab contains a series of related panels.
· The **HOME TAB,** selected in this example, contains multiple panels including **DRAW, MODIFY, LAYERS, ANNOTATION,** and **BLOCK.**

You can pull a panel off the ribbon interface. The line panel was removed from the home tab by **CLICKING AND DRAGGING** the panel towards the middle of the AutoCAD window.

Minimize the Ribbon Panels to **PANEL BUTTONS** by **CLICKING** the **SMALL ARROW BUTTON** to the right of the last tab.

Minimize the Ribbon Panels to **PANEL TITLES** by **CLICKING** the **SMALL ARROW BUTTON** to the right of the last tab.

Minimize the Ribbon Panels to **TABS** by **CLICKING** the **SMALL ARROW BUTTON** to the right of the last tab.

Pan

· When you draw in AutoCAD, your drawings are limited by the size of the screen. The **PAN** command allows you to slide your drawing around on the screen in the same way you could slide a piece of paper around your drafting table.

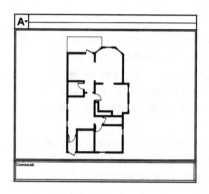 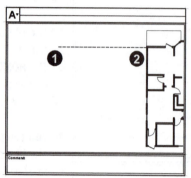

· The **PAN** command slides your drawing around on the screen without changing the size of the drawing on the screen.
· Type the command **PAN** and press **ENTER**.
· Your mouse cursor will change to a **HAND**. With the mouse, **CLICK AND DRAG** in your drawing. You will notice that the drawing follows your cursor around the screen.
· Press the **ENTER** or **ESCAPE** key to end the Pan command.

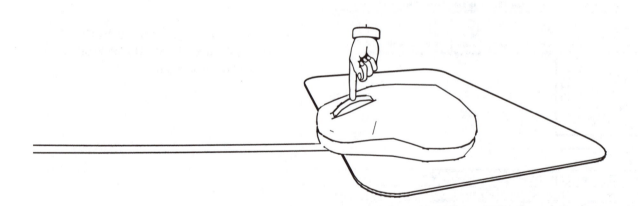

Pan with the Mouse

· You can also start the **PAN** command with the scroll wheel on your mouse. The scroll wheel is also a mouse button. With the mouse scroll wheel, **CLICK AND DRAG** in your drawing. You will notice that the drawing follows your cursor around the screen.
· The **PAN** command automatically ends when you release the scroll wheel button.

Zoom

· When you draw in AutoCAD, your drawings are limited by the size of the screen. The **ZOOM** command allows you to move closer to and farther away from elements in your drawing.

Zoom Window

· Zoom window allows you to enlarge a specific part of your drawing by drawing a window around it.

· Type the command **ZOOM** and press **ENTER**.
· **Step 1:** The zoom command asks you for the first corner of the zoom window. Drag the AutoCAD cursor to the top left of the area you want to enlarge and **CLICK ONCE**.
· **Step 2:** The zoom command asks you for the second corner of the zoom window. Drag the AutoCAD cursor to the location on the screen where you want the lower right corner of the area you want to enlarge and **CLICK ONCE**.

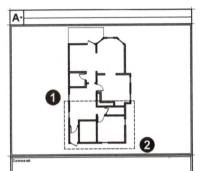
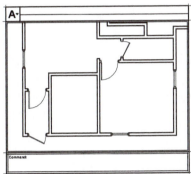

Zoom Extents

· Enlarges or shrinks your drawing to fit entirely on the screen.

· Type the command **ZOOM** and press **ENTER**.
· Type the command **EXTENTS** and press **ENTER**.

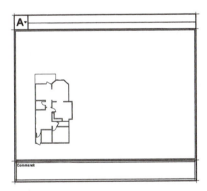
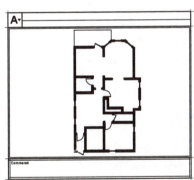

Zoom with the Mouse

· Use the scroll wheel on your mouse to enlarge or shrink your drawing dynamically.

· The scroll wheel on your mouse is also a button. If you **DOUBLE CLICK** on the scroll wheel, AutoCAD will perform the **ZOOM EXTENTS** command.

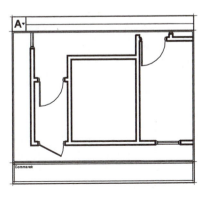
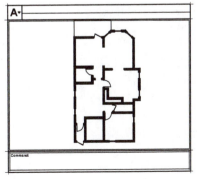

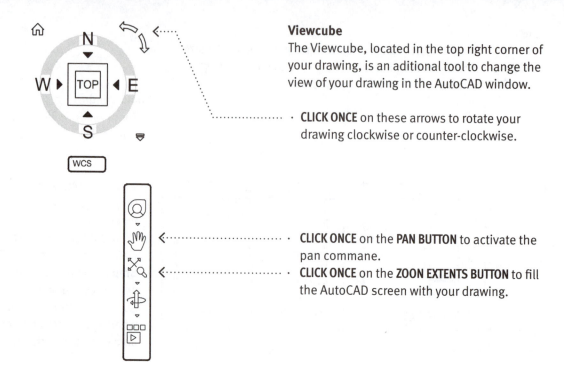

Viewcube

The Viewcube, located in the top right corner of your drawing, is an aditional tool to change the view of your drawing in the AutoCAD window.

· **CLICK ONCE** on these arrows to rotate your drawing clockwise or counter-clockwise.

· **CLICK ONCE** on the **PAN BUTTON** to activate the pan commane.

· **CLICK ONCE** on the **ZOON EXTENTS BUTTON** to fill the AutoCAD screen with your drawing.

Guide for Success

I encourage new AutoCAD users to practice drawing as soon as possible. Consider the following challenges to help you through this book.

· Draw the examples/projects provided at the end of each chapter.
· Draw a room in your home.
· Draw a design project you have already drawn by hand.

Companion Download

The following websites feature the companion download for this book: www.fairchildbooks.combook.cms?bookid=179 or www.DDFDbook.com/download

· Download learning exercises to practice different drawing tools covered in this book.
· Download sheet templates to start almost any type of drawing.
· Download sample plans, elevations, and sections to see how professionals draw using AutoCAD.

CHAPTER 2
Drawing Lines and Shapes

Lines, circles, and arcs are the fundamental building blocks of all design drawings. By the end of this chapter you will have a strong understanding of the means and methods to draw these elements in AutoCAD.

Consider the following questions as you work through this chapter:

· What are the relationships between fundamental manual drawing skills and their AutoCAD command equivalents?
· How are drawing units configured in an AutoCAD drawing?
· What is drawing precision, and what tools help you achieve it in an AutoCAD drawing?

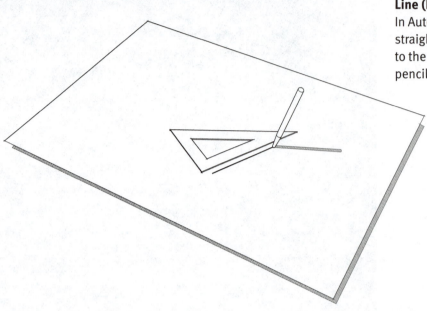

Line (Pencil)

In AutoCAD, you use the **LINE** command to draw straight lines. The manual drafting equivalent to the **LINE** command is drawing a line with a pencil and a straight edge.

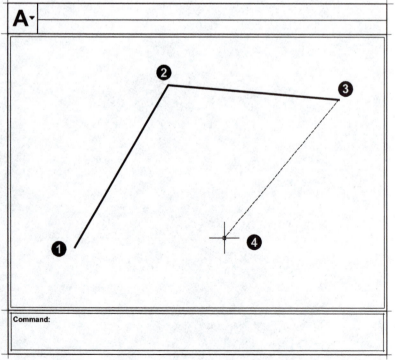

Drawing Your First Lines in AutoCAD

- Open AutoCAD on your computer.
- Using the keyboard, type the command **LINE** and press **ENTER**.
- **Step 1**: Using the mouse, **CLICK ONCE** in the lower left of the AutoCAD drawing area. As you move the drawing cursor around the screen, notice how AutoCAD shows you a straight line.
- **Step 2**: **CLICK ONCE** in the drawing area of AutoCAD following the diagram on the left.
- **Step 3**: **CLICK ONCE** in the drawing area of AutoCAD following the diagram on the left.
- **Step 4**: Press **ENTER** on the keyboard to end the **LINE** command.

Erase (Eraser)

In AutoCAD, you use the **ERASE** command to erase lines that are no longer needed or were drawn in error.

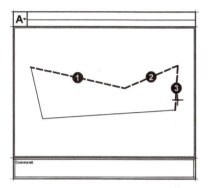

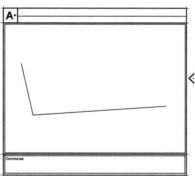

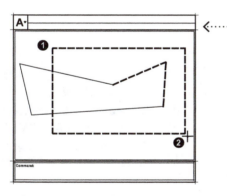

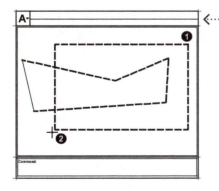

Erasing Lines in Your Drawing

· Type the command **ERASE** and press enter. In the command prompt (at the bottom of AutoCAD), the erase command prompts you to select the objects you want to erase. For now, we will cover the easier methods to select objects in AutoCAD.

· **Method 1:** To erase all the lines in your drawing, type the command **ALL** and press **ENTER**. Press **ENTER** to complete the erase command.

· **Method 2:** To erase selected lines in your drawing, **CLICK ONCE** on the lines you want to erase, one at a time. When you are finished selecting lines to erase, press **ENTER**.

· **Method 3:** Draw a **WINDOW SELECTION** around the items you want to erase. Every line or object that is completely within this window will be selected (and erased).

· To draw a **WINDOW SELECTION, CLICK ONCE** on the left side of the objects you want to erase. As you drag the mouse to the right, you will see a window on the screen. **CLICK ONCE** on the second corner of the window. When you are finished selecting lines to erase, press **ENTER**.

· **Method 4:** Draw a **CROSSING SELECTION** that touches the items you want to erase. Every line or object that this crossing selection touches will be added to the selection (and erased).

· **CLICK ONCE** on the right side of the objects you want to erase. As you drag the mouse to the left, you will see a window on the screen. **CLICK ONCE** on the second corner of the window. When you are finished selecting lines to erase, press **ENTER**.

Ortho (Parallel Bar Line, T Square)

In AutoCAD, you use Ortho to draw horizontal and vertical lines much the same as you use a parallel bar or T square on a drafting table to draw horizontal and vertical lines.

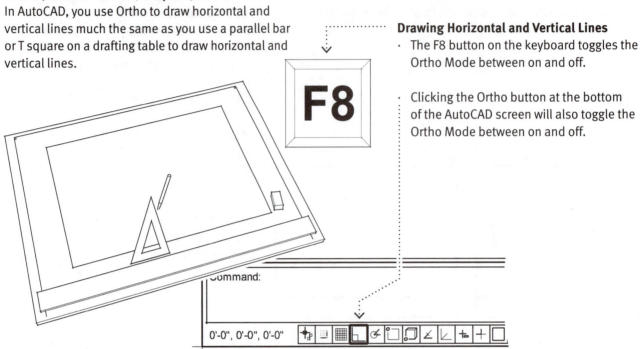

Drawing Horizontal and Vertical Lines

· The F8 button on the keyboard toggles the Ortho Mode between on and off.

· Clicking the Ortho button at the bottom of the AutoCAD screen will also toggle the Ortho Mode between on and off.

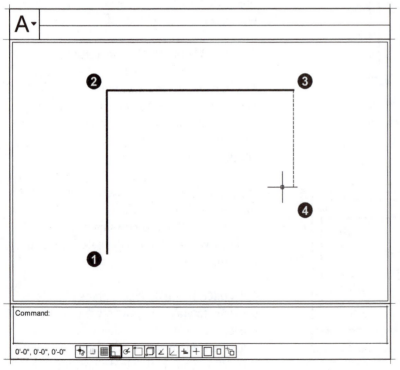

· Using the keyboard, type the command **LINE** and press **ENTER**.

· **Step 1a**: Using the mouse, **CLICK ONCE** in the lower left of the AutoCAD drawing area. As you move the drawing cursor around the screen, notice how AutoCAD shows you a straight line.

· **Step 1b**: Press **F8** on the keyboard. As you move the drawing cursor around the screen, notice how AutoCAD now shows you only horizontal and vertical lines.

· **Step 2**: **CLICK ONCE** in the drawing area of AutoCAD following the diagram on the left.

· **Step 3**: **CLICK ONCE** in the drawing area of AutoCAD following the diagram on the left.

· **Step 4**: Press **ENTER** on the keyboard to end the **LINE** command.

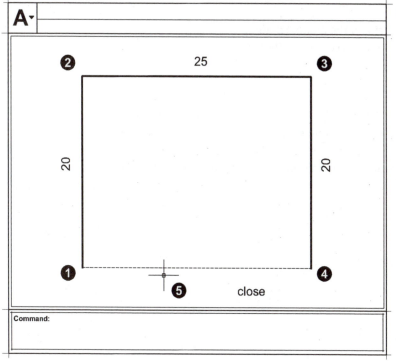

Drawing Lines at a Specific Distance

- Using the keyboard, type the command **LINE** and press **ENTER**.
- **Step 1**: **CLICK ONCE** in the lower left of the AutoCAD drawing area. Press **F8** on the keyboard to turn Ortho Mode on.
- **Step 2**: Drag the AutoCAD cursor upward on the screen. Type **20** on the keyboard and press **ENTER**.
- **Step 3**: Drag the AutoCAD cursor to the right on the screen. Type **25** on the keyboard and press **ENTER**.
- **Step 4**: Drag the AutoCAD cursor downward on the screen. Type **20** on the keyboard and press **ENTER**.
- **Step 5**: Type **CLOSE** on the keyboard and press **ENTER**.

- The Close command draws a line from the last point entered to the first point. (In our drawing, the Close command created a line from Step 4 to Step 1.)

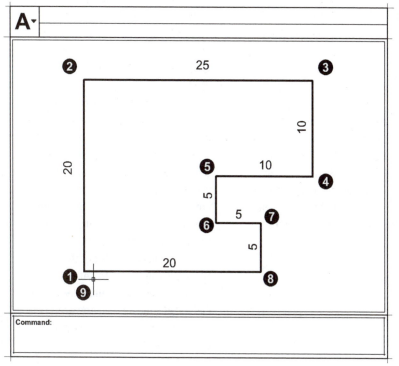

Drawing Exercise

- Practice drawing lines at specific distances by redrawing the sketch to the left.

- Erase everything in your drawing before you begin this drawing.

Drawing Circles

In AutoCAD, you use the **CIRCLE** command to draw a circle. The manual drafting equivalent to the **CIRCLE** command is drawing a circle with a compass. We will look at the three most common methods to draw a circle in AutoCAD.

Circle

Unless you specify otherwise, Auto-CAD will draw a circle the same way you draw a circle with a compass. You will need to know the center of the circle and the length of the radius.

Two-Point Circle

When you draw a two-point circle, you are actually drawing a line that repre-sents the diameter of the circle.

Three-Point Circle

When you draw a three-point circle, you are actually defining three points that are on the edge of the circle. This method is used infrequently.

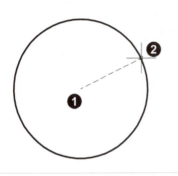
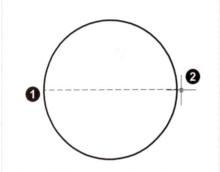
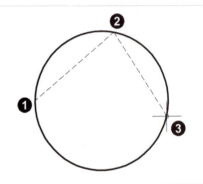

- Type the command **CIRCLE** and press **ENTER.**
- **Step 1: CLICK ONCE** in the drawing area where you want the center of your circle.
- **Step 2**: Drag the AutoCAD cursor in any direction on the screen. Type **15** on the keyboard and press **ENTER.** In this example, **15** is the radius of the circle.

- Type the command **CIRCLE** and press **ENTER.**
- Type the command **2P** and press **ENTER.** (This is your way to tell AutoCAD you want to draw a two-point circle.)
- **Step 1: CLICK ONCE** in the draw-ing area where you want the left edge of your circle.
- **Step 2**: Drag the AutoCAD cur-sor in the right direction on the screen. Type **30** on the keyboard and press **ENTER.** In this example, **30** is the diameter of the circle.

- Type the command **CIRCLE** and press **ENTER.**
- Type the command **3P** and press **ENTER.** (This is your way to tell Auto-CAD you want to draw a three-point circle.)
- **Step 1: CLICK ONCE** in the drawing area where you want the first edge of your circle.
- **Step 2:** Move the AutoCAD cur-sor in any direction on the screen and **CLICK ONCE** in the drawing area where you want the second edge of your circle. (You will not see any-thing on the screen until you mouse click the second point of the circle.)
- **Step 3**: Drag the AutoCAD cursor in any direction on the screen and **CLICK ONCE** in the drawing area where you want the third edge of your circle.

Drawing Rectangles and Polygons

You can increase your drafting speed by allowing AutoCAD to help you create specific kinds of shapes like **RECTANGLES** and **POLYGONS**. You can use the rectangle and polygon command to create equilateral triangles, squares, pentagons, and hexagons.

Rectangle

AutoCAD will draw a rectangle or square when you provide the location of two opposite corners. (You are drawing the diagonal of the rectangle.)

Inscribed Polygon

An inscribed polygon can have three or more sides and will fit inside a specified circle.

Circumscribed Polygon

A circumscribed polygon can have three or more sides and will fit outside a specified circle.

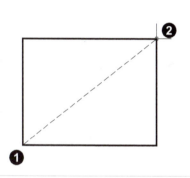
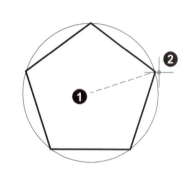
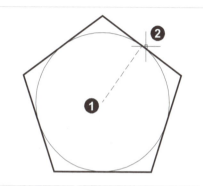

- Type the command **RECTANGLE** and press **ENTER**.
- **Step 1:** **CLICK ONCE** in the drawing area where you want the lower left corner of your rectangle.
- **Step 2:** Drag the AutoCAD cursor up and to the right. **CLICK ONCE** in the drawing area where you want the upper right corner of your rectangle.

Alternate for Specific Sized Rectangles

- Type the command **RECTANGLE** and press **ENTER**.
- **Step 1:** **CLICK ONCE** in the drawing area where you want the lower left corner of your rectangle.
- **Step 2:** On the keyboard, type **@10,30** and press **ENTER**. AutoCAD will draw a rectangle that is **10** units wide and **30** units tall.
  (Change the 10 and the 30 to draw rectangles of other sizes.)

- Type the command **POLYGON** and press **ENTER**.
- AutoCAD will ask you how many sides you want for your polygon. Type the command **5** and press **ENTER**.
- **Step 1:** **CLICK ONCE** in the drawing area where you want the center of your polygon.
  AutoCAD will ask you if you want to create an inscribed or circumscribed polygon. Type the letter **I** (for inscribed) and press **ENTER**.
- **Step 2:** Drag the AutoCAD cursor to the right on the screen. Type **30** on the keyboard and press **ENTER**.

- You have created a five-sided polygon that sits inside a circle with a radius of 30 inches.

- Type the command **POLYGON** and press **ENTER**.
- AutoCAD will ask you how many sides you want for your polygon. Type the command **5** and press **ENTER**.
- **Step 1:** **CLICK ONCE** in the drawing area where you want the center of your polygon.
  AutoCAD will ask you if you want to create an inscribed or circumscribed polygon. Type the letter **C** (for circumscribed) and press **ENTER**.
- **Step 2:** Drag the AutoCAD cursor to the right on the screen. Type **30** on the keyboard and press **ENTER**.

- You have created a five-sided polygon that sits outside a circle with a radius of 30 inches.

Drawing Arcs

The **ARC** command allows us to draw part of a circle. The manual drafting equivalent to the **ARC** command is drawing a circle, semicircle, or arc with a compass. We will look at the three most common methods to draw an **ARC** in AutoCAD.

Arc – Three Points

Unless you specify otherwise, Auto-CAD will draw an arc based on three points along the arc.

Arc – Center, Start, End

Using the Center option, AutoCAD will draw an arc the same way you draw with a compass. You will need to know the center of the arc, the start point, and the end point.

Arc – Start, Center, End

This is a variation on the previous method of drawing an arc. You will need to know the start of the arc, the center point, and end point.

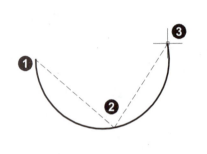

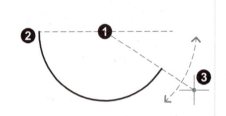

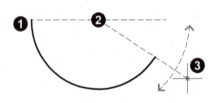

- Type the command **ARC** and press **ENTER**.
- **Step 1**: CLICK ONCE in the drawing area where you want the first point of your arc.
- **Step 2**: Drag the AutoCAD cursor in any direction on the screen. **CLICK ONCE** in the drawing area where you want the second point of your arc.
- **Step 2**: Drag the AutoCAD cursor in any direction on the screen. **CLICK ONCE** in the drawing area where you want the third (end) point of your arc.

- Type the command **ARC** and press **ENTER**.
- Type the letter **C** (for center) and press **ENTER**. (This is your way to tell AutoCAD you want to draw an arc by its center.)
- **Step 1**: CLICK ONCE in the drawing area where you want the center of your arc.
- **Step 2**: CLICK ONCE in the drawing area where you want the start of your arc.
- **Step 3**: CLICK ONCE in the drawing area where you want the end of your arc.

- Type the command **ARC** and press **ENTER**.
- **Step 1**: CLICK ONCE in the drawing area where you want the start of your arc.
- Type the letter **C** (for center) and press **ENTER**.
- **Step 2**: CLICK ONCE in the drawing area where you want the center of your arc.
- **Step 3**: CLICK ONCE in the drawing area where you want the end of your arc.

Drawing Ellipses

An ellipse looks like a stretched circle. AutoCAD creates the shape of an ellipse by two axes that define its length and width. The longer axis is called the major axis, and the shorter axis is called the minor axis.

Ellipse – Two Axes

Unless you specify otherwise, Auto-CAD will draw an ellipse based on the length of the two axes.

Ellipse – Center, Axis, Axis

AutoCAD can draw an ellipse based on the center point and the length of the two axes.

Ellipse – Angled

AutoCAD can draw an ellipse tilted on an angle. The angle of an ellipse is set by the first axis you draw.

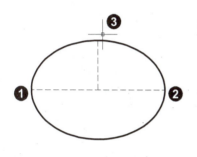 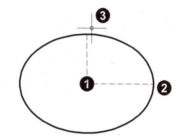 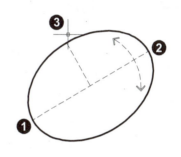

- Type the command **ELLIPSE** and press **ENTER**.
- **Step 1**: CLICK ONCE in the drawing area where you want the start of your first axis.
- **Step 2**: Drag the AutoCAD cursor in any direction on the screen. **CLICK ONCE** in the drawing area where you want the end of your first axis.
- **Step 3**: Drag the AutoCAD cursor in any direction on the screen. **CLICK ONCE** in the drawing area where you want the end of your second axis.

- You can specify distances in the **ELLIPSE** command the same way you specify distances in other commands, like line and circle.

- Type the command **ELLIPSE** and press **ENTER**.
- Type the letter **C** (for center) and press **ENTER**. (This is your way to tell AutoCAD you want to draw an ellipse by its center.)
- **Step 1**: CLICK ONCE in the drawing area where you want the center of your ellipse.
- **Step 2**: Drag the AutoCAD cursor in any direction on the screen. **CLICK ONCE** in the drawing area where you want the end of your first axis.
- **Step 3**: Drag the AutoCAD cursor in any direction on the screen. **CLICK ONCE** in the drawing area where you want the end of your second axis.

- Type the command **ELLIPSE** and press **ENTER**.
- **Step 1**: CLICK ONCE in the drawing area where you want the start of your first axis.
- **Step 2**: Drag the AutoCAD cursor in any direction on the screen. **CLICK ONCE** in the drawing area where you want the end and angle of your first axis.
- **Step 3**: Drag the AutoCAD cursor in any direction on the screen. **CLICK ONCE** in the drawing area where you want the end of your second axis.

- The axes in an ellipse are always perpendicular to each other.

- You can also use the Rotate command to change the angle of an ellipse you have already drawn.

Object Snaps

In a good AutoCAD drawing, lines connect to each other at precise points (the end of a line, middle of a line, or intersection of two lines). Object snaps allow you to start or end lines at a precise point relative to something you have already drawn.

Using Object Snaps

Object snaps can be activated during most AutoCAD commands. While you are in a command, hold down the **SHIFT** key and **RIGHT CLICK** to activate the Object Snap menu. Select the desired object snap and continue with your command.

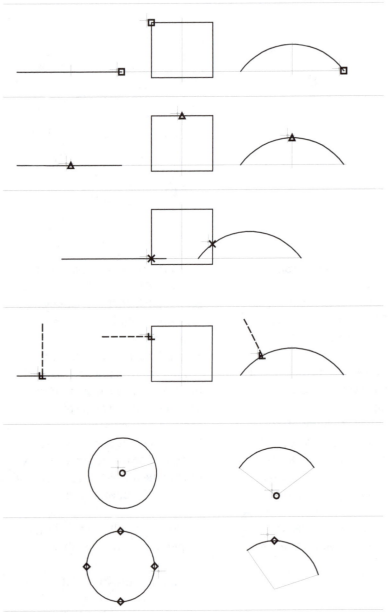

· Endpoint – Snaps to the endpoint of a line, circle, or arc. Also snaps to the closest corner of a square, rectangle, or polygon. Endpoint can be used as the first or second point when drawing a line.

· Midpoint – Snaps to the midpoint of a line or arc. Also snaps to the midpoint of any side of a square, rectangle, or polygon. Midpoint can be used as the first or second point when drawing a line.

· Intersection – Snaps to the intersection between any two of the following: line, arc, circle, square, rectangle, or polygon. Intersection can be used as the first or second point when drawing a line.

· Perpendicular – Snaps to create a new line that is perpendicular to a line, arc, circle, square, rectangle, or polygon. Perpendicular is mostly used as the second point when drawing a line.

· Center – Snaps to the center of an arc or circle. Center can be used as the first or second point when drawing a line.

· Quadrant – Snaps to one of the four quadrants of an arc or circle. Quadrant can be used as the first or second point when drawing a line.

Running Object Snaps

Object snaps can be set to activate automatically as you draw in Auto-CAD. (You do not need to use the shift right-click method described on the previous page).

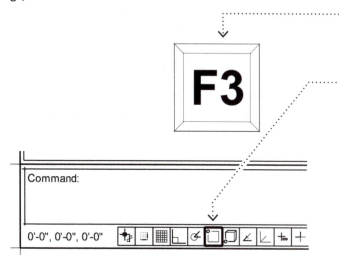

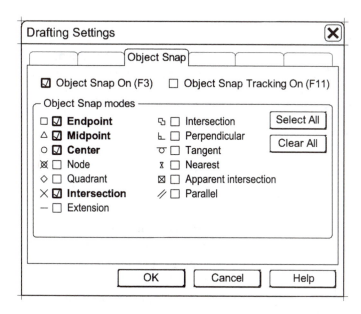

- Pressing the **F3** button on the keyboard toggles the Running Object Snap mode between on and off.

- Clicking the Snap button at the bottom of the AutoCAD screen will also toggle the Running Object Snap mode between on and off.

Setting the Running Object Snaps
When you use running object snaps, it is important to be specific about which object snap modes you want turned on.

· Type the command **OSNAP** and press **ENTER**.
· **UNCHECK** the Object Snap Tracking On option.
· Check on the following modes: **ENDPOINT, MIDPOINT, CENTER,** and **INTERSECTION**.
· **CLICK OK.**
· These four running object snaps will increase your accuracy and productivity for almost everything you draw in AutoCAD.
· Use the **SHIFT RIGHT-CLICK** method if you need to activate a different object snap.

· It is recommended that you do not draw with the perpendicular or nearest running object snaps turned on. These two object snaps (in Running Object Snap mode) are responsible for 90 percent of all drawing inaccuracies.

Drawing Precision

There are many things to consider when evaluating the craft of a manually drafted drawing. For example, you must keep your lead or pencil sharp, maintain a clear and legible line weight, and draw line length with precision. Similarly, the extra time you spend now to master these skills in AutoCAD will help you tremendously when you start your first drawing.

Setting the Drawing Units

Most likely, you will want to draw in AutoCAD using feet and inches or the metric system. AutoCAD allows you to draw using either unit of measure.

· We will use feet and inches as the primary drawing units in this book.

· To set the drawing units in AutoCAD, type **UNITS** and press **ENTER**.

· **Feet and Inches** – Set the Length Type to **ARCHITECTURAL** and the Length Precision to **1/32"**.

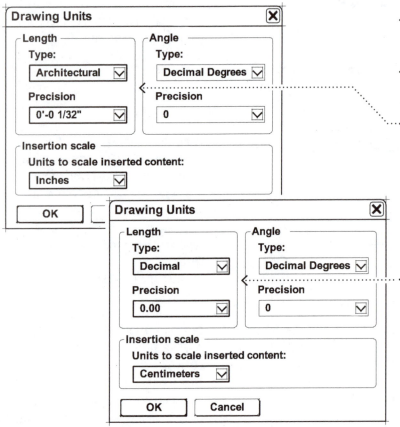

· **Metric** – Set the Length Type to **DECIMAL** and the Length Precision to **0.00**.

Using Feet and Inches

In a good AutoCAD drawing, lines are drawn at precise lengths (i.e., 1'-6"). If you are precise when drawing lines in AutoCAD, you will find huge benefits at later stages in your project.

· Pressing the **SPACE BAR** in AutoCAD is the same as pressing **ENTER**. Use the hyphen (-) instead of pressing the space bar when entering units.

Methods to enter 2' 6"
· type **30"** and press enter
· type **2.5'** and press enter
· type **2'6"** and press enter
· type **2'-6"** and press enter

Methods to enter 2' 6½"
· type **30.5"** and press enter
· type **2'6-1/2"** and press enter

UNDO

Using the Undo Command

The **UNDO** command allows you to step backward in your drawing and undo the last command. For example, if you erased a line that you did not want to erase, the Undo command would put that line back in your drawing. AutoCAD will undo all the way back to the point when you opened your drawing.

Undo Quickly

· The quickest way to use the Undo command is to press the **CTRL** key and the letter **Z** at the same time (**CTRL+Z**). This will undo the most recent command.
· You can use **CTRL+Z** multiple times to undo a series of commands.
· The shortcut for the Redo command is **CTRL+Y**. This will redo your last undo.

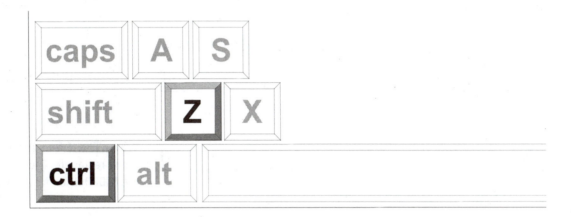

Undo Multiple Steps

The Undo command also allows you to undo several steps at once. This is helpful if you know that you want to undo the last five commands.

· Type the command **UNDO** and press **ENTER**.

· AutoCAD will prompt you for the number of commands you want to undo. Type **5** and press **ENTER**. AutoCAD will undo the last five commands.

· If you want to undo back to the point when you opened your drawing, ask AutoCAD to undo an extremely large number of commands (e.g., 10,000).

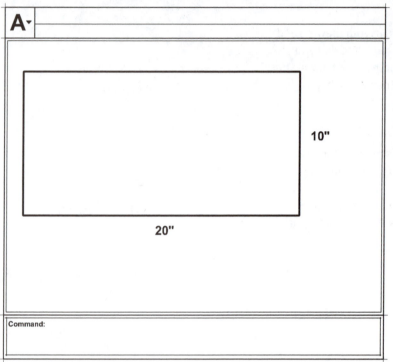

Learning Exercise

The following exercise will help you better understand drawing shapes and lines using object snaps. There are additional exercises available for download at: www.fairchildbooks.com/book.cms?bookid=179

· Open a new AutoCAD drawing
· Set your **UNITS** to **ARCHITECTURAL**.
· Draw a **RECTANGLE 20"** wide by **10"** high.

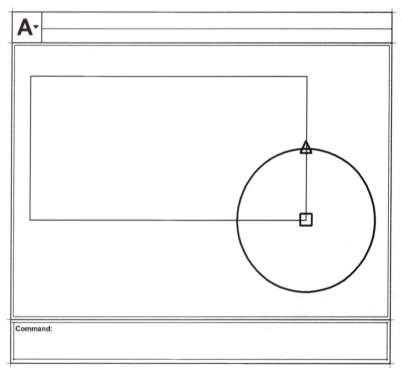

· Draw a **CIRCLE** from the lower right **ENDPOINT** of the rectangle. The radius of the circle is the **MIDPOINT** of the rectangle.

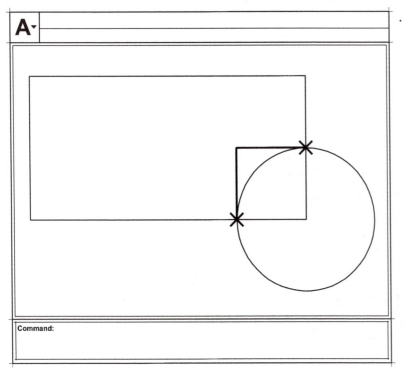

· Draw two lines that start at the **INTERSECTION** of the circle and the rectangle.

Command:

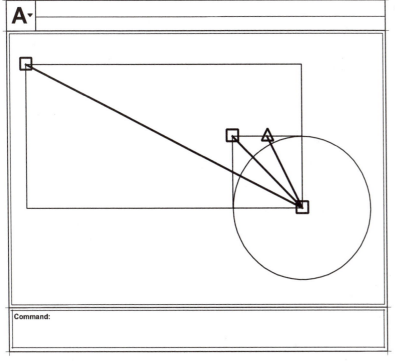

· Draw three lines using the **ENDPOINT** and **MID-POINT** object snaps.

Command:

Companion Download
The companion download contains several AutoCAD drawings that allow you to test your understanding of drawing lines and shapes in AutoCAD.

Look inside the Learning Exercises folder for these files.

The following websites feature the companion download for this book: www.fairchildbooks.combook.cms?bookid=179 or www.DDFDbook.com/ch2

CHAPTER 3
Modifying Lines and Shapes

If you have ever typed a letter on a typewriter, you understand how word processing software like Microsoft Word saves you time and energy during the editing process. This chapter introduces many of the editing commands in AutoCAD. These concepts and commands will help you more efficiently edit your design drawings.

Consider the following questions as you work through this chapter:

· What are the different editing tools in AutoCAD, and how do they relate to their manual drawing equivalents?
· How much longer does it take you to draw in AutoCAD versus drawing by hand?
· How much longer does it take you to edit your drawings in AutoCAD versus editing your hand drawings?

Move

There is no efficient manual equivalent to the **MOVE** command in AutoCAD. If you need to move lines on a manually drafted drawing, you must erase the lines and re-draw them in their new location. The **MOVE** command allows you to literally pick the lines up off the paper and place them in a new location on the paper.

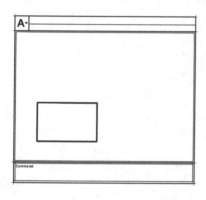 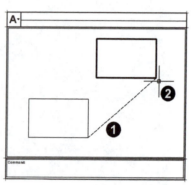

Moving Lines in Your Drawing

· Type the command **MOVE** and press enter.
· The Move command asks you to select the objects you want to move. You can select objects to move using the exact same selection methods we discussed with the Erase command in Chapter 2.
· Select the lines in your drawing that you would like to move (we selected the entire rectangle in the example to the left). When you are finished selecting lines to move, press **ENTER**.
· **Step 1:** The Move command asks you for the base point of your move. **ENDPOINT** snap (shift + right click) to the lower right corner of the rectangle.
· **Step 2:** The Move command asks you for the second point of your move. Drag the AutoCAD cursor to the location on the screen where you want the lower right corner of the rectangle and **CLICK ONCE**.

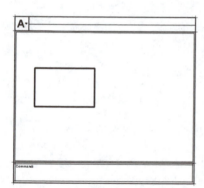

Move a Specific Distance

· Type the command **MOVE** and press **ENTER**.
· Select the lines in your drawing that you would like to move and press **ENTER**.
· **Step 1:** Click anywhere on the screen. Turn Ortho on by pressing the **F8** key.
· **Step 2:** Drag the AutoCAD cursor in the right direction on the screen. Type **20** on the keyboard and press **ENTER**.

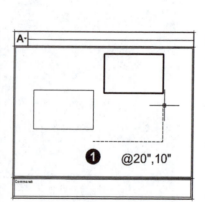

Move a Distance Over and Up

· Type the command **MOVE** and press **ENTER**.
· Select the lines in your drawing that you would like to move and press **ENTER**.
· **Step 1:** Click anywhere on the screen. Turn Ortho on by pressing the **F8** key.
· **Step 2:** Drag the AutoCAD cursor to the right on the screen. Type **@20",10"** on the keyboard and press **ENTER**.
· The horizontal distance is 20" and the vertical distance is 10".

Copy

There is no efficient manual equivalent to the **COPY** command in AutoCAD. Many designers use trace (translucent paper) to redraw lines and then move the trace around as an overlay to their original drawing. The **COPY** command allows you to literally pick the lines up off the paper and copy them in a new location on the paper. We use the **COPY** command the same way we use the **MOVE** command.

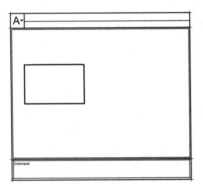

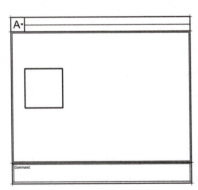

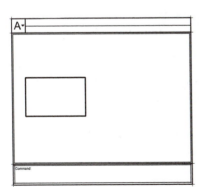

Copy a Specific Distance

· Type the command **COPY** and press **ENTER**.
· The copy command asks you to select the objects you want to copy. Selection methods are discussed with the Erase command in Chapter 2.
· Select the lines in your drawing that you would like to copy (we selected the entire rectangle in the example to the left). When you are finished selecting lines to copy, press **ENTER**.
· **Step 1**: The Copy command asks you for the base point of your copy. Click anywhere on the screen. Turn Ortho on by pressing the **F8** key.
· **Step 2**: The Copy command asks you for the second point of your copy. Drag the AutoCAD cursor in the right direction on the screen. Type **20"** on the keyboard and press **ENTER**.
· Press **ENTER** to end the Copy command.

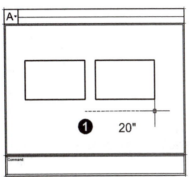

Multiple Copy a Specific Distance

New to AutoCAD 2012, you can now make multiple copies of objects in the drawing.
· Type the command **COPY** and press **ENTER**.
· Select the lines in your drawing that you would like to move and press **ENTER**.
· **Step 1**: Click anywhere on the screen. Turn Ortho on by pressing the **F8** key.
· **Step 2**: Drag the AutoCAD cursor in the right direction on the screen. Type **10"** on the keyboard and press **ENTER**.
· **Step 3**: Drag the AutoCAD cursor to the right on the screen. Type **20"** and press **ENTER**.
· Press **ENTER** to end the Copy command.

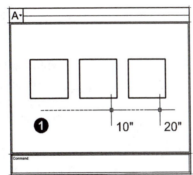

Copy a Distance Over and Up

· Type the command **COPY** and press **ENTER**.
· Select the lines in your drawing that you would like to move and press **ENTER**.
· **Step 1**: Click anywhere on the screen. Turn Ortho on by pressing the **F8** key.
· **Step 2**: Drag the AutoCAD cursor in the right direction on the screen. Type **@20",10"** on the keyboard and press **ENTER**.
· Press **ENTER** to end the Copy command.

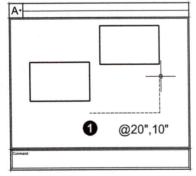

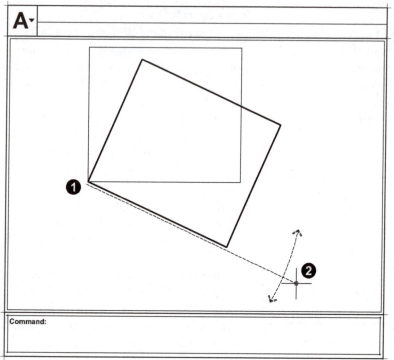

Rotating Lines in Your Drawing

There is no efficient manual equivalent to the **ROTATE** command in AutoCAD. The **ROTATE** command allows you to rotate lines around a pivot point and place them in a new location on the paper.

· Type the command **ROTATE** and press **ENTER**.
· The rotate command asks you to select the objects you want to copy. Select the lines in your drawing that you would like to rotate (we selected the entire rectangle in the example to the left). When you are finished selecting lines to rotate, press **ENTER**.
· **Step 1:** The Rotate command asks you for the base point of your rotate (this is really the pivot point of your rotation). **ENDPOINT** snap to the lower left corner of the rectangle.
· **Step 2:** The Rotate command asks you to specify the rotation angle. Drag the AutoCAD cursor to the right and up and down to see your rectangle dynamically rotate. **CLICK ONCE** when you find the desired angle.

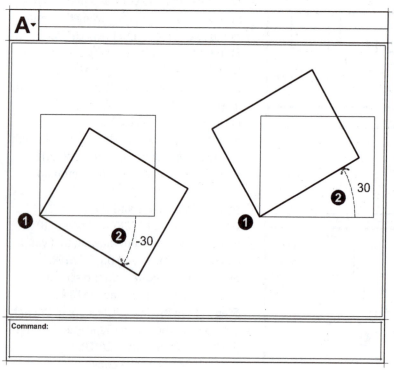

Rotating Lines at a Specific Angle

The rotation shown in the example above is not very precise. We can precisely rotate a line or lines at a specific angle.

· Type the command **ROTATE** and press **ENTER**.
· Select the lines in your drawing that you would like to rotate and press **ENTER**.
· **Step 1:** The Rotate command asks you for the base point of your rotation. **ENDPOINT** snap to the lower left corner of the rectangle.
· **Step 2:** The Rotate command asks you to specify the rotation angle. Type **-30** on the keyboard and press **ENTER**.

· Positive angles (e.g., **30**) in AutoCAD rotate objects counterclockwise.

· Negative angles (e.g., **-30**) in AutoCAD rotate objects clockwise.

Mirroring/Reflecting Lines in Your Drawing

The **MIRROR** command allows you to make a mirror image of (or flip) a line or group of lines in your drawing. This is the same concept as taking a drawing on translucent paper and folding the paper along a line. The lines you see through the back of the paper are the mirror image.

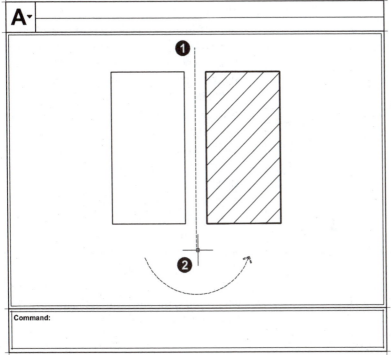

Mirroring Lines in Your Drawing

The **MIRROR** command requires that you draw an imaginary mirror line to reflect your lines.

· Type the command **MIRROR** and press **ENTER**.
· The Mirror prompt asks you to select the objects you want to mirror. Select the lines in your drawing that you would like to mirror (we selected the left rectangle in the example to the left). When you are finished selecting lines to mirror, press **ENTER**.
· **Step 1:** The Mirror prompt asks you for the first point of your mirror line. (In our example, the mirror line is represented as a dashed line. This line does not always exist in your drawing.) **CLICK ONCE** to the right of the rectangle.
· **Step 2:** The Mirror prompt asks you for the second point of your mirror line. Turn Ortho on by pressing the **F8** key. Drag the AutoCAD cursor downward and **CLICK ONCE**.
· The Mirror prompt asks if you would like to delete the source objects (it is really asking if you want to delete the original rectangle). Type the letter **N** (for no) on the keyboard and press **ENTER**.

Examples of Mirrored Lines

· The mirror is extremely useful when working on floor plans and elevations. It allows you to duplicate large portions of your drawing without having to re-draw them.

· When you mirror a line or group of lines you can choose to delete or keep the original objects.

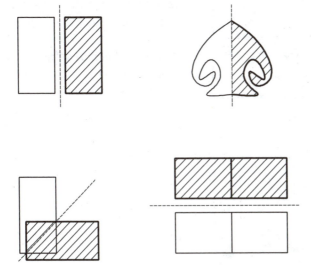

Stretch

Use **STRETCH** to select endpoints and move their location in your drawing. The lines that are connected to those endpoints are automatically adjusted.

Stretching Lines in Your Drawing

The Stretch command requires that you draw a **CROSSING WINDOW** around the endpoints that you want to change. The remaining endpoints in your drawing remain unchanged.

- Type the command **STRETCH** and press **ENTER**.
- The stretch prompt asks you to select the objects to stretch (it is really asking you to draw a crossing window over the endpoints that you want to stretch). Select the lower right endpoint of the rectangle by drawing a **CROSSING WINDOW**.
- **Step 1: CLICK ONCE** to the right and below the lower right corner of the rectangle.
- **Step 2: CLICK ONCE** to the left and above the lower right corner of the rectangle and press **ENTER**.
- **Step 3:** The stretch prompt asks you for the base point of your stretch. **ENDPOINT** snap to the lower right corner of the rectangle.
- **Step 4:** The stretch prompt asks you for the second point of your stretch. Drag the AutoCAD cursor to the location on the screen where you want the lower right corner of the new stretched shape and **CLICK ONCE**.

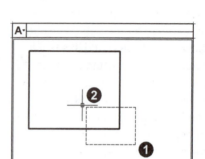
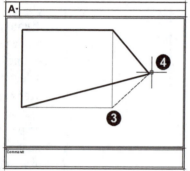

- Try using Ortho (Click the **ORTHO** button or press **F8**) to stretch the same rectangle, as indicated in the diagrams to the left.

- Notice the difference between stretching the bottom right corner and stretching the bottom right and top right corners.

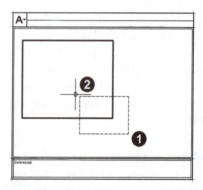
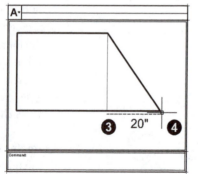

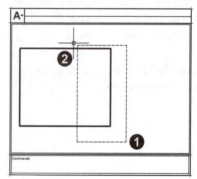
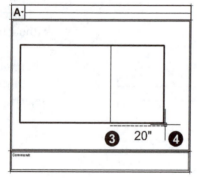

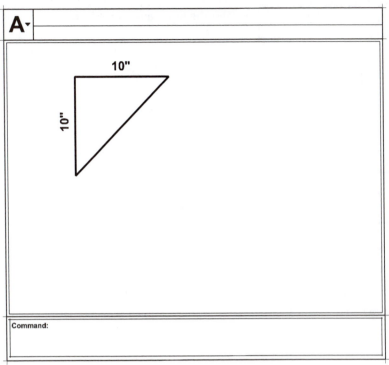

Command:

Learning Exercise

Using the commands discussed in Chapters 1–3, draw and edit the sketches to the left. There are additional exercises available for download at books.dougseidler.com.

· Set your drawing units to architectural (feet and inches).

· Draw a triangle with a left and top side 10" long.

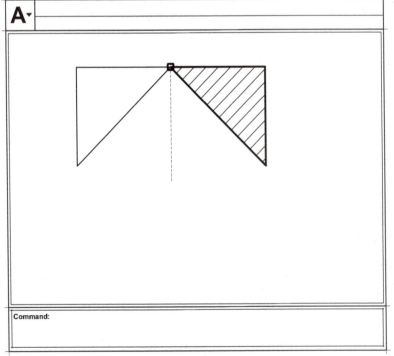

Command:

· **MIRROR** the triangle about the top right **END-POINT.**

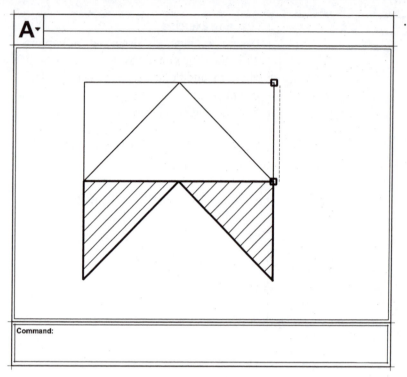

· **COPY** the two triangles down **10"**.

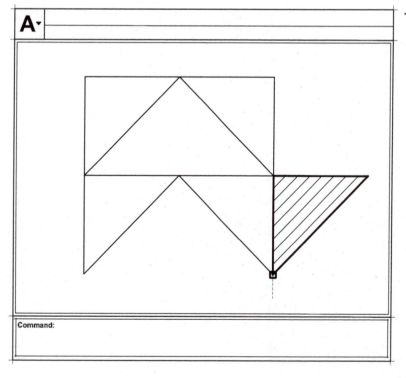

· **MIRROR** the bottom right triangle about the bottom right **ENDPOINT**.

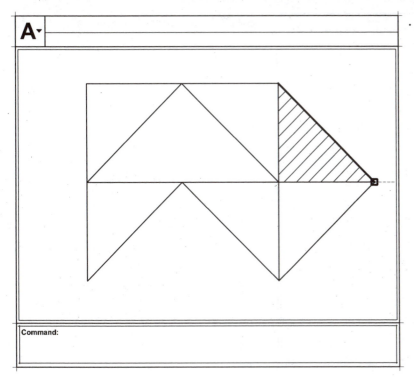

· **MIRROR** the bottom right triangle about the top right **ENDPOINT**.

Command:

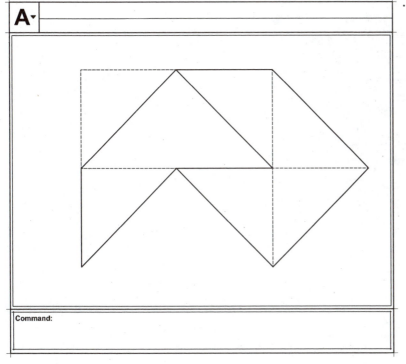

· **ERASE** the dashed lines.

Command:

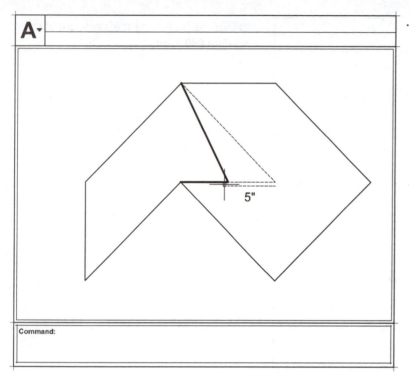

· **STRETCH** the indicated endpoint **5"** to the left.

Companion Download

The companion download contains several AutoCAD drawings that allow you to test your understanding of modifying lines and shapes in AutoCAD.

Look inside the Learning Exercises folder for these files.

The following websites feature the companion download for this book: www.fairchildbooks.combook.cms?bookid=179 or www.DDFDbook.com/ch3

CHAPTER 4
Drawing with Accuracy and Speed

In the previous three chapters you learned the AutoCAD equivalent to many of the skills you already possess from your experience with manual drawing. The concepts and commands in this chapter will be new to you if you have not previously used a digital drawing program. That said, you will use the commands introduced in this chapter more frequently than any of the other commands discussed in this book.

Consider the following questions as you work through this chapter:

- How can the concepts and commands in this chapter help me draw more efficiently?
- Many of the commands in this chapter involve a combination of multiple manual drawing skills. What manual drawing skills would you combine to achieve the same result as the commands discussed in this chapter?

Polyline

A polyline is really just a series of connected lines that are grouped together. This means that when you select any single segment within a polyline, AutoCAD will select the entire polyline. You will find many instances when polylines increase your drawing efficiency (some by the end of this chapter).

· Drawing with the Polyline command (**PLINE**) is the exact same as drawing with the Line command. The resulting lines look and behave the same, with the single exception that they are joined together.

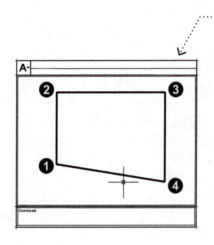

· Type the command **PLINE** and press **ENTER**.
· **Step 1**: Using the mouse, **CLICK ONCE** in the lower left of the AutoCAD drawing area.
· **Steps 2–4**: **CLICK ONCE** in the AutoCAD drawing area, following the diagram on the left.
· Type **CLOSE** and press **ENTER** on the keyboard to end the Polyline command and to close your shape.

Grips

· The blue squares at the endpoints and midpoints of lines are called grips. These grips show up when you select a line or shape before you start a command (e.g., move, copy, or erase).
· By clicking on a grip, you can stretch the selected object.

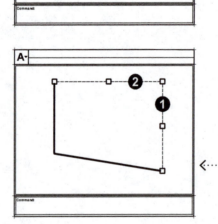

More About Polylines

· When you select a single line segment in a polyline, the entire polyline is selected.

· Polylines have grips only at the endpoints of line segments.

More About Lines

· When you select a single line segment in a series of lines, only the individually selected line is highlighted.

· Lines have grips at the endpoints and the midpoints of line segments.

Editing Polylines

The **PEDIT** command allows you to change the width of polylines, convert lines to polylines, and join lines to an existing polyline. Although there are more options available in the **PEDIT** command, we will focus on the three most used commands.

Changing Lines to Polylines	Joining Lines to a Polyline	Changing the Width of a Polyline

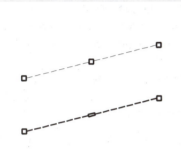

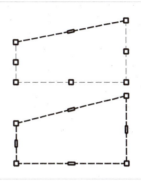

Changing Lines to Polylines

· Type the command **PEDIT** and press **ENTER**.
· Select a single line in your drawing that you would like to convert to a polyline (AutoCAD will allow you to select only one line).
· The **PEDIT** prompt asks you if you would like to turn the selected line into a polyline. Type the letter **Y** (for yes) and press **ENTER**.
· Press **ENTER** or **ESCAPE** to exit the **PEDIT** command.

Joining Lines to a Polyline

· Type the command **PEDIT** and press **ENTER**.
· **SELECT** a single line or polyline in your drawing (AutoCAD will allow you to select only one line).
· If you selected a line, the **PEDIT** prompt asks you if you would like to turn the selected line into a polyline. Type the letter **Y** (for yes) and press **ENTER**.
· **CLICK ONCE** on the **JOIN** option in the dynamic input window.
· **SELECT** the lines you would like to join to your originally selected line or polyline. Press **ENTER** when you have finished selecting lines. Note: AutoCAD will join only lines that share endpoints.
· Press **ENTER** or **ESCAPE** to exit the **PEDIT** command.

Changing the Width of a Polyline

· Type the command **PEDIT** and press **ENTER**.
· Select a single line or polyline in your drawing.
· If you selected a line, the **PEDIT** prompt asks you if you would like to turn the selected line into a polyline. Type the letter **Y** (for yes) and press **ENTER**.
· **CLICK ONCE** on the **WIDTH** option in the dynamic input window.
· Type a new width on the keyboard (i.e., **2"**) and press **ENTER**.
· Press **ENTER** or **ESCAPE** to exit the **PEDIT** command.

· Setting the width of a polyline to **0** will return the line to its original thickness.

· Some people use polyline widths as line weights when drawing plans and sections in AutoCAD. A more common method for drawing with line weight is discussed in Chapter 5.

Trim

The **TRIM** command allows you to precisely trim the end of a line, polyline, circle, or arc based on its intersection with a second line (or cutting edge).

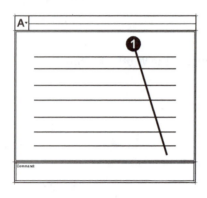

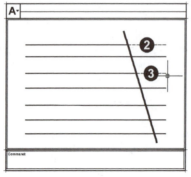

- Type the command **TRIM** and press **ENTER**.
- **Step 1: CLICK ONCE** on the line, polyline, arc, or circle that you want to use as a cutting edge and press **ENTER**.
- **Step 2: CLICK ONCE** on the first line that you want to trim. AutoCAD will erase the portion of that line that extends beyond the cutting edge.
- **Step 3: CLICK ONCE** on the second line that you want to trim.
- Press **ENTER** or **ESCAPE** to exit the **TRIM** command.

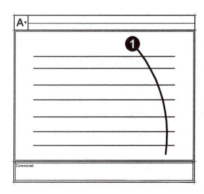

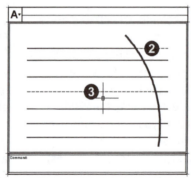

Controlling the Trim

- When you click on a line that you want to trim, AutoCAD will trim relative to the cutting edge. You are telling AutoCAD which part of the line you want to trim or erase.

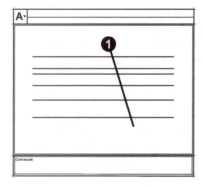

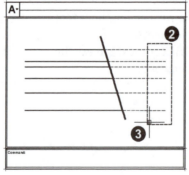

Trimming Multiple Lines

- You can draw a **CROSSING SELECTION** over a series of lines to trim them all at once. This is quicker than individually selecting the lines that you want to trim.

Extend

The **EXTEND** command allows you to precisely extend the end of a line, polyline, circle, or arc based on its intersection with a second line (or projection edge).

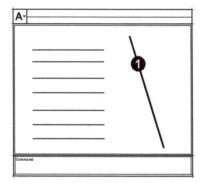
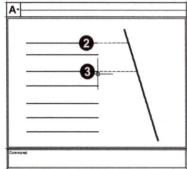

- Type the command **EXTEND** and press **ENTER**.
- **Step 1**: **CLICK ONCE** on the line, polyline, arc, or circle that you want to use as a projection edge and press **ENTER**.
- **Step 2**: **CLICK ONCE** on the first line that you want to extend. AutoCAD will extend that line to the projection edge.
- **Step 3**: **CLICK ONCE** on the second line that you want to extend.
- Press **ENTER** or **ESCAPE** to exit the **EXTEND** command.

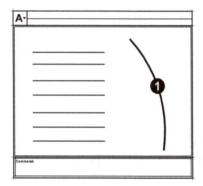
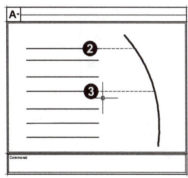

Controlling the Extend

- AutoCAD allows you to extend a line in two directions. Click on the side of the midpoint in the direction that you would like to extend.

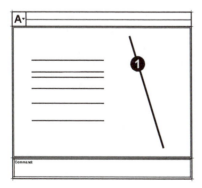
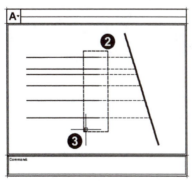

Extending Multiple Lines

- You can draw a **CROSSING SELECTION** over a series of lines to extend them all at once. This is quicker than individually selecting the lines that you want to extend.

Offset

The **OFFSET** command creates a parallel line or a concentric circle a set distance from an existing line, arc, or circle. This command is mostly used to set the thickness of walls in floor plans.

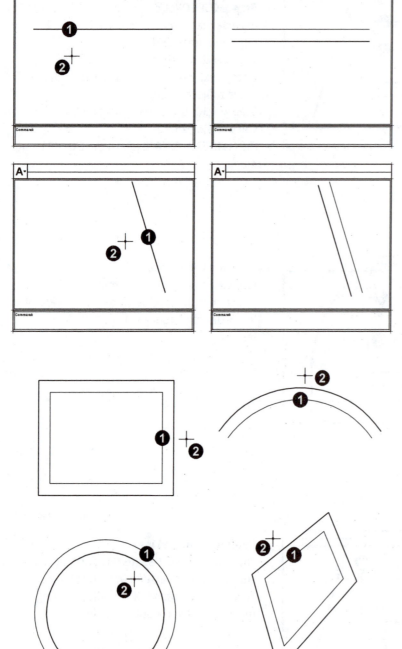

Offsetting Lines

· Type the command **OFFSET** and press **ENTER**.
· Type the distance you want to offset lines (e.g., **6"**) and press **ENTER**.
· **Step 1: CLICK ONCE** on the line, polyline, arc, or circle that you want to offset.
· **Step 2: CLICK ONCE** on the side of the line where you want to create the parallel line.
· AutoCAD allows you to offset multiple objects without restarting the **OFFSET** command. Press **ENTER** or **ESCAPE** to exit the **OFFSET** command.

· AutoCAD will remember your last offset distance when you start the **OFFSET** command. If you want to keep this distance you can press **ENTER** rather than entering the distance again.

· You can draw an entire floor plan with Line, Offset, Trim, and Extend.

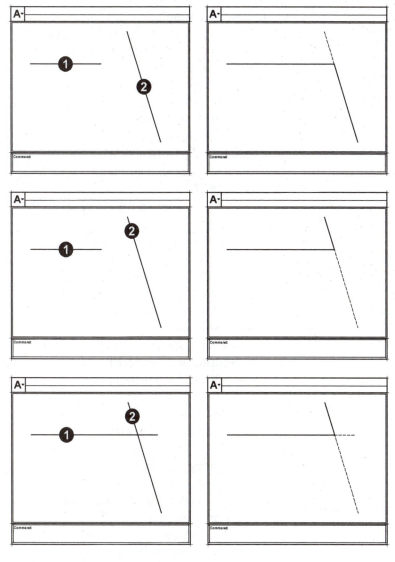

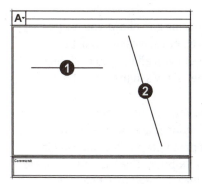

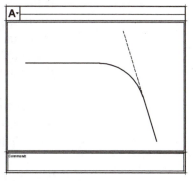

Fillet

The **FILLET** command is a combination of the Trim and Extend commands. It will extend two lines to their exact intersection and trim the portions of the line that are beyond the intersection.

· Type the command **FILLET** and press **ENTER**.
· **Step 1**: **CLICK ONCE** on the first line that you want to connect.
· **Step 2**: **CLICK ONCE** on the second line that you want to connect.

· The fillet command automatically ends after you select the second line. You can press the **SPACEBAR** or **ENTER** key to repeat the **FILLET** command.

· Notice the relationship between the point where you select a line and the portion of the line that AutoCAD keeps when filleting two lines.

· You can fillet two lines, arcs, or polylines.

Radius Fillet

Setting a **RADIUS** in the Fillet command will provide a curved or radius connection between the lines.

· Type the command **FILLET** and press **ENTER**.
· Type the letter **R** (for radius) and press **ENTER**. Enter the value of the radius (e.g., **5"**) and press **ENTER**.
· **Step 1**: **CLICK ONCE** on the first line that you want to connect.
· **Step 2**: **CLICK ONCE** on the second line that you want to connect.

· The Fillet command remembers the previously set radius. Set the **RADIUS** back to **0** when you want a non-radius fillet.

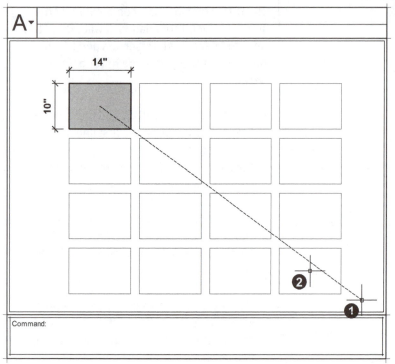

Rectangular Array

The rectangular array command allows you to quickly create duplicates of an original object in a grid pattern.

- Type the command **ARRAY** and press **ENTER**.
- Select the lines in your drawing that you would like to array (we selected the entire rectangle in the example to the left). When you have finished selecting lines to array, press **ENTER**.
- From the dynamic input menu select **RECTAN-GULAR**.
- **Step 1:** Drag the AutoCAD cursor in the direction on the screen where you want to array the selected lines. AutoCAD will dynamically add to the array as you drag your cursor. **CLICK** when you see the quantity of lines you want in the array.
- **Step 2:** Drag the AutoCAD cursor to adjust the spacing between each item in the array.
- Press **ENTER** to accept the array.

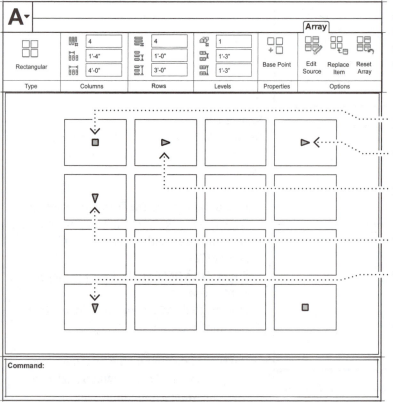

Adjusting a Rectangular Array

In AutoCAD 2012, you can adjust the properties of an array after you initially create it in your drawing.

- To adjust an Rectangular Array, **CLICK ONCE** on any item in the array.
- The Move grip allows you to move all of the items in the array as a single object.
- The Column Count grip allows you to change the total number of columns in the array.
- The Column Spacing grip allows you to change the distance between each column in the array.
- The Row Spacing grip allows you to change the distance between each row in the array.
- The Row Count grip allows you to change the total number of rows in the array.

- **Ribbon Tip:** You can also modify the Column Spacing, Column Count, Row Spacing, and Row Count parameters in the Array tab in the AutoCAD Ribbon. The Array tab is visible when you click on an associative array.

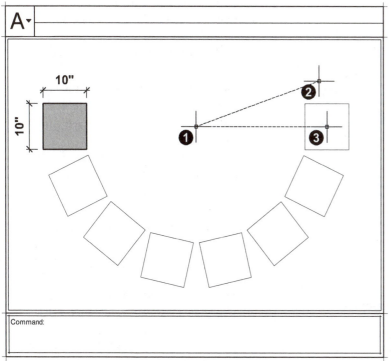

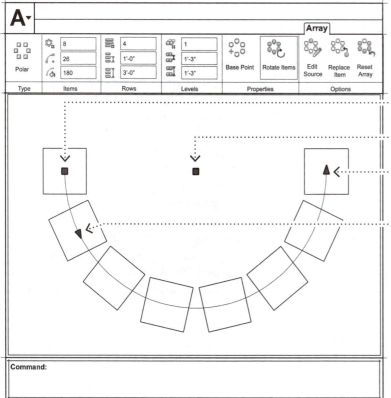

Polar Array

The Polar Array command allows you to quickly create duplicates of an original object in a radial pattern.

- Type the command **ARRAY** and press **ENTER**.
- Select the lines in your drawing that you would like to array (we selected the entire rectangle in the example to the left). When you have finished selecting lines to array, press **ENTER**.
- From the dynamic input menu select **POLAR**.
- **Step 1: CLICK ONCE** at the center point of the array with the AutoCAD cursor. The previously selected objects will be rotated about this center point.
- **Step 2:** Drag the AutoCAD cursor to adjust the quantity of items in the array. **CLICK** when you see the quantity of items you want in the array.
- **Step 3:** Drag the AutoCAD cursor to specify the fill angle for the arrayed items. **CLICK** when you see the desired fill angle or type the fill angle and press **ENTER**.
- Press **ENTER** to accept the array.

Adjusting a Polar Array

- To adjust a Polar Array, **CLICK ONCE** on any item in the array.
- The Stretch Radius grip allows you to adjust the radius of the array.
- The Move grip allows you to move all of the items in the array as a single object.
- The Item Count / Fill Angle grip allows you to modify the fill angle which also modifies the number of items in the array.
- The Angle Between Items grip allows you to modify the angle between each item in the array.

- **Ribbon Tip:** You can also modify the Stretch Radius, Angle Between Items, Item Count, and Fill Angle parameters in the Array tab in the AutoCAD Ribbon. The Array tab is visible when you click on an associative array.

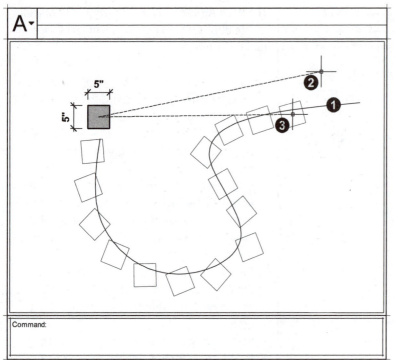

Path Array

New to AutoCAD 2012, the path array evenly distributes selected objects along a path.

- Type the command **ARRAY** and press **ENTER**.
- Select the lines in your drawing that you would like to array (we selected the entire rectangle in the example to the left). When you have finished selecting lines to array, press **ENTER**.
- From the dynamic input menu select PATH.
- **Step 1: CLICK ONCE** on the path curve for the array (we selected the spline in the example to the left).
- **Step 2:** Drag the AutoCAD cursor to adjust the quantity of items in the array. **CLICK** when you see the quantity of items you want in the array.
- **Step 3:** Drag the AutoCAD cursor to specify the fill angle for the arrayed items. **CLICK** when you see the desired fill angle or type the fill angle and press **ENTER**.
- Press **ENTER** to accept the array.

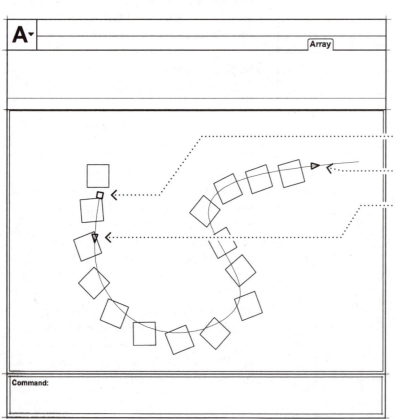

Adjusting a Path Array

- To adjust a Path Array, **CLICK ONCE** on any item in the array.
- The Move grip allows you to move all of the items in the array as a single object.
- The Item Count grip allows you to modify the number of items in the array.
- The Item Spacing grip allows you to modify the distance between each item in the array.

- **Ribbon Tip:** You can also modify the Item Spacing and Item Count parameters in the Array tab in the AutoCAD Ribbon. The Array tab is visible when you click on an associative array.

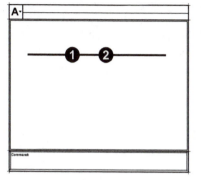
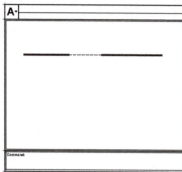

Break

The Break command splits a single line into two separate lines.

- Type the command **BREAK** and press **ENTER**.
- **Step 1: CLICK ONCE** on the line that you want to break. (This point will be one edge of the break in the line.)
- **Step 2: CLICK ONCE** on the line where you want the second edge of the break.

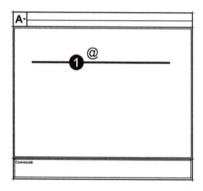
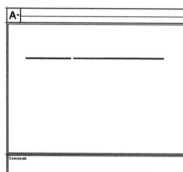

Alternate Break Method

You can break a line into two lines without introducing a gap between the lines.

- Type the command **BREAK** and press **ENTER**.
- **CLICK ONCE** on the line that you want to break.
- Instead of clicking for the second point of the break, type the character **@** and press **ENTER**.

- AutoCAD will break the line into two lines at the point where you first clicked on the line.

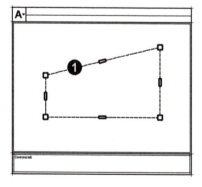
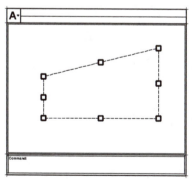

Explode

You can explode a rectangle or polyline into a series of lines. The Explode command will separate a set of lines into individual lines. This command should be used with caution.

- Type the command **EXPLODE** and press **ENTER**.
- **CLICK ONCE** on the polyline or rectangle that you want to explode.
- Press the **ENTER** key to complete the command.

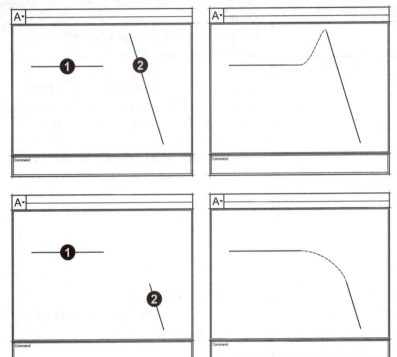

Blend

New to AutoCAD 2012, the blend tool creates smooth transitions between non-closed objects. For example, the blend tool can transition between two different lines or between a line and an arc.

- **TYPE** the command **BLEND** and press **ENTER**.
- **Step 1: CLICK ONCE** on the first line that you want to blend.
- **Step 2: CLICK ONCE** on the second line that you want to blend.
- The **BLEND** command automatically ends after you select the second line. You can **PRESS** the **SPACEBAR** or **ENTER** key to repeat the **BLEND** command on a second set of objects.

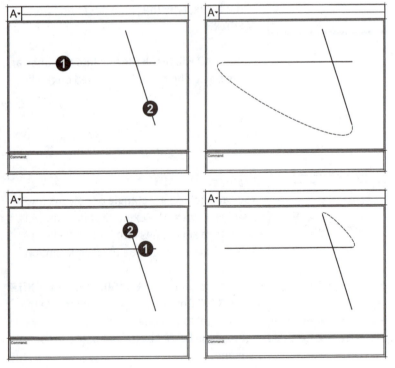

- The **BLEND** tool starts the blend from the endpoint closest to where you click on a line or arc.
- In the examples to the left, two different blends are created using the same initial lines.
- Notice the relationship between the click points on each and the location of the blend.

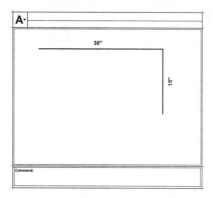

Learning Exercise

Using the commands discussed in this and previous chapters, draw and edit the sketches to the left. There are additional exercises available for download at http://fairchildbooks.com/books.cms?bookId=179

· Set your drawing units to architectural (feet and inches).
· Draw a horizontal line **30"** in length and a vertical line **15"** in length.

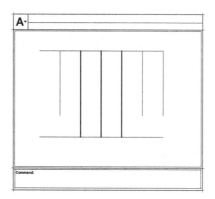

· **OFFSET** the vertical line in **5"** increments to the left.
· **OFFSET** the horizontal line **20"**.

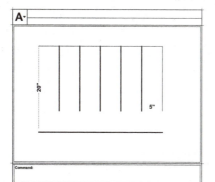

· **EXTEND** the three lines shown in the sketch to the left.

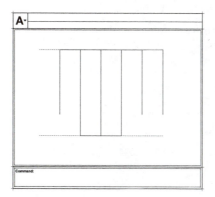

· **TRIM** the dashed lines shown in the sketch to the left.

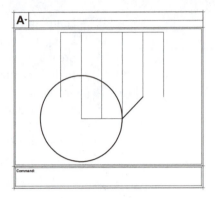

· Draw the **CIRCLE** and angled **LINE** using **OBJECT SNAPS**.

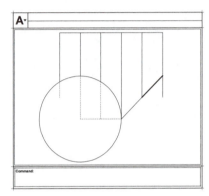

· **TRIM** the dashed lines shown in the sketch to the left.
· Extend the diagonal line to the left, as shown in the sketch.

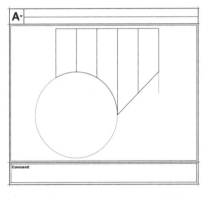

· **TRIM** the dashed line and circle shown in the sketch to the left.

Companion Download

The companion download contains several AutoCAD drawings that allow you to test your understanding of the drawing and editing commands discussed in this chapter.

Look inside the Learning Exercises folder for these files.

The following websites feature the companion download for this book: www.fairchildbooks.combook.cms?bookid=179 or www.DDFDbook.com/ch4

Design Drawings

CHAPTER 5
Organizing Plans, Sections, and Elevations

In the previous four chapters you were introduced to the technical tools you need to successfully complete drawings in AutoCAD. In this chapter we look at drawing fundamentals that will turn your AutoCAD drawings into design drawings. These skills include line weight, drawing presentation, and drawing organization.

Consider the following questions as you work through this chapter:
· How can layers help you organize your drawings?
· How can layers help you control line weight in your drawings?
· How are layers used differently in plan, section, and elevation drawings?

Line Weight

Clear and legible line weight will communicate your design better than any combination of AutoCAD commands. You have most likely been introduced to line weight in a manual drafting studio, conceptual drawing studio, or design studio. These drawing conventions existed long before AutoCAD. It is important to understand how to draw in AutoCAD using these conventions.

· When drafting by hand, you adjust line thickness by adjusting the type of lead in your pencil or by adjusting the pressure applied to the paper.
· In AutoCAD, you adjust line thickness by selecting different colors for different kinds of lines.

Red (Color 1)

Yellow (Color 2)

Green (Color 3)

Heavy Lines

· These lines are used to delineate objects (in plan or section) that are cut through.
· In AutoCAD use Red (Color 1), Yellow (Color 2), or Green (Color 3).

Cyan (Color 4)

Blue (Color 5)

Medium and Light Lines

· These lines are used to delineate a change in plane or a corner (in elevation).
· In a floor plan, these lines can represent furniture or casework.
· In AutoCAD use Cyan (Color 4) or Blue (Color 5).

Magenta (Color 6)

White (Color 7)

Light Lines

· These lines are used to delineate a change in color, material, or surface.
· In a floor plan, these lines can represent a transition from carpeting to wood flooring. In elevation, these lines can represent crown molding or trim around a door.
· In AutoCAD use Magenta (Color 6) or White (Color 7).

Dark Grey (Color 8)

Light Grey (Color 9)

Very Light Lines

· These lines are used to delineate surface texture or material patterns.
· In a floor plan, these lines can represent a wood or tile floor material.
· In AutoCAD use Dark Gray (Color 8) or Light Gray (Color 9).

HIDDEN2 (Color 5)

CENTER2 (Color 5)

Hidden and Center Line Types

· Hidden lines are used to delineate major objects that are above the floor cutting plane or objects that are hidden behind other objects in your drawing. In AutoCAD, use line type **HIDDEN2**.

· Center lines are used to delineate the centerline of objects like doors, windows, or building structure. In AutoCAD, use line type **CENTER2**.

Selecting Colors in AutoCAD

In AutoCAD, you adjust line thickness by selecting different colors for different kinds of lines. The Select Color dialog box is the primary place you will select colors in AutoCAD.

- AutoCAD recognizes 255 colors. Each of these colors is a potentially different line weight. As you have seen on the previous page, you will use only nine of these colors.

The AutoCAD Color Index is separated into sections.

- **COLOR 10** to **COLOR 249** are represented in this section. Disregard these colors when drawing in AutoCAD.

- **COLOR 1** to **COLOR 9** are represented in this section. From left to right, you can click on the desired color in this section to correspond to the different line weights on the previous page.

- **COLOR 250** to **COLOR 255** are represented in this section. These colors will produce various shades of gray when used with solid hatches.

- You can type the color name or number directly into the color input box. If you select a color by clicking directly on the color swatch, the color name will populate in this box.

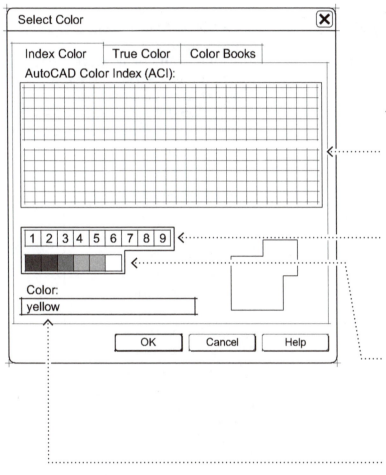

Hatch Solids

- **COLOR 250** through **COLOR 254** print as different values of gray and are used for solid poché.
- Poché (also refered to as Hatching in AutoCAD) is discussed in Chapter 8.

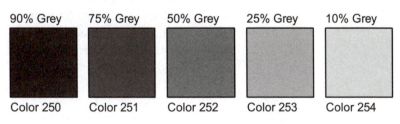

90% Grey	75% Grey	50% Grey	25% Grey	10% Grey
Color 250	Color 251	Color 252	Color 253	Color 254

Drawing with Layers

Layers serve three primary purposes in AutoCAD.

· **Line Weight** – Lines inherit their **COLOR** and **LINETYPE** from the layer on which they are drawn. By changing the color of the furniture layer, AutoCAD will automatically change the color of all the lines in this layer.

· **Organization** – Layers help categorize and organize lines based on what they represent in your drawings (e.g., doors, walls, etc.).

· **Visibility** – You can turn off layers to print different versions of your floor plan.

Layer Properties Manager

The Layer Properties Manager allows you to set up and modify all the layers in your drawing.

· Type the command **LAYER** and press **ENTER** to open the Layer Properties Manager.

· The **NEW LAYER** button creates a new layer in your drawing.

· The **DELETE LAYER** button will delete the currently selected layer. You cannot delete layers that have lines on them.

· The **SET CURRENT** button will set the selected layer to current. All new lines are drawn on the layer set to current.

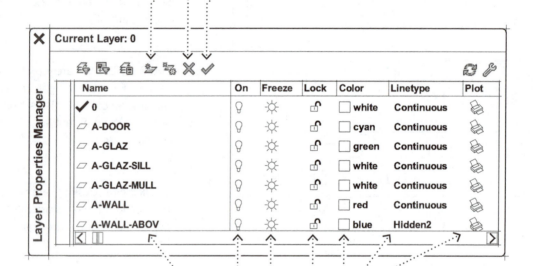

· **Name** – **CLICK ONCE** on the layer name to rename the layer.

· **On** – **CLICK ONCE** on the light bulb icon to turn the layer **ON** or **OFF**.

· **Freeze** – **CLICK ONCE** on the sunshine/ snowflake icon to **THAW** or **FREEZE** the layer. Objects on locked layers are not visible and cannot be modified.

· **Lock** – **CLICK ONCE** on the lock bulb icon to **LOCK** or **UNLOCK** the layer. Objects on locked layers are visible but cannot be modified.

· **Plot / No Plot** – **CLICK ONCE** on the printer icon to modify if the selected layer will print.

· **Line type** – **CLICK ONCE** on the line type to modify the line type for all objects on that layer.

· **Color** – **CLICK ONCE** on the color swatch to modify the color for all objects on that layer. Use Colors 1 through 9 for lines and Colors 250 through 254 for solid hatches.

Properties Panel

The **PROPERTIES PANEL** is located in the **HOME TAB** of the AutoCAD ribbon. This panel allows you to modify the properties for any object in AutoCAD (including line color and line type).

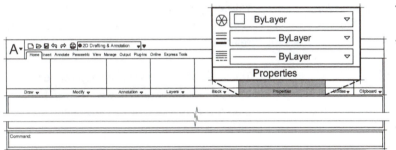

- Good AutoCAD drawings assign properties to layers, not individual objects (or lines).
- It may be tempting to change the color of lines in your drawing using the Properties panel. You will save time later in your project if you create and use layers to control the color of lines in your drawing.
- In your drawing, 99 percent of the objects should have ByLayer assignments for color and line type. (The term ByLayer means the objects get their color and line type from their layer.)

Layers Panel

The **LAYERS PANEL** is located in the **HOME TAB** of the AutoCAD ribbon. This panel allows you to move any object in AutoCAD to a specific layer.

Setting the Current Layer

The layer displayed in the Layers panel is the current layer. Any objects drawn in AutoCAD will be automatically placed on this layer.

- The current layer in this example is **A-WALL**.
- You can change the current layer by clicking the down arrow to the right of the current layer and selecting the desired layer.

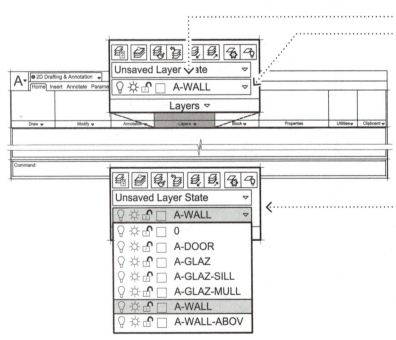

Changing an Object's Layers

It is easy to change an object to a new layer.

- Select a line (or any other object) in your drawing. The layer displayed in the Layers panel will change to the layer assigned to the line you selected.
- You can change the selected line's layer by clicking the down arrow to the right of the current layer and selecting the desired layer.
- Press the **ESCAPE** key twice to deselect the line and continue drawing.

Floor Plans

Floor plans are a horizontal section taken through a house or building. They are usually cut 3'–6' above the floor but may vary according to the project. This imaginary line is referred to as the cutting plane.

· This horizontal plane slices through walls, doors, windows, and columns. Below the slice, we see furniture, flooring material, countertops, and so on.

· When drawing a floor plan in AutoCAD, you will categorize lines based on what they represent in your drawing and based on their relative thickness.

· The scale of the drawing will determine the appropriate number of line weights. A floor plan drawn at 1/4" = 1'-0" only needs four different line weights.

· There may be different layers in your Auto-CAD drawing that have the same color. For example, the furniture layer and the counter-top layer may share the same color because you want them to print with the same line weight.

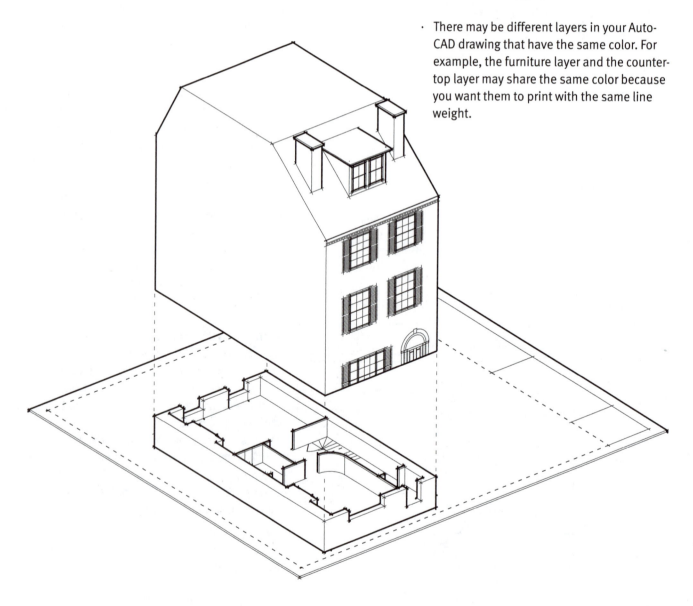

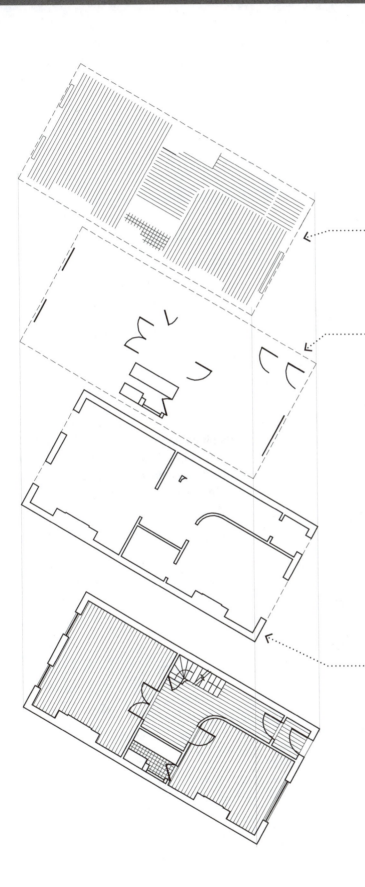

Typical Floor Plan Layers

The following represents typical floor plan layers and appropriate layer colors. Many offices set their own office standards for layer names and layer colors.

· Understanding the concepts illustrated below will allow you to adapt to any office environment.

Very Light Lines

· **A-Floor-Hatch:** Color 8 or Color 9.
These lines typically represent material patterns or scale of material. This should not visually distract from the overall drawing.

Medium Lines

· **A-Door:** Color 3 or Color 4.
The number of lines drawn is determined by the scale of the drawing. (Refer to page 62 for examples of doors drawn at different scales.)

· **A-Window:** Color 3 or Color 4.
The number of lines drawn is determined by the scale of the drawing. (Refer to page 63 for examples of windows drawn at different scales.)

· **A-Furn:** Color 5 or Color 6.
The abbreviation **FURN** is short for furniture.

· **A-Case:** Color 5 or Color 6.
The abbreviation **CASE** is short for casework. This layer can include cabinets and built-ins.

Heavy Lines

· **A-Wall:** Color 1 or Color 2.
Some designers prefer to draw interior and exterior walls with different line weights.
A-Wall-Intr: Color 2 (interior walls).
A-Wall-Extr: Color 1 (exterior walls).

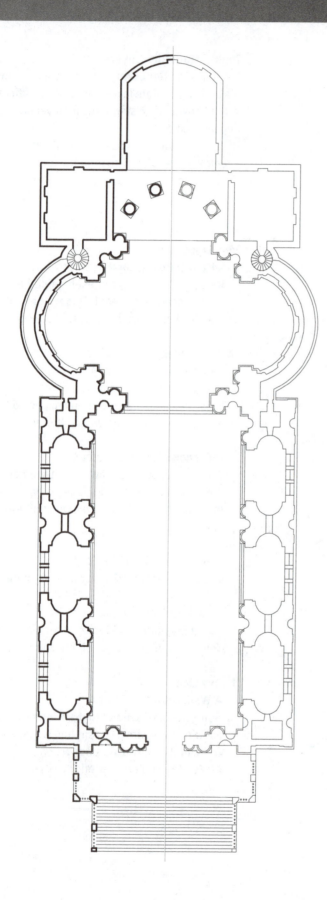

The Plan Cut and Line Weight
When drawing floor plans, you need to clearly identify the difference between solid mass (or walls) and void (or rooms).

· The right side of this floor plan was drawn with a single line weight and does not emphasize the horizontal section cut. In this drawing, it is difficult to identify space.

· The left side of this floor plan was drawn with a hierarchy of lines to convey the spatial properties of this church. In this drawing, the contrast between mass and void is clearer than in the previous drawing.

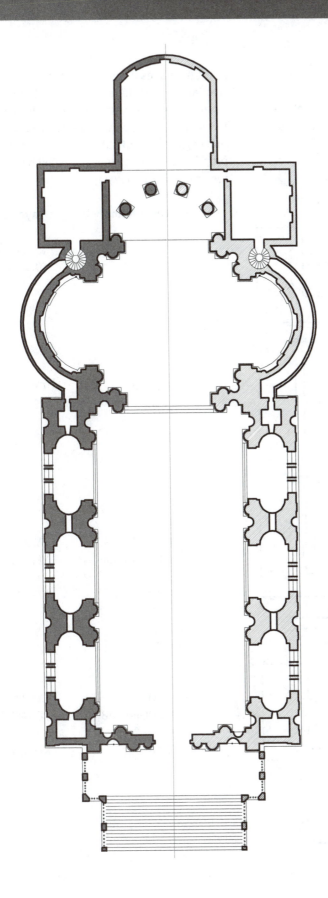

Poché

Solid tone can be added to a drawing to add contrast between the mass and the void. In AutoCAD you can add poché with the hatch command, which is discussed in Chapter 8.

· The left side of this floor plan uses a solid tone to communicate space by creating contrast between the walls and the space of this church. The tone in this drawing is a solid hatch pattern and is Color 252.

· The right side of this floor plan uses multiple angled lines to communicate space by creating contrast between the walls and the space of this church. The tone in this drawing is an ANSI31 hatch pattern with a scale of 45. The hatch layer is set to Color 9.

Il Redentore, Venice, Italy, begun 1576, Andrea Palladio
drawing by Kristine Mortensen.

Quantity Not Quality

When you draw by hand, the detail you include in your drawing is limited by the scale of the drawing. A 1/16"=1'-0" floor plan is too small for you to draw a doorjamb. However, a 1/2"=1'-0" enlargement of the same floor plan is large enough to show a doorjamb.

AutoCAD makes it easy to zoom in closer to the doorjamb and include precise detail without regard for the scale of the drawing. However, it is important to apply hand-drafting logic to drawings created in AutoCAD. Include the appropriate number of lines (or detail) based on the scale of your drawing.

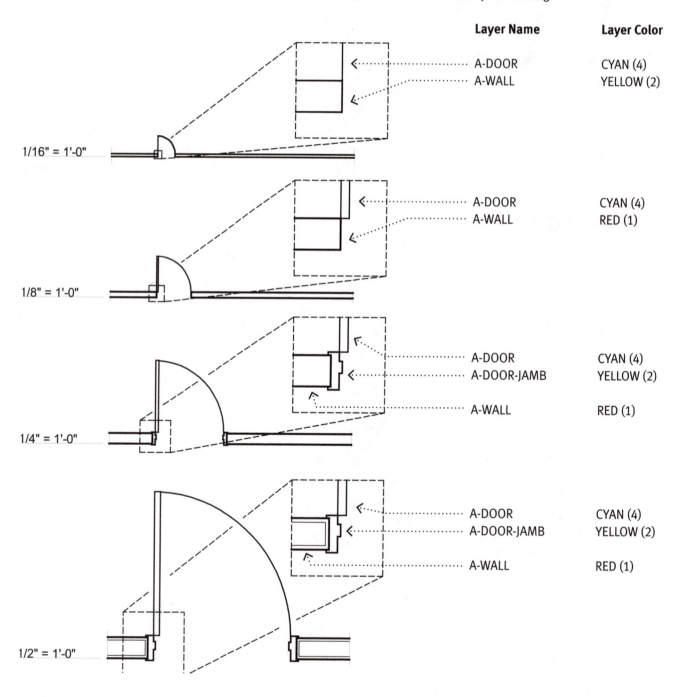

	Layer Name	Layer Color
1/16" = 1'-0"	A-DOOR	CYAN (4)
	A-WALL	YELLOW (2)
1/8" = 1'-0"	A-DOOR	CYAN (4)
	A-WALL	RED (1)
1/4" = 1'-0"	A-DOOR	CYAN (4)
	A-DOOR-JAMB	YELLOW (2)
	A-WALL	RED (1)
1/2" = 1'-0"	A-DOOR	CYAN (4)
	A-DOOR-JAMB	YELLOW (2)
	A-WALL	RED (1)

As stated, AutoCAD makes it easy to zoom in closer to the doorjamb and include precise detail without regard for the scale of the drawing. Care should be taken not to add too much detail that will clutter the drawing. Notice the extra information drawn in the larger scale plans.

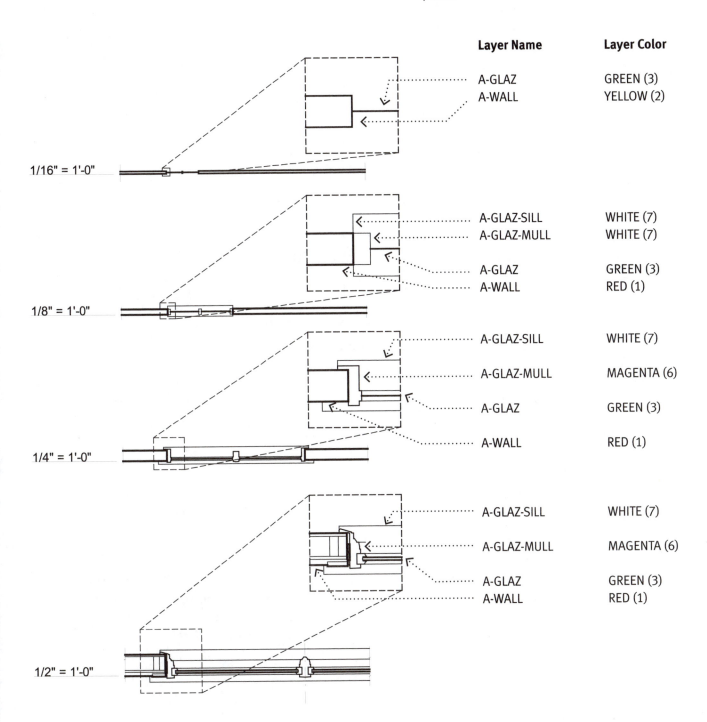

Layer Name	Layer Color
A-GLAZ	GREEN (3)
A-WALL	YELLOW (2)

1/16" = 1'-0"

Layer Name	Layer Color
A-GLAZ-SILL	WHITE (7)
A-GLAZ-MULL	WHITE (7)
A-GLAZ	GREEN (3)
A-WALL	RED (1)

1/8" = 1'-0"

A-GLAZ-SILL	WHITE (7)
A-GLAZ-MULL	MAGENTA (6)
A-GLAZ	GREEN (3)
A-WALL	RED (1)

1/4" = 1'-0"

A-GLAZ-SILL	WHITE (7)
A-GLAZ-MULL	MAGENTA (6)
A-GLAZ	GREEN (3)
A-WALL	RED (1)

1/2" = 1'-0"

Building Sections

Building sections are vertical slices through a house or building. They are usually cut through the entire building but may vary according to the project. This imaginary line is referred to as the cutting plane.

· This vertical plane slices through walls and windows. Building sections should not be cut through columns. Beyond the slice, we see wall openings, windows, doors, wall material, and so on.

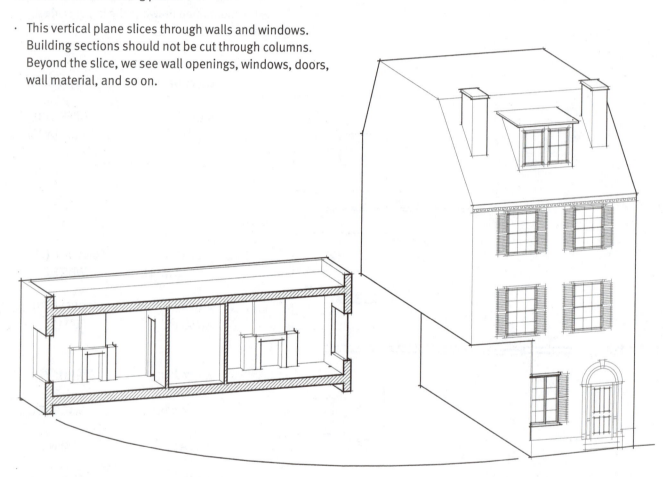

· When drawing a building section in Auto-CAD, you will categorize lines based on their relative thickness.

· The scale of the drawing will determine the appropriate number of line weights. A section drawn at 1/4"=1'-0" only needs four different line weights.

Typical Building Section Layers

The following represents typical section layers and appropriate layer colors. Many offices set their own office standards for layer names and layer colors.

· Understanding the concepts illustrated below will allow you to adapt to any office environment.

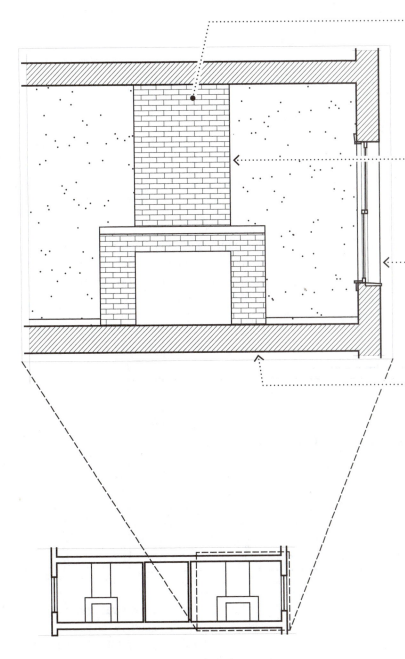

Very Light Lines

· **A-Sect-XLight:** Color 8 or Color 9.
These lines typically represent material patterns or scale of material. These lines should not visually distract from the overall drawing.

Light Lines

· **A-Sect-Light:** Color 6 or Color 7.
These lines typically represent a change in material on a wall or surface. This can include wood trim around a door or opening.

Medium Lines

· **A-Sect-Medium:** Color 4 or Color 5.
These lines are used to delineate a change in plane, a corner in elevation, or an opening in a wall. They are also referred to as profile lines.

Heavy Lines

· **A-Sect-Dark:** Color 1 or Color 2.
These lines are used to delineate objects that are being sliced through, including walls and windows.

· **A-Sect-Floor:** Color 1.
Some designers add a separate layer to draw the floor or ground in section. The ground layer should be as dark or darker than the darkest line in your drawing.

Section Cut and Line Weight

Just like the floor plan, when drawing sections you need to clearly identify the difference between solid mass (or walls) and void (or space).

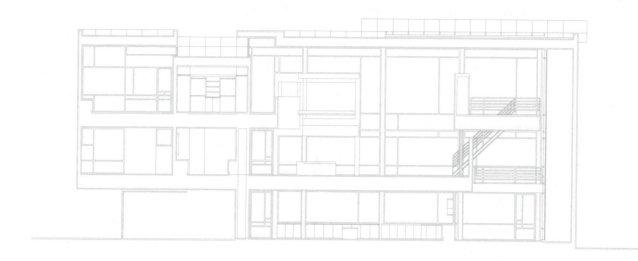

· The building section above was drawn with
a single line weight and does not emphasize
the section cut. In this drawing it is difficult
to identify space.

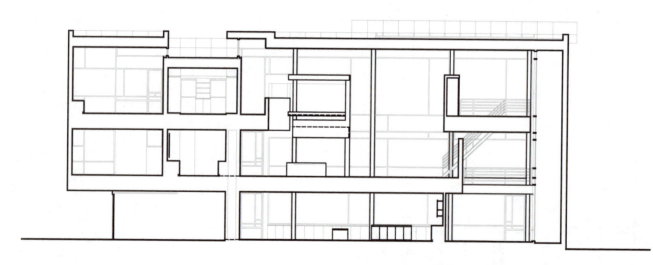

Rachofsky House, Dallas, TX, 1991–96, Richard Meier
drawing by Lori Anderson Wier. Reprinted with permission
of Richard Meier & Partners Architects LLP.

· The building section above was drawn with
a hierarchy of lines to convey the spatial
properties of this house. In this drawing, the
contrast between mass and void is clearer
than in the previous drawing.

Poché

Solid tone can be added to a drawing to show contrast between the mass and the void. In AutoCAD you can add poché with the Hatch command, which is discussed in Chapter 8.

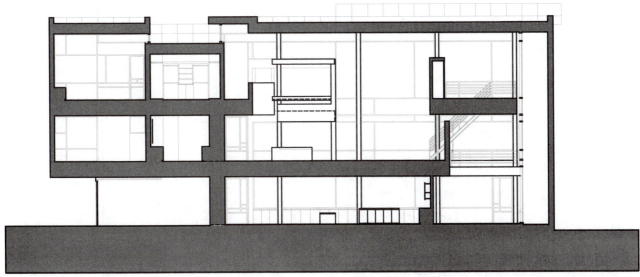

· The building section above uses a solid tone to communicate the space inside this home. The tone in this drawing is a solid hatch pattern and is Color 252.

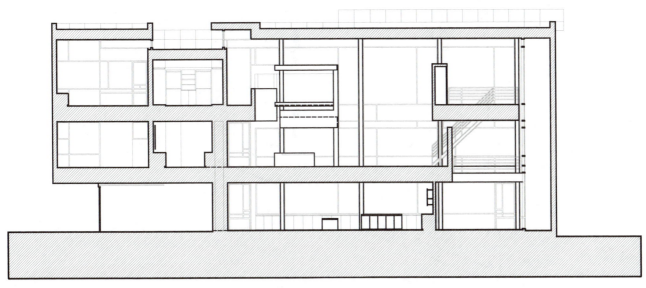

· The building section above uses multiple angled lines to communicate the space inside this home. The tone in this drawing is an ANSI31 hatch pattern with a scale of 45. The hatch layer is set to Color 9.

Building Elevations and Interior Elevations

Unlike sections, elevations do not require that we cut through the building or house. Elevations are two-dimensional drawings that describe what surfaces will look like after the project is built.

- Interior elevations usually describe a single wall in a room
  (Preferred scale: 1/4"=1'-0").
- Exterior (or Building) Elevations usually describe a single side of the building
  (Preferred scale: 1/4"=1'-0" or 1/8" = 1'-0").

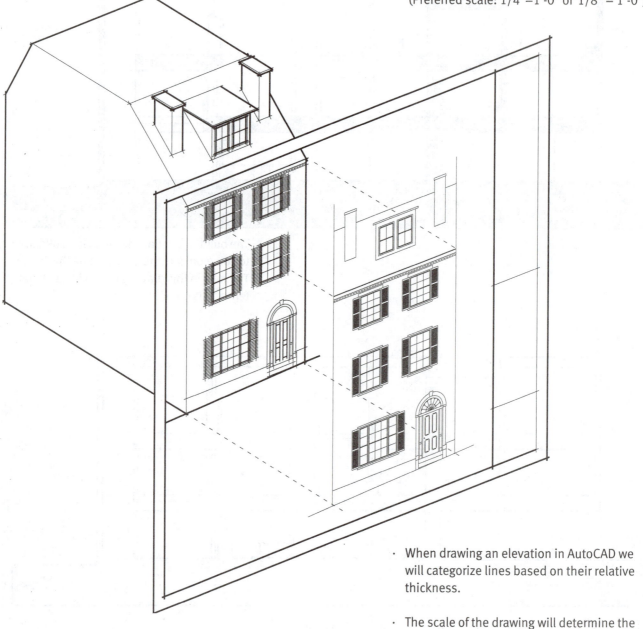

- When drawing an elevation in AutoCAD we will categorize lines based on their relative thickness.

- The scale of the drawing will determine the appropriate number of line weights. An elevation drawn at 1/4" = 1'-0" only needs four distinct line weights.

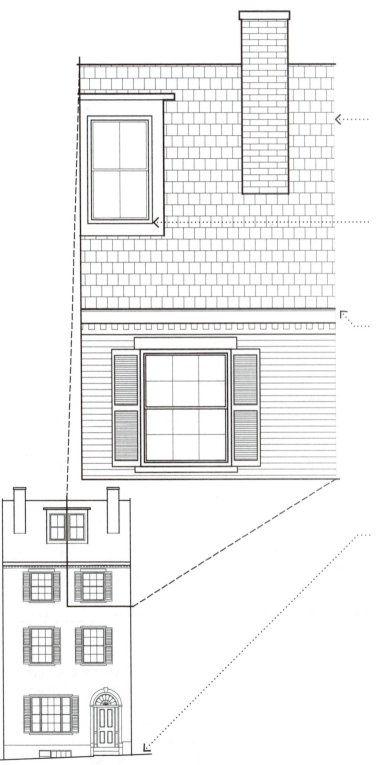

Typical Elevation Layers

The following represents typical elevation layers and appropriate layer colors. Many offices set their own office standards for layer names and layer colors.

· Understanding the concepts illustrated below will allow you to adapt to any office environment.

Very Light Lines

· **A-Elev-XLight:** Color 8 or Color 9.
These lines typically represent material patterns or scale of material. These lines should not visually distract the overall drawing.

Light Lines

· **A-Elev-Light:** Color 6 or Color 7.
These lines typically represent a change in material on a wall or surface. This can include wood trim around a door or opening.

Medium Lines

· **A-Elev-Medium:** Color 4 or Color 5.
These lines are used to delineate a change in plane, a corner in elevation, or an opening in a wall. They are also referred to as profile lines.

Heavy Lines

· **A-Elev-Dark:** Color 1 or Color 2.
These lines are used to delineate the perimeter of the elevation.

· **A-Elev-Floor:** Color 1.
Some designers add a separate layer to draw the floor or ground in their elevations. The ground layer should be as dark as or darker than the darkest line in your drawing.

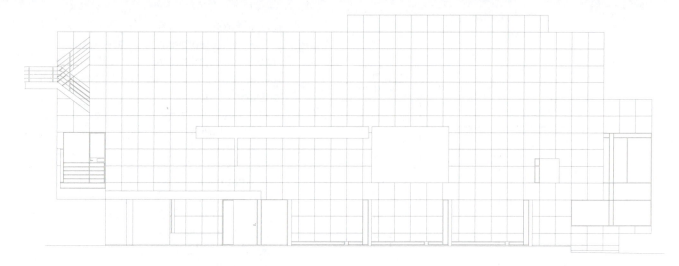

Elevation Line Weight

When drawing elevations you need to clearly indicate the difference between lines that identify a change in plane and lines that identify a change in surface material.

· This elevation was drawn with just a couple of line weights and does not emphasize the edges of surfaces. In this drawing, it is difficult to identify depth.

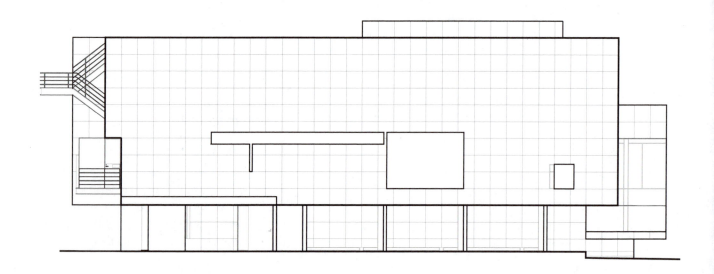

East Elevation, Rachofsky House, Dallas, TX, 1991–96, Richard Meier drawing by Cheri Kotsiopoulos. Reprinted with permission of Richard Meier & Partners Architects LLP.

· This elevation was drawn with a hierarchy of lines to convey the depth of this house elevation. In this drawing, the contrast between the edges of surfaces and lines that define a change in surface material is clearer than in the previous drawing.

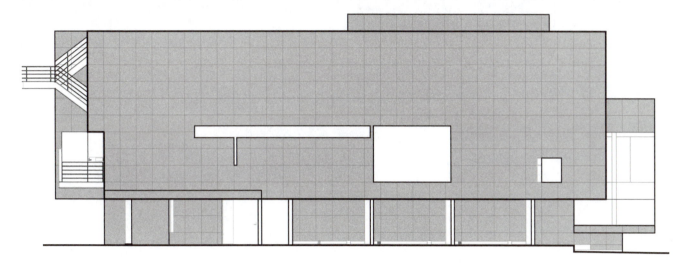

Poché

Solid tone can be added to an elevation to add contrast between the mass and the void or to communicate material. In AutoCAD you can add poché with the Hatch command, which is discussed in Chapter 8.

· This elevation uses a solid tone to communicate material by creating contrast between the walls and the windows of this house. The tone in this drawing is a solid hatch pattern and is Color 253.

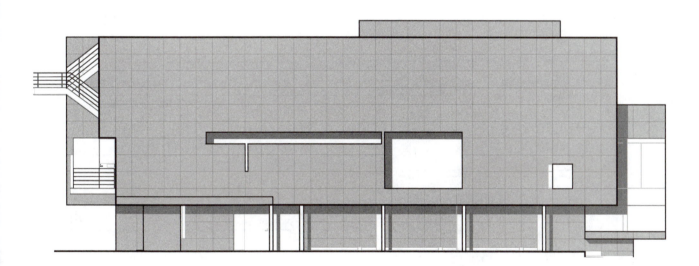

· In addition to the tone used in the elevation at the top of this page, this elevation further communicates depth by adding shadow with a solid tone. The shadow tone in this drawing is a solid hatch pattern and is Color 252.

The Interior Elevation/Section and Line Weight

Often, you will use a section/interior elevation to identify both interior finishes and spatial relationship in a design project. Just like the floor plan, you need to clearly identify the difference between solid mass (or walls) and void (or space).

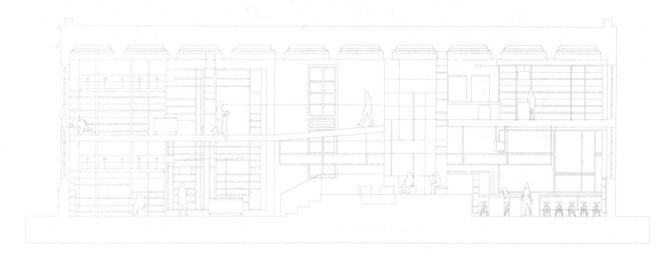

· The section/elevation above was drawn with a single line weight and does not emphasize the section cut or the depth of interior space. In this drawing it is difficult to identify space.

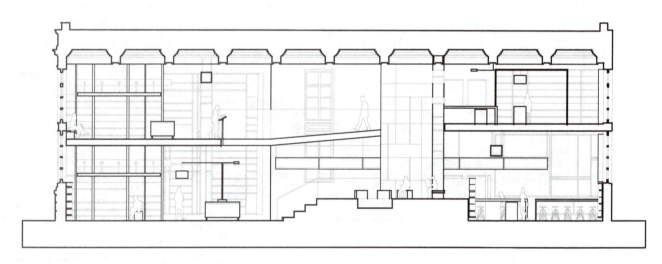

Interior Elevation, Master's Thesis Project, 2006, Lori Anderson Wier, New England School of Art and Design at Suffolk University.

· The section/elevation above was drawn with a hierarchy of lines to convey the spatial properties of this design. In this drawing, the contrast between mass, void, and spatial depth is clearer than in the previous drawing.

Poché

Solid tone can be added to a drawing to show contrast between the mass and the void. In AutoCAD you can add poché with the Hatch command, which is discussed in Chapter 8.

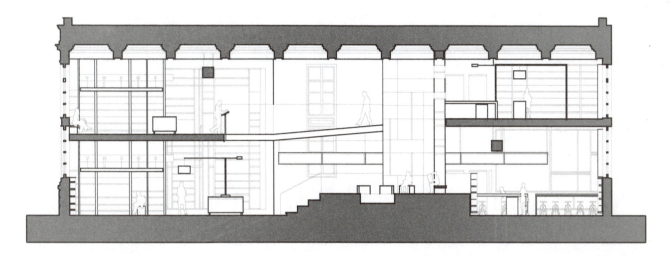

· The section/elevation above uses a solid tone to communicate the space inside this design. The tone in this drawing is a solid hatch pattern and is Color 252.

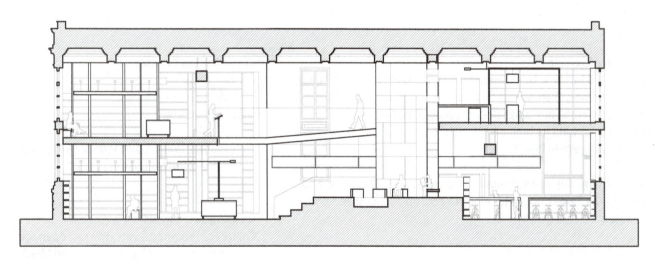

· The building section above uses multiple angled lines to communicate the space inside this design. The tone in this drawing is an ANSI31 hatch pattern and is Color 9.

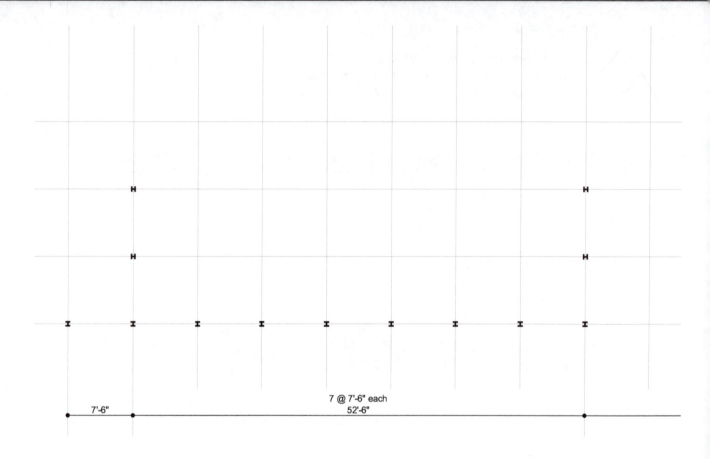

7 @ 7'-6" each
52'-6"

7'-6"

Learning Exercise

Completed in 1949, the Eames House represents one of 25 "Case Study" homes. The Case Study House Program, commissioned by *Arts and Architecture* magazine, challenged architects to design homes that could be built and furnished with building technologies used during World War II.

At the end of this and subsequent chapters, you will complete portions of the Eames House to reinforce concepts discussed during the chapter.

Creating Your Drawing

· Open AutoCAD.
· Save the new drawing as **DDFD-EAMES.DWG**

· Set your drawing's **UNIT LENGTH** to **ARCHITECTURAL** and **UNIT PRECISION** to **1/32"**.

Creating Your Layers

Create the following layers. You can open the layer manager by typing the command **LAYER** and pressing **ENTER**.

· **S-GRID**   Color 9
· **S-COL**   Color 3
· Set the current layer to **S-GRID**

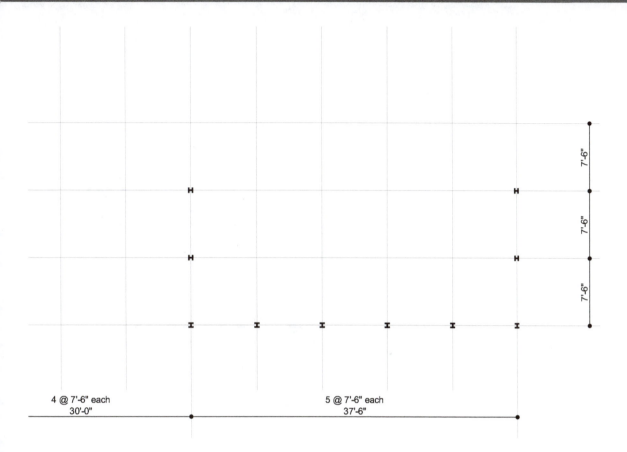

4 @ 7'-6" each
30'-0"

5 @ 7'-6" each
37'-6"

7'-6"

7'-6"

7'-6"

Drawing the Structural Grid

· Draw a horizontal line **140'-0"** in length.

· Offset this horizontal line two times by **7'-6"**.

· Draw a vertical line **36'-0"** in height.

· Use the **OFFSET** or **ARRAY** command to create the remaining vertical lines.

Drawing the Columns

· The structural columns in this house are 5"×5" w-flanges (I beams).
· Set the current layer to **S-COL**
· Draw a 5"×5" square. If you used the rectangle command, explode the rectangle.
· Erase the left and right side of the square and draw a vertical line between the midpoints of the top and bottom edge.

· Use the copy, rotate, and move commands to position the columns to match the drawing above.

· Save your drawing.

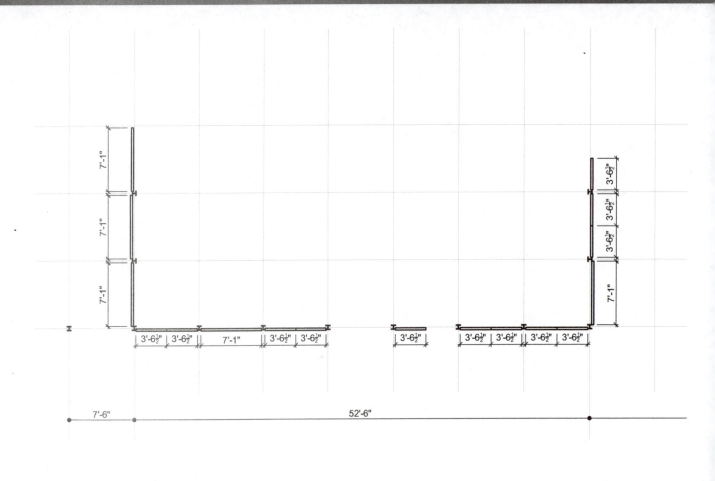

Creating Your Layers

Create the following layers.

· **A-GLAZ**   Color 4
· Set the current layer to **A-GLAZ**

Drawing the Exterior Window Panels

· Draw a rectangle **3'–6-1/2"** wide × **3"** thick.

· Draw a second rectangle **7'–1"** wide × **3"** thick.

· Use the copy, rotate, and move commands to position the windows to match the drawing above.

· Save your drawing.

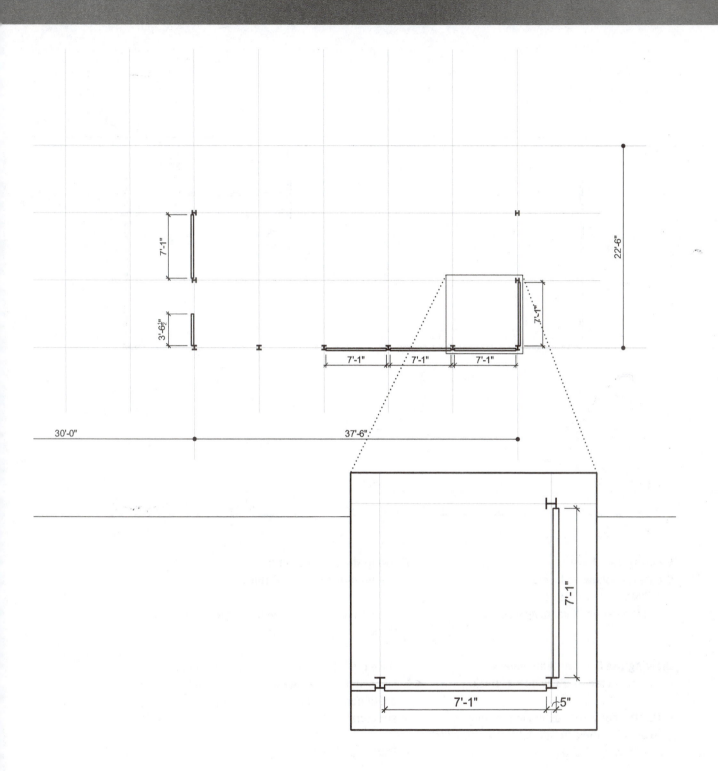

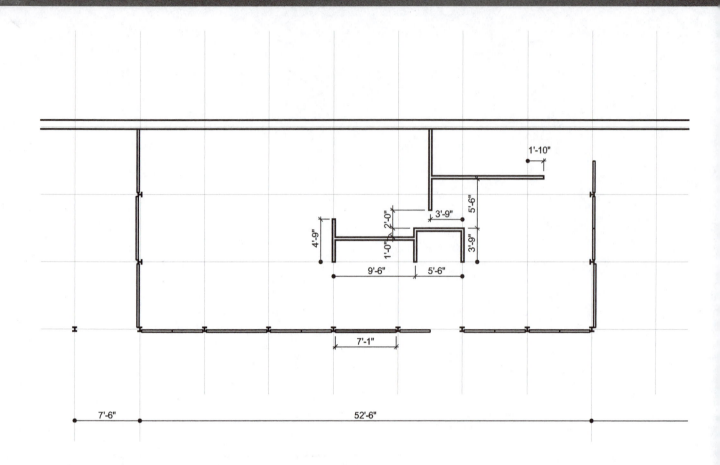

Creating Your Layers

Create the following layers.

- **A-WALL**   Color 1
- Set the current layer to **A-WALL**

Drawing the Exterior Wall Panels

- Draw a rectangle **7'1"** wide × **3"** thick.

- Use the copy, rotate, and move commands to position the exterior wall panels to match the drawing above.

Drawing the Interior Walls

- The interior walls are 4" thick.

- The retaining wall (top wall in drawing) is 12" thick.

- Draw the interior walls to match the dimensions in the drawing above. Interior walls are dimensioned from or centered on the structural grid.

- Save your drawing.

Congratulations, you have completed the learning exercise for this chapter.

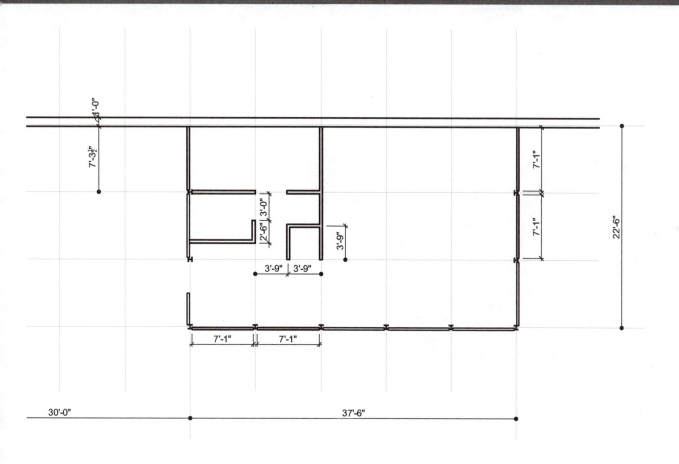

Companion Download

The companion download contains additional AutoCAD drawings that allow you to test your understanding of using layers in AutoCAD.

Look inside the Learning Exercises folder for these files.

You may also want to review the drawings located in the Sample Drawings folder to see how professionals draw in AutoCAD.

The following websites feature the companion download for this book: www.fairchildbooks.combook.cms?bookid=179 or www.DDFDbook.com/ch5

CHAPTER 6
Drawing and Printing to Scale

This chapter discusses the process of printing your digital drawing. In AutoCAD, you create and save a separate layout for each sheet that you need to print. This allows you to quickly print your drawings in the future and at a moment's notice.

The concepts discussed in this chapter are the most challenging AutoCAD concepts. The best way to master these concepts (like most things in life) is through practice, trial, and error. When you draw by hand, you know the scale of your drawing before you begin drawing. You use an architectural scale to reduce the drawing proportionally to fit on the sheet of paper.

In AutoCAD you draw everything at full scale or real world scale. The advantage to this new method of working is that you can complete a drawing and then determine what size paper and what scale you want to print your drawing. The disadvantage for new learners is that it can be frustrating to struggle with printing when you know how easy it would be to complete the same drawing by hand.

Consider the following questions as you work through this chapter:
· What do you need to know about a manual drawing before you start to draw?
· What do you need to know about your digital drawing before you set up a layout?

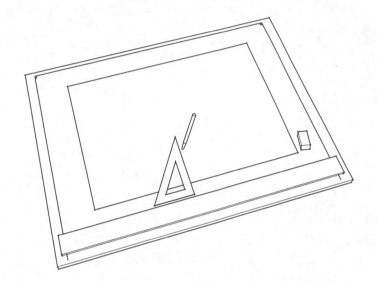

· When drawing by hand you use an architectural scale to draw a reduced drawing at a measurable size.
(Like 1/8"=1'-0")
· When drawing in AutoCAD you draw at real world size (full scale) and AutoCAD will reduce it to the appropriate scale.

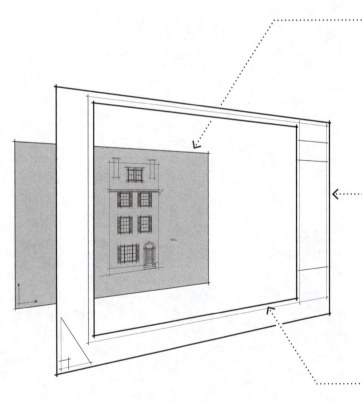

Paper Space versus Model Space

AutoCAD has two different areas that you will use to create scaled drawings.

Model Space

· **MODEL SPACE** (or the Model tab) is the place in AutoCAD where we draft 95 percent of our lines.
· While in Model Space, you draft at true world scale. True world scale means if you are drafting a room that is 30'-6" wide by 20'-0" deep in Model Space you will draft your lines 30'-6" wide by 20'-0" deep.

Paper Space / Layout View

· The **LAYOUT VIEW** (Layout1, Layout2, and Layout3 tabs) is the place in AutoCAD where you set up the sheets you are going to print or plot.
· Anything that you draft in your Layout View will print the same size as you drafted it. Therefore, if you add 1/8" tall text to your layout view, this text will measure 1/8" tall on your printed sheet.

Viewport

· The opening (or window) you see in the Layout View is called a **VIEWPORT**. Viewports allow you to see through your Layout View to the project you drafted in Model Space.

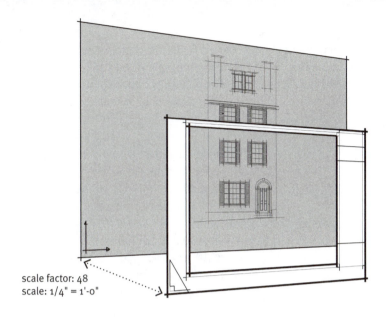

scale factor: 48
scale: 1/4" = 1'-0"

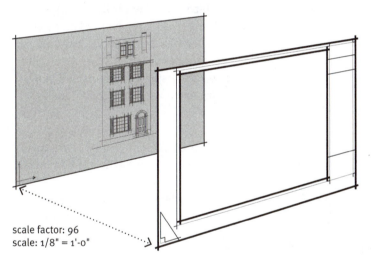

scale factor: 96
scale: 1/8" = 1'-0"

AutoCAD Scale Factors

The Scale Factor concept is unique to AutoCAD. In this diagram, the Scale Factor represents the distance between Model Space and the layout view. If you move Model Space farther back, then the drawing in your layout view will get smaller. If you move Model Space closer, then the drawing in your layout view will get larger.

· For a drawing/viewport to be scaled 1/4" = 1'-0", the scale factor is **48.**
· For a drawing/viewport to be scaled 1/8" = 1'-0", the scale factor is **96.**

· As you increase the scale factor, you are increasing the distance between Model Space and Paper Space which decreases the printed size of your drawing.

The following is a list of drawing scales and their AutoCAD scale factors:

Drawing Scale	Scale Factor
3"=1'-0"	4
1 1/2"=1'-0"	8
1"=1'-0"	12
3/4"=1'-0"	16
1/2"=1'-0"	24
3/8"=1'-0"	32
1/4"=1'-0"	48
3/16"=1'-0"	64
1/8"=1'-0"	96
3/32"=1'-0"	128
1/16"=1'-0"	192
1/32=1'-0"	384

Plot Styles

When you print a drawing, AutoCAD uses line color to determine the line weight it sends to the printer. The plot style (CTB file) is the file where you set the relationship between line color and line weight. For example, the CTB file tells AutoCAD to pring red lines .0210" thick.

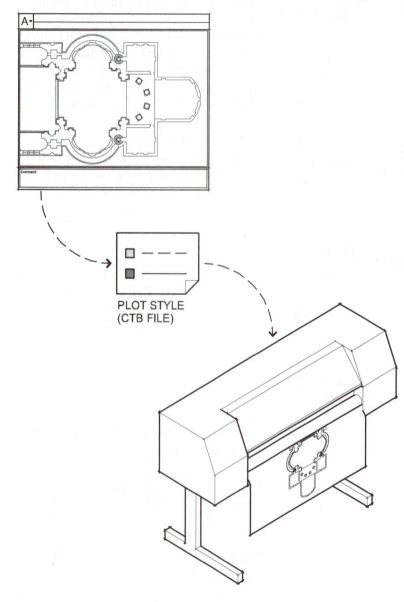

PLOT STYLE
(CTB FILE)

· There is no national (or international) standard for line weights and colors.
· This book uses a custom plot style (DDFD-Full.ctb) that can be installed on any computer.

· Because the plot style is installed on the computer and not saved with your drawing, you should take this file with you if you are plotting on a new computer.

· It is easy to add additional plot styles to AutoCAD when you need to print drawings created with a different color standard than you use for your projects.

Color Dependent Versus Named Plot Style

There are two different types of plot styles in AutoCAD. While this book will focus on using the color dependent plot style, it is important that you understand what a named plot style is and how to convert it to a color dependent plot style.

· Each AutoCAD drawing can be set up for either a CTB file or an STB file but not both.

Color Dependent Plot Style (CTB file)

· This plot style determines line thickness based solely on the color of the line in your drawing.
. CTB files are the easiest to implement and the most commonly used in offices.

Named Plot Styles (STB)

· Recent versions of AutoCAD have included a new method to plot called **NAMED PLOT STYLES**.
· This plot style determines line thickness based on the layer that the line is drawn on. For example, a line on the door layer will print a specified thickness regardless of its color.
· Because this new method is not widely adopted in the profession, this book will only discuss **COLOR DEPENDENT PLOT STYLE (CTB)**.

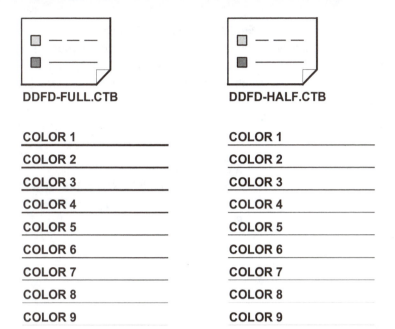

DDFD-FULL.CTB

| COLOR 1 |
| COLOR 2 |
| COLOR 3 |
| COLOR 4 |
| COLOR 5 |
| COLOR 6 |
| COLOR 7 |
| COLOR 8 |
| COLOR 9 |

DDFD-HALF.CTB

| COLOR 1 |
| COLOR 2 |
| COLOR 3 |
| COLOR 4 |
| COLOR 5 |
| COLOR 6 |
| COLOR 7 |
| COLOR 8 |
| COLOR 9 |

CTB Files

There are two different versions of the CTB file that are compatible with the line colors described in this book.

· **DDFD-FULL.CTB** is used to print 95 percent of your drawings and will print the line weight at full thickness.

· **DDFD-HALF.CTB** reduces each line weight by 50 percent and is useful when printing a reduced drawing at 11"×17" or 8.5"×11".

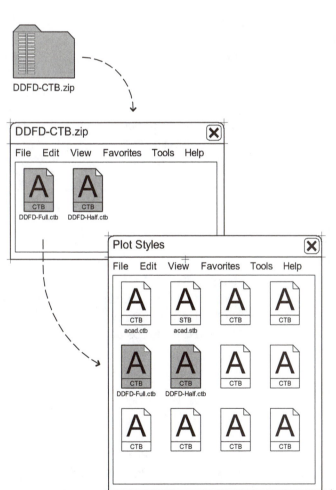

DDFD-CTB.zip

Installing a New CTB File

· Download this book's **CTB** files from our web site: www.DDFDbook.com/ctb

· Double click on the file you downloaded (DDFD-CTB.zip). This opens the zipped folder which contains this book's CTB files.

· Open AutoCAD.
· Type the command **STYLESMANAGER** and press **ENTER.** This command will open the location on your computer where AutoCAD stores (and looks for) plot styles.

· Copy DDFD-Full.ctb and DDFD-Half.ctb from the **ZIPPED FOLDER** to the **PLOT STYLES FOLDER** on your computer.
· Close and open AutoCAD

Drawing Templates

The companion download for this textbook contains multiple drawing templates. Download these drawing templates at: www.DDFDbook.com/ch6

Selecting a Drawing Template

Select the template that matches your sheet size and architectural scale. Each template is named to help you identify its sheet size and architectural scale.

- · AutoCAD version compatability
- · Sheet size
- · Architectural scale (1/4"=1'-0")
- · Sheet orientation (**PORTRAIT** or **LANDSCAPE**) or sheet type (**CDS** for construction drawings or **PRESENTATION**).

DDFD2010 11X17 - 1-4 INCH - PORTRAIT

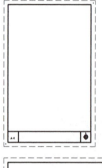

11"×17" templates

- · DDFD2010 11x17 - 1-2 Inch - Portrait.dwt
- · DDFD2010 11x17 - 1-4 Inch - Portrait.dwt
- · DDFD2010 11x17 - 1-8 Inch - Portrait.dwt

- · DDFD2010 11x17 - 1-2 Inch - Landscape.dwt
- · DDFD2010 11x17 - 1-4 Inch - Landscape.dwt
- · DDFD2010 11x17 - 1-8 Inch - Landscape.dwt

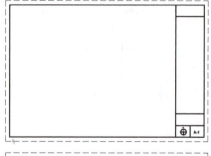

24"×36" templates

- · DDFD2010 24x36 - 1-2 Inch - CDs.dwt
- · DDFD2010 24x36 - 1-4 Inch - CDs.dwt
- · DDFD2010 24x36 - 1-8 Inch - CDs.dwt

- · DDFD2010 24x36 - 1-2 Inch - Presentation.dwt
- · DDFD2010 24x36 - 1-4 Inch - Presentation.dwt
- · DDFD2010 24x36 - 1-8 Inch - Presentation.dwt

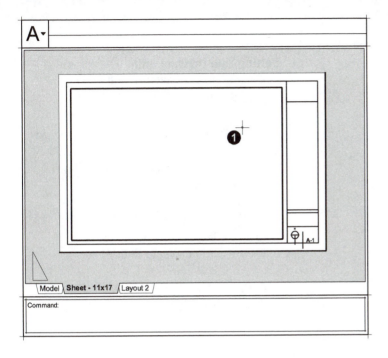

Drawing to Scale in the Layout Tab

Now that you have selected and opened a drawing template you can draw in either the **MODEL TAB** or the **LAYOUT TAB**.

· Drawing in the **LAYOUT TAB** (inside the activated viewport) is easier for some designers that are new to AutoCAD because it closely resembles drawing on a drafting table.

· To start your drawing, **DOUBLE CLICK** inside the viewport (step 1).
· Draw lines at real world scale and AutoCAD will automatically scale them based on the architectural scale of your template.

Drawing to Scale in the Model Space

· Your drawing exists in both the **LAYOUT TAB** and the **MODEL TAB**.
· After you are comfortable drawing inside the viewport, click the **MODEL TAB** to see how your drawing looks in model space.

· If you do not see your drawing when you switch to model space, type **ZOOM** and press **ENTER** the type the letter **E** and press **ENTER**.

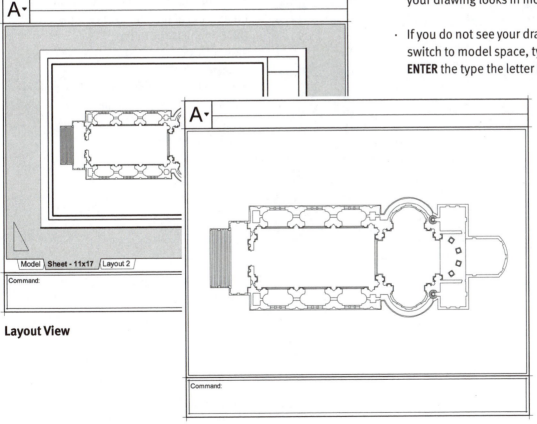

Layout View

Model Space View

Creating Custom Layouts in AutoCAD

The following guide will take you through the process of setting up a custom layout in AutoCAD.

Setting Your Drawing Units

· Set your **UNITS** to **ARCHITECTURAL** and your precision to **1/32"**.

Creating Your Layers

Create the following layers. You can open the layer manager by typing the command **LAYER** and pressing **ENTER**.

· **TB-BORDER**   Color 1
· **TB-TEXT**   Color 4
· **TB-VIEWPORT**   Color 31, NoPlot
· Set the current layer to **TB-BORDER**.

· The TB prefix in these layer names is an abbreviation for Title Block.

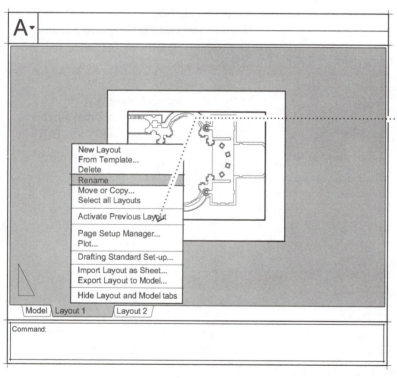

Creating Your First Layout

· The **MODEL** and **LAYOUT** tabs are located at the bottom of the AutoCAD window. **CLICK ONCE** on the **LAYOUT 1** tab.
· **RIGHT CLICK** on the **LAYOUT 1** tab and select **RENAME**.
· Rename the layout to match the size of the drawing sheet you would like to set up. For example, you could rename the layout to **SHEET – 11×17** and click **OK**.

Standard Paper Sizes

When you start a hand drawing you need to know what size paper you are going to use. When you set up a digital drawing for printing, you need to know what paper sizes are available.

· This chapter has several guides to set up different size title blocks. Refer to the charts on this page to determine your sheet size and where each guide starts in this chapter.

Standard Paper Sizes

The following paper sizes are available for most laser and ink jet printers.

· ANSI A/Letter	8½" × 11"	(see tabloid setup, page 90)
· Legal	8½" × 14"	(see tabloid setup, page 90)
· ANSI B/Tabloid	11" × 17"	page 90

Small Format Printers

· Most ink jet and laser printers will print Letter and Legal size paper. Some will also print Tabloid (11" × 17") paper.

Large Format Paper Sizes

The following paper sizes are available for most large format printers and plotters.

· ANSI B/Tabloid	11" × 17"	page 90
· ANSI C	17" × 22"	
· ANSI D	22" × 34"	
· ANSI E	34" × 44"	
· ARCH C	18" × 24"	page 92
· ARCH D	24" × 36"	page 94
· ARCH E	36" × 48"	
· ARCH E1	30" × 42"	

Large Format Printers

· Large format printers (plotters) print a variety of sizes. All allow you to load individual sheets of paper. Some allow you to load a roll of paper.

· When printing to a large format printer, it is important to identify the width of the printer. If the printer is 24" wide then the largest paper you can print on is restricted to a maximum of 24" in one direction. For example, with a 24" roll of paper you can print 18" × 24" and 24" × 36" but not 30" × 42".

11" × 17" – Setting Up a Tabloid-Sized Sheet

This sheet size is most commonly used for construction administration sketches or smaller residential projects. The tabloid and portrait layout both have a 0.5" margin which is compatible with most laser and inkjet printers.

11" x 17" Sheet with .5" margin

Portrait Layout

· Set the current layer to **TB-BORDER**.

· Using the **RECTANGLE** command, draw a rectangle that is **11"** wide and **17"** tall. This rectangle will most likely extend into the grey area of the layout. You will adjust this on the next page when you select the page size for your drawing.

· **OFFSET** the rectangle **0.5"** to the inside. This new rectangle represents the margins required by your printer. (With most printers, you cannot print to the edge of the paper.)

· **ERASE** the first **RECTANGLE**. (You do not need this rectangle anymore.)

· Complete your title sheet so it matches the image to the left.

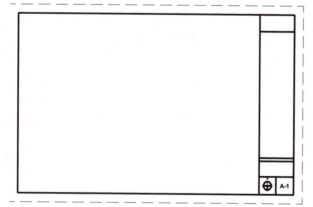

11" x 17" Sheet with .5" margin

Landscape Layout

· Set the current layer to **TB-BORDER**.

· Using the rectangle command, draw a **RECTANGLE** that is **17"** wide and **11"** tall. This rectangle will most likely extend into the grey area of the layout. You will adjust this on the next page when you select the page size for your drawing.

· **OFFSET** the rectangle **0.5"** to the inside. This new rectangle represents the margins required by your printer. (With most printers, you cannot print to the edge of the paper.)

· **ERASE** the first **RECTANGLE**. (You do not need this rectangle anymore.)

· Complete your title sheet so it matches the image to the left.

PAGE SETUP MANAGER/ANSI B

Set Up Your Page to Print

The **PAGE SETUP MANAGER** allows you to specify page layout and plotting device settings for each layout in your drawing. The page setup settings that you specify are stored within the layout, making it easy for you to print.

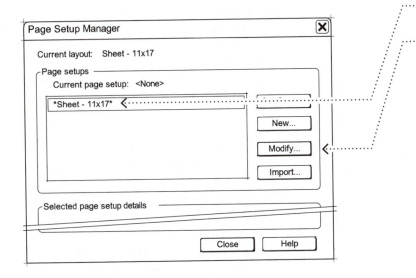

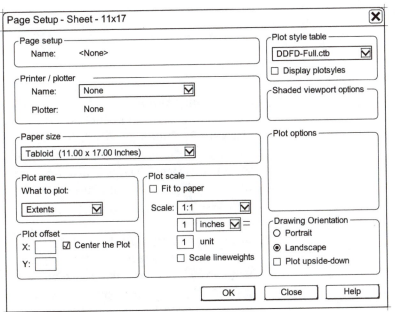

- Type **PAGESETUP** and press **ENTER** to open the page setup manager.
- **CLICK ONCE** on ***SHEET – 11×17*** (your sheet may have a different name).
- Click the **MODIFY** button.

Follow the steps below to complete the setup for your layout.

Printer / Plotter
- Select the printer you want use for this drawing. Printers installed on your computer are available for selection.

Paper Size
- This selection box will show paper sizes that are available for the printer you selected. Select **TABLOID** or **ANSI B**.

Plot Area
- This selection box allows you to customize what you want AutoCAD to print. Select **EXTENTS**.

Plot Offsets
- Place a checkmark in the **CENTER THE PLOT** box.

Plot Scale
- Uncheck **FIT TO PAPER**. (If you do check this option, you will prevent your drawing from printing to scale.)
- Select **1:1** from the drop-down list.

Plot Style Table (Pen Assignments)
- Select **DDFD-FULL.CTB**.

Drawing Orientation
- Select **LANDSCAPE** or **PORTRAIT** to match the orientation of your sheet.

- **CLICK ONCE** the **OK** button to close the page setup dialog box.
- **CLICK ONCE** the **CLOSE** button to close the page setup manager dialog box.

- Finish setting up your viewport on page 96.

18" × 24" – Setting Up an ARCH C-Sized Sheet

This sheet size is most commonly used for presentation drawings and construction documents. Most large format printers can print a 24" wide piece of paper and require a 0.75" margin.

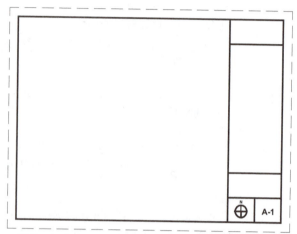

18" x 24" Construction Document Sheet with .75" margin

Construction Document Layout
- Set the current layer to **TB-BORDER**.
- Using the **RECTANGLE** command, draw a rectangle that is **24"** wide and **18"** tall. This rectangle will most likely extend into the grey area of the layout. You will adjust this on the next page when you select the page size for your drawing.
- **OFFSET** the rectangle **0.75"** to the inside. This new rectangle represents the margins required by your printer. (With most printers, you cannot print to the edge of the paper.)
- **ERASE** the first rectangle. (You do not need this rectangle anymore.)
- Complete your title sheet so it matches the image to the left, using lines, circles, and text.

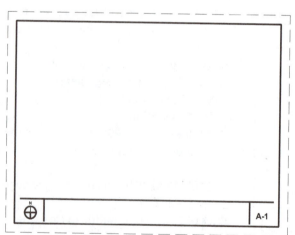

18" x 24" Presentation Drawing Sheet with .75" margin

Design Drawing Layout
- Set the current layer to **TB-BORDER**.
- Using the **RECTANGLE** command, draw a rectangle that is **24"** wide and **18"** tall. This rectangle will most likely extend into the grey area of the layout. You will adjust this on the next page when you select the page size for your drawing.
- **OFFSET** the rectangle **0.75"** to the inside. This new rectangle represents the margins required by your printer. (With most printers, you cannot print to the edge of the paper.)
- **ERASE** the first rectangle. (You do not need this rectangle anymore.)
- Complete your title sheet so it matches the image to the left.

Set Up Your Page to Print

The **PAGE SETUP MANAGER** allows you to specify page layout and plotting device settings for each layout in your drawing. The page setup settings that you specify are stored within the layout, making it easy for you to print.

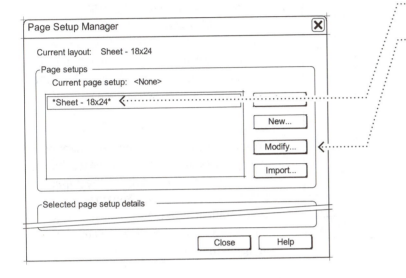

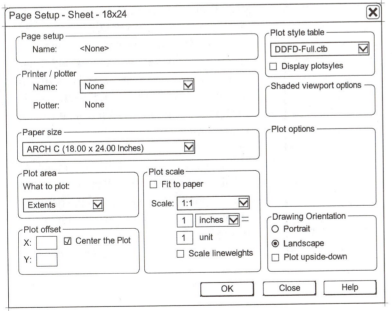

· Type **PAGESETUP** and press **ENTER** to open the page setup manager.
· Click once on ***SHEET – 18×24*** (your sheet may have a different name).
· Click the **MODIFY** button.

Follow the steps below to complete the setup for your layout.

Printer/Plotter

· Select the printer you want use for this drawing. Printers installed on your computer are available for selection.

Paper Size

· This selection box will show paper sizes that are available for the printer you selected. Select **ARCH C.**

Plot Area

· This selection box allows you to customize what you want AutoCAD to print. Select **EXTENTS.**

Plot Offsets

· Place a checkmark in the **CENTER THE PLOT** box.

Plot Scale

· Uncheck **FIT TO PAPER.** (If you do check this option, you will prevent your drawing from printing to scale.)
· Select **1:1** from the drop-down list.

Plot Style Table (pen assignments)

· Select **DDFD-FULL.CTB.**

Drawing Orientation

· Select **LANDSCAPE** or **PORTRAIT** to match the orientation of your sheet.

· **CLICK ONCE** the **OK** button to close the page setup dialog box.
· **CLICK ONCE** the **CLOSE** button to close the page setup manager dialog box.

· Finish setting up your viewport on page 96.

24" × 36" – Setting Up an ARCH D-Sized Sheet

This sheet size is most commonly used for presentation drawings and construction documents. Most large format printers can print a 24" wide piece of paper and require a 0.75" margin.

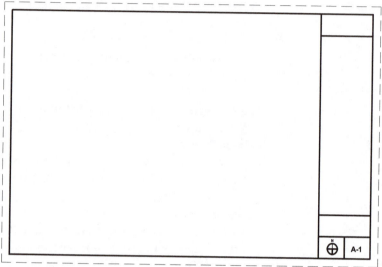

24" x 36" Construction Document Sheet with .75" margin

Construction Document Layout

· Set the current layer to **TB-BORDER.**
· Using the **RECTANGLE** command, draw a rectangle that is **36"** wide and **24"** tall. This rectangle will most likely extend into the grey area of the layout. You will adjust this on the next page when you select the page size for your drawing.
· **OFFSET** the rectangle **0.75"** to the inside. This new rectangle represents the margins required by your printer. (With most printers, you cannot print to the edge of the paper.)
· **ERASE** the first rectangle. (You do not need this rectangle anymore.)
· Complete your title sheet so it matches the image to the left.

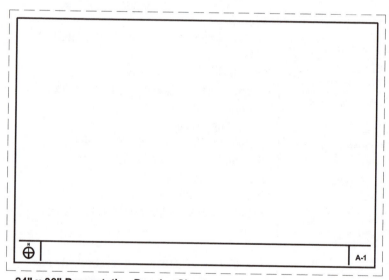

24" x 36" Presentation Drawing Sheet with .75" margin

Design Drawing Layout

· Set the current layer to **TB-BORDER.**
· Using the **RECTANGLE** command, draw a rectangle that is **36"** wide and **24"** tall. This rectangle will most likely extend into the grey area of the layout. You will adjust this on the next page when you select the page size for your drawing.
· **OFFSET** the rectangle **0.75"** to the inside. This new rectangle represents the margins required by your printer. (With most printers, you cannot print to the edge of the paper.)
· **ERASE** the first rectangle. (You do not need this rectangle anymore.)
· Complete your title sheet so it matches the image to the left.

Set Up Your Page to Print

The **PAGE SETUP MANAGER** allows you to specify page layout and plotting device settings for each layout in your drawing. The page setup settings that you specify are stored within the layout, making it easy for you to print.

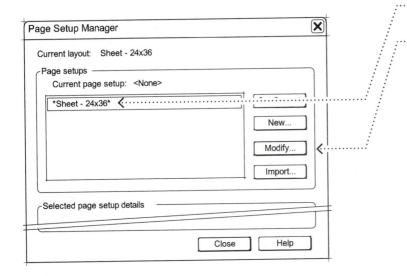

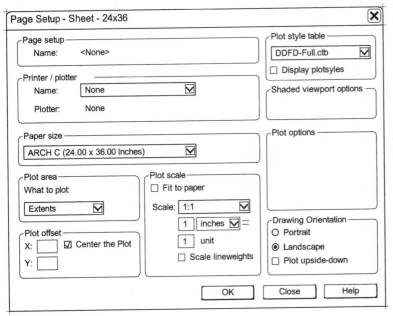

· Type **PAGESETUP** and press **ENTER** to open the page setup manager.
· Click once on ***SHEET – 24×36*** (your sheet may have a different name).
· Click the **MODIFY** button.

Follow the steps below to complete the setup for your layout.

Printer/Plotter

· Select the printer you want use for this drawing. Printers installed on your computer are available for selection.

Paper Size

· This selection box will show paper sizes that are available for the printer you selected. Select **ARCH D**.

Plot Area

· This selection box allows you to customize what you want AutoCAD to print. Select **EXTENTS**.

Plot Offsets

· Place a checkmark in the **CENTER THE PLOT** box.

Plot Scale

· Uncheck **FIT TO PAPER**. (If you do check this option, you will prevent your drawing from printing to scale.)
· Select **1:1** from the drop-down list.

Plot Style Table (pen assignments)

· Select **DDFD-FULL.CTB**.

Drawing Orientation

· Select **LANDSCAPE** or **PORTRAIT** to match the orientation of your sheet.

· **CLICK ONCE** the **OK** button to close the page setup dialog box.
· **CLICK ONCE** the **CLOSE** button to close the page setup manager dialog box.

· Finish setting up your viewport on page 96.

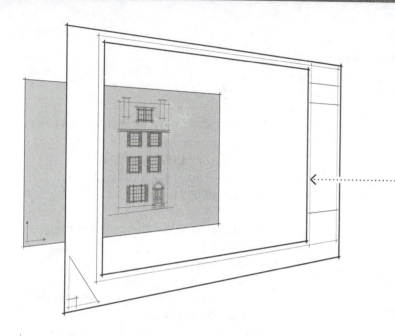

Adjusting an existing Viewport

You may have noticed the viewport in your layout. If you have already started your drawing in modelspace, you can most likely see some or all of your drawing inside the viewport.

· Viewports act like a window and allow you to see through your Layout View to Model Space.

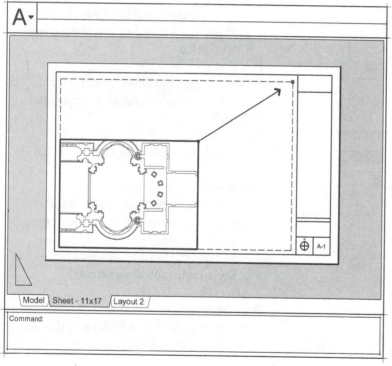

· **CLICK ONCE** on the frame of the viewport and move it to layer **TB-VIEWPORT**.

· Stretch the existing viewport in your layout to fill your title sheet (use the stretch command or clicking on the viewport's grips). In this example the viewport is stretched to about 1/8" inside the drawing portion of the title sheet.
· It is important that the viewport does not overlap any other lines in your drawing.
· **ERASE** any construction lines used to create your viewport or title sheet.

Creating a new Viewport

You can add multiple viewport to a layout with the **VIEWPORT** command. The steps below will add an additional viewport to your layout.

· Type the command **MVIEW** and press **ENTER**.
· **CLICK ONCE** in the drawing area where you want the lower left corner of your viewport.
· Drag the AutoCAD cursor up and to the right.
· **CLICK ONCE** in the drawing area where you want the upper right corner of your viewport.

Set the scale for your Viewport
The final step in setting up a custom layout is
to set the scale for the viewport you created.

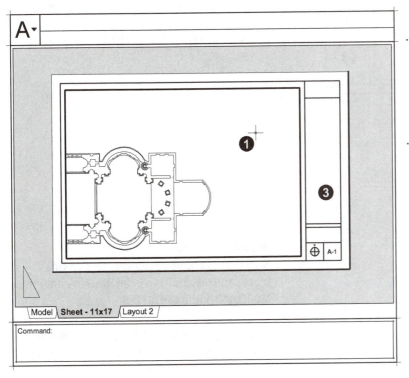

· **Step 1:** Activate the viewport in your layout
by **DOUBLE CLICKING** inside the viewport.
Clicking the Model/Paper button at the bottom of the AutoCAD screen will also activate
and de-activate the viewport.

· Type the command **ZOOM** and press **EN-
TER.** Type the letter **E** and press **ENTER.** This
performs a zoom extents which scales your
drawing to fit the viewport.

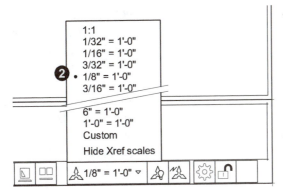

· **Step 2:** Select the scale of your drawing from
the annotative scale selection box in the bottom right corner of AutoCAD. As you select
different scales, your drawing (in model
space) will enlarge or shrink inside the viewport.

· **Step 3:** De-activate the viewport by **DOUBLE
CLICKING** outside the viewport.

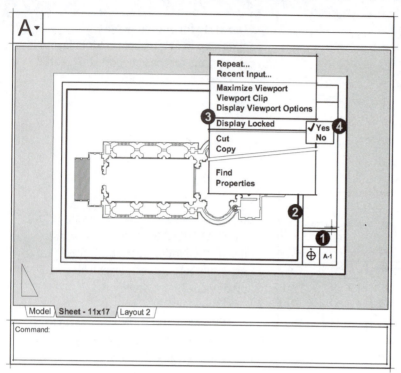

Locking your Viewport

By locking the viewport, you will protect the scale of your drawing from accidentally changing as you work on your drawing.

· **Step 1:** De-activate the viewport by **DOUBLE CLICKING** outside the viewport.

· **Step 2: CLICK ONCE** on the viewport's frame then **RIGHT CLICK** on the viewport's fram.

· **Steps 3-4:** Go to **DISPLAY LOCKED** and select **YES**.

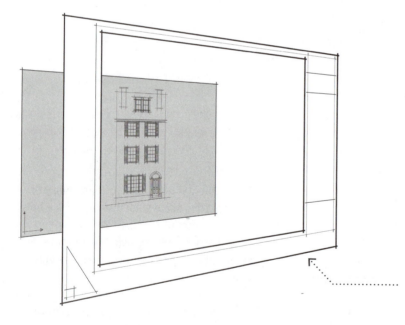

Drawing to Scale

Now that you have set up your layout, title block, and viewport, you can draw in either the **MODEL TAB** or the **LAYOUT TAB**.

· Drawing in the **LAYOUT TAB** (inside the activated viewport) is easier for some designers that are new to AutoCAD because it closely resembles drawing on a drafting table.

· **DOUBLE CLICK** inside the viewport and begin drawing your plan, section, or elevation.
· Draw lines at real world scale and AutoCAD will scale them to the scale of your viewport.

· Your drawing exists in both the **LAYOUT TAB** and the **MODEL TAB**. Remember the analogy of the window view back from the layout to the model tab.

Plotting a Layout/Drawing
When you print a layout, AutoCAD will remember the settings in the Page Setup Manager.

· Type the command **PLOT** and press **ENTER** to open the plot dialog box.

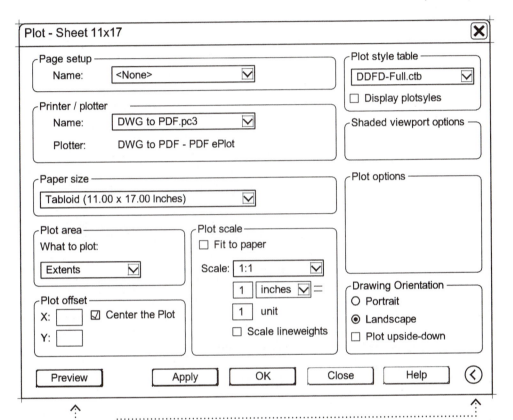

Plot - Sheet 11x17 ☒

Page setup
Name: <None> ▽

Printer / plotter
Name: DWG to PDF.pc3 ▽
Plotter: DWG to PDF - PDF ePlot

Paper size
Tabloid (11.00 x 17.00 Inches) ▽

Plot area
What to plot:
Extents ▽

Plot offset
X: [ ] ☑ Center the Plot
Y: [ ]

Plot scale
☐ Fit to paper
Scale: 1:1 ▽
1 inches ▽ =
1 unit
☐ Scale lineweights

Plot style table
DDFD-Full.ctb ▽
☐ Display plotsyles

Shaded viewport options

Plot options

Drawing Orientation
○ Portrait
◉ Landscape
☐ Plot upside-down

Preview   Apply   OK   Close   Help   ◁

· Verify that the plotter and plot style are properly set. In this example AutoCAD's **DWG TO PDF** plotter was selected. This will create a PDF file of your AutoCAD drawing.

· If you cannot see the right portion of the plot dialog box (includin the plot style table), click the arrow at the bottom right of the plot dialog box.

· **CLICK** the **PREVIEW** button to see a preview of your print. While in the preview screen, you can zoom and pan around your drawing to check line weight and text fonts.

· If everything looks okay in the preview, press the **ESCAPE** key **ONCE** and then click the **OK** button to print your drawing.

· If you need to make a change to the plot settings, press the **ESCAPE** key **ONCE**, make the changes, and then **CLICK** the **PREVIEW** button again.

· If you need to make a change to your drawing, press the **ESCAPE** key **TWICE** to exit the Plot dialog box. After you have made your adjustments, start over at the top of this page.

Learning Exercise

In this chapter exercise, you will set up a layout to print the floor plan you began in the previous chapter.

Open Your Drawing

· Open AutoCAD.
· Open the drawing you created in the previous chapter: **DDFD-EAMES.DWG**

Creating Your Layers

Create the following layers.

· **TB-VIEWPORT**   Color 31 NoPlot
· **TB-BORDER**   Color 1
· **TB-TEXT**   Color 5
· Set the current layer to **TB-BORDER.**

Drawing Your Layout

· Using the guides in this chapter, create an 18" × 24" landscape layout to match the drawing above.

· Save your drawing.

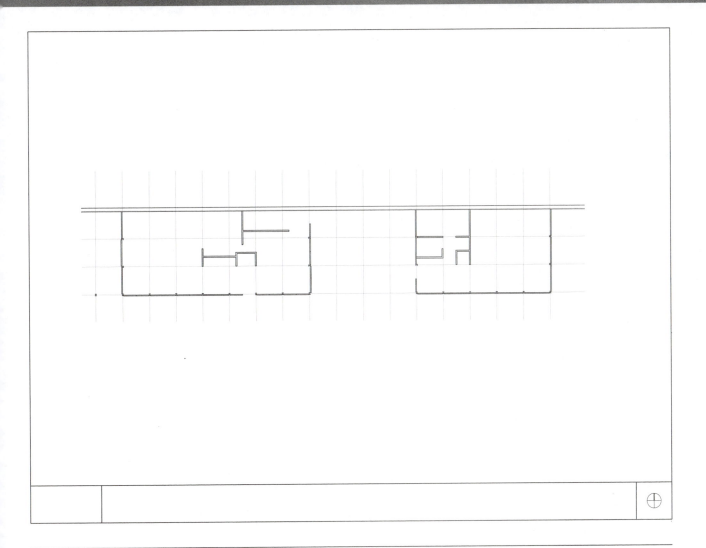

Set the scale for your drawing

· Set the annotative scale of your drawing to **1/8"=1'-0"**.

· Using the guides in this chapter, set the scale of your viewport to **1/8"=1'-0"**.

· Lock the viewport.

· Save your drawing.

· Congratulations, you have completed the learning exercise for this chapter.

CHAPTER 7
Text Styles and Sizes

Adding text to your drawing in AutoCAD is similar to using word processing software, with one exception: In a word processing program you control the height of text with the font size. Twelve-point Arial text will always print the same height—regardless of the word processing software and regardless of the printer.

In AutoCAD, text height is measure in inches (or millimeters if you are drawing in metric). Most designers include text like room names and drawing symbols in model space because it simplifies adjusting the position of the text within the drawing.

Text height is determined by the desired printed text height and the scale of your drawing. For example, if you want your text to print 1/8" tall and your drawing is scaled at 1/16" = 1'-0" then your text will be to 2'-0" tall in model space. Prior to AutoCAD 2010, designers had to manually set this text height for every drawing. Starting in AutoCAD 2010, AutoDesk introduced annotative text which manages the relationship between model space text height and paper text height.

This chapter will introduce both methods of adding text to your drawing including key charts to help you master adding text to your AutoCAD drawings.

Drawing Scale and Text Size

Text in digital drawings should be sized appropriately and consistently across all sheets and architectural drawing scales in a drawing set. Understanding the relationship between drawing scale and text size in AutoCAD requires observation of drawings at different scales with similar text.

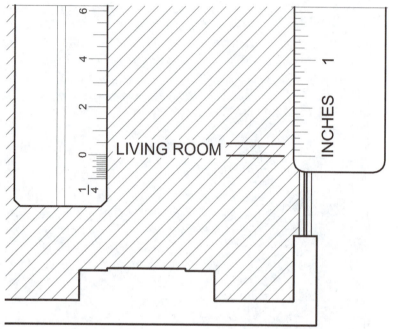

PLAN - 1/4"=1'-0"

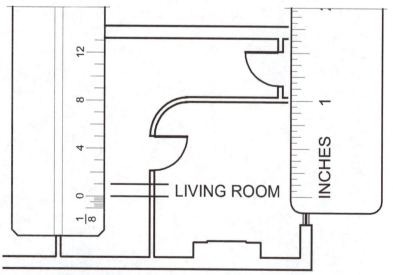

PLAN - 1/8"=1'-0"

· If you are working on a presentation drawing, the text must be legible from a few feet away.
· If you are working on construction drawings, the text must be legible from a few inches away.
· In general, text should be added to your drawing in **MODEL SPACE**.

Text Height 1/4" = 1'-0"
· The floor plan to the left is printed at **1/4"=1'-0"**.
· The text label "living room" measures 1/8" tall with a ruler. This is the paper text height.
· The text label "living room" measures 6" tall with an architectural scale. This is the model text height, or, the height of the text in model space.

Text Height 1/8" = 1'-0"
· The floor plan to the left is printed at **1/8"=1'-0"**.
· The text label "living room" measures 1/8" tall with a ruler. This is the paper text height.
· The text label "living room" measures 12" tall with an architectural scale. This is the model text height, or, the height of the text in model space.

· As the architectural drawing scale is reduced smaller (in this example from 1/4"=1'-0" to 1/8"=1'-0"), the model text height is increased (in this example from 6" to 12").

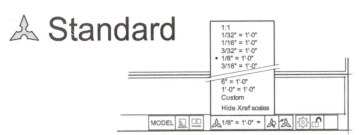

Annotative Text Height

· When you add text to your drawings in model space, you will draw it at an enlarged size so that it will print consistently through your presentation or drawing set.

· The annotative symbol indicates that the text in your drawing is adjusted to the drawing's annotative scale.

· Set the annotative scale of your drawing to match the architectural scale of your drawing (in this example, the annotative scale is set to 1/8"=1'-0"). AutoCAD will use this annotative scale to calculate the appropriate model space text height.

· Use 1/4" paper text height for title blocks and presentation drawing titles.
· Use 1/8" paper text height for notes in most design drawings.
· Use 3/32" paper text height for construction documents.

Manually Calculating Text Height

· Prior to AutoCAD 2010, designers need to manually calculate text height. Multiply the desired printed text height (1/8") by the scale factor for the current drawing scale (48, 96, 192, and so on) to get the appropriate text height: **1/8"× 96 = 12"**

· Use the chart to the left to determine the appropriate text height for imperial scaled drawings.

Drawing Scale	Scale Factor	Paper Text Height		
		1/4"	1/8"	3/32"
		Model Text Height		
3"=1'-0"	4	1"	1/2"	3/8"
1 1/2"=1'-0"	8	2"	1"	3/4"
1"=1'-0"	12	3"	1-1/2"	1-1/8"
3/4"=1'-0"	16	4"	2"	1-1/2"
1/2"=1'-0"	24	6"	3"	2-1/4"
3/8"=1'-0"	32	8"	4"	3"
1/4"=1'-0"	48	12"	6"	4-1/2"
3/16"=1'-0"	64	1'-4"	8"	6"
1/8"=1'-0"	96	2'-0"	12"	9"
3/32"=1'-0"	128	2'-8"	1'-4"	12"
1/16"=1'-0"	192	4'-0"	2'-0"	1'-6"
1/32=1'-0"	384	8'-0"	4'-0"	3'-0"

Drawing Scale	Scale Factor	Paper Text Height		
		6mm	3mm	2.5mm
		Model Text Height		
1:10	10	60mm	30mm	25mm
1:20	20	120mm	60mm	50mm
1:50	50	300mm	150mm	125mm
1:100	100	600mm	300mm	250mm

· Use the chart to the left to determine the appropriate text height for metric scaled drawings.

Text Styles

Text styles allow you to define different text font preferences in your AutoCAD drawing. You will need to set up at least one text style before you add text to you drawing.

· There are two types of fonts available in AutoCAD: AutoCAD fonts and TrueType fonts.

AutoCAD Fonts

· AutoCAD fonts have an .shx extension.
· The weight of an AutoCAD font is determined by the color of its layer. This behavior is the same as the relationship between line color and line weight.

AUTOCAD FONTS				
TXT.SHX	ABCDEFGHIJKLMNOPQRSTUVWXYZ	1234567890	COLOR 7
SIMPLEX.TXT	ABCDEFGHIJKLMNOPQRSTUVWXYZ	1234567890	
TXT.SHX	ABCDEFGHIJKLMNOPQRSTUVWXYZ	1234567890	COLOR 5
SIMPLEX.TXT	ABCDEFGHIJKLMNOPQRSTUVWXYZ	1234567890	

TRUE TYPE FONTS		
ARIAL	ABCDEFGHIJKLMNOPQRSTUVWXYZ	1234567890
ARIAL (BOLD)	**ABCDEFGHIJKLMNOPQRSTUVWXYZ**	**1234567890**
CITY BLUEPRINT	ABCDEFGHIJKLMNOPQRSTUVWXYZ	1234567890
COUNTRY BLUEPRINT	ABCDEFGHIJKLMNOPQRSTUVWXYZ	1234567890

TrueType Fonts

· TrueType fonts have a TT icon and are available in all Windows programs, including Word Perfect and Microsoft Word.
· The weight of a TrueType font is determined by the font style setting (bold, italic, and so on).
· Some fonts, like city blueprint and country blueprint, cannot print bold in AutoCAD and are difficult to read in presentations and construction drawings.

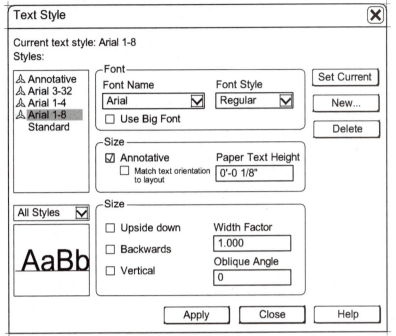

Adding a Text Style

The Text Style dialog box allows you to create and modify text styles in the current drawing. Text styles are stored separately in each Auto-CAD drawing.

· Set your drawing's **UNIT LENGTH** to **ARCHITEC-TURAL** and **UNIT PRECISION** to **1/32"**.
· Type the command **STYLE** and press **ENTER**. This opens the Text Style dialog box (left).

· **CLICK** the **NEW** button. Type the style name **ARIAL 1-8** and press **ENTER**.
· From the **FONT NAME** drop-down list, select **ARIAL**.
· **CHECK** the **ANNOTATIVE** option.
· Set the **PAPER TEXT HEIGHT** to **1/8"**.

Create two additional text styles:
· **ARIAL 1-4** - **PAPER TEXT HEIGHT: 1/4"**
· **ARIAL 3-32** - **PAPER TEXT HEIGHT: 3/32"**

· **CLICK ONCE** on the **ARIAL 1-8** style and **CLICK** the **SET CURRENT** button.
· **CLICK ONCE** the **CLOSE** button.

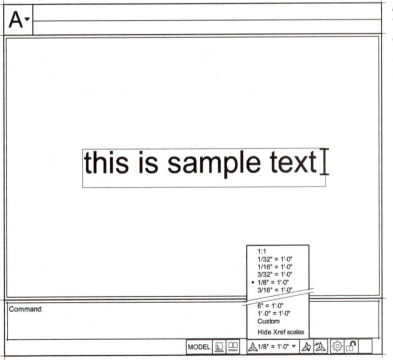

Adding Text

The **TEXT** command allows you to add text to your drawing. We will add a line of text to a drawing scaled at 1/8" = 1'-0".
· Set your drawing's **ANNOTATIVE SCALE** to **1/8"=1'-0"**.
· Type the command **TEXT** and press **ENTER**.
· **CLICK ONCE** in AutoCAD where you want to start your text. (You can move the text location in your drawing after you complete the **TEXT** command.)
· AutoCAD prompts you for the text rotation. Type **0** and press **ENTER**.
· Type **THIS IS SAMPLE TEXT** and press **ENTER**.
· Press **ENTER** one more time to end the Text command.

Adding Multiline Text

The **MTEXT** command allows you to add multi-line text to your drawing. We will add text to a drawing scaled at 1/8" = 1'-0".

· Set your drawing's **ANNOTATIVE SCALE** to **1/8"=1'-0"**.

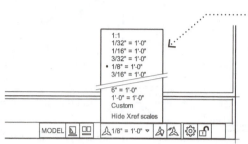

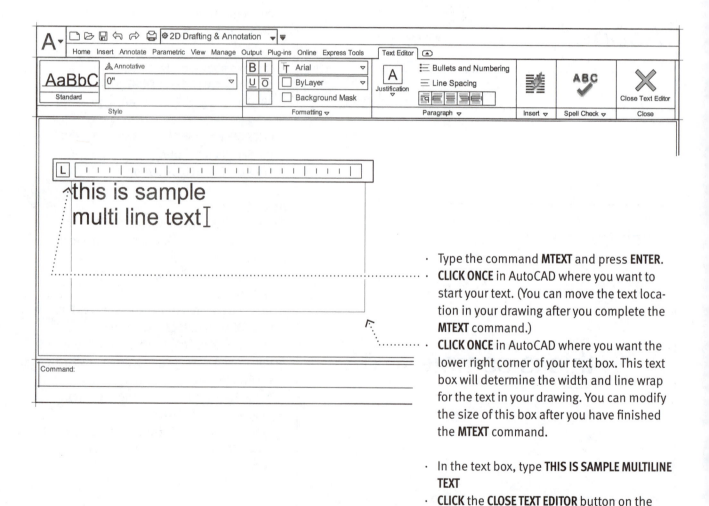

· Type the command **MTEXT** and press **ENTER**.
· **CLICK ONCE** in AutoCAD where you want to start your text. (You can move the text location in your drawing after you complete the **MTEXT** command.)
· **CLICK ONCE** in AutoCAD where you want the lower right corner of your text box. This text box will determine the width and line wrap for the text in your drawing. You can modify the size of this box after you have finished the **MTEXT** command.

· In the text box, type **THIS IS SAMPLE MULTILINE TEXT**
· **CLICK** the **CLOSE TEXT EDITOR** button on the right side of the **TEXT EDITOR RIBBON** to end the Multiline Text command.

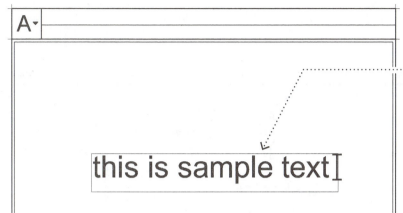

Editing Text

The **DDEDIT** command allows you to edit text and multiline text in your drawing.

- Type the command **DDEDIT** and press **ENTER**.
- **CLICK ONCE** on the text that you want to edit.
- If you are editing **SINGLE LINE TEXT**, complete your text edits and press **ENTER**.
- If you are editing **MULTILINE TEXT**, complete your text edit and click the **OK** button.
- Press **ENTER** one more time to end the **DDEDIT** command.

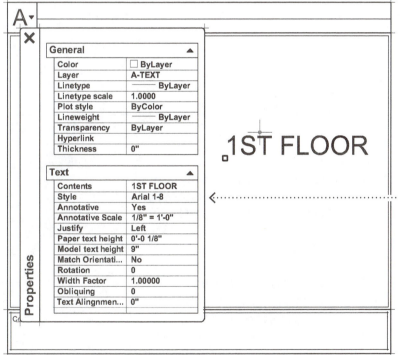

Editing Paper Text Height

- You can change the height of text in your drawing by changing the text style in the Properties Palette.
- To open the Properties Palette, type **CH** and press **ENTER**.
- **CLICK ONCE** on the text that you want to modify.
- The Text section of the palette displays the text's Style, Justification, Height, Rotation, and Width Factor.
- Changing the **TEXT STYLE** to **ARIAL 1-4**, **ARIAL 1-8**, or **ARIAL 1-32**.
- Press the **ESCAPE** key twice to deselect the text and end the text modification.

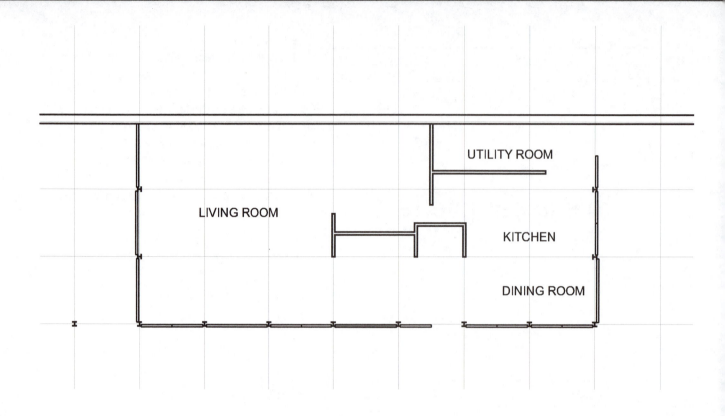

Learning Exercise

In this chapter exercise, you will add the text labels to the floor plan you began in the previous chapters.

Open Your Drawing

· Open AutoCAD.
· Open the drawing you created in the previous chapter:
  DDFD-EAMES.DWG

Creating Your Layers

Create the following layers:

· **A-TEXT**   Color 5
· Set the current layer to **A-TEXT**.

Adding a Text Style

· Open the Text Style manager and add the following annotative text styles to your drawing: **ARIAL 3-32**, **ARIAL 1-8**, and **ARIAL 1-4**.

· Save your drawing.

Adding Text Labels to Your Plan

· In model space, set the annotative scale of your drawing to **1/8"=1'-0"**
· Using the **TEXT** command, add the appropriate labels to your drawing to match the drawing above. Use the text style **ARIAL 1-8** for these text labels.

· Save your drawing.

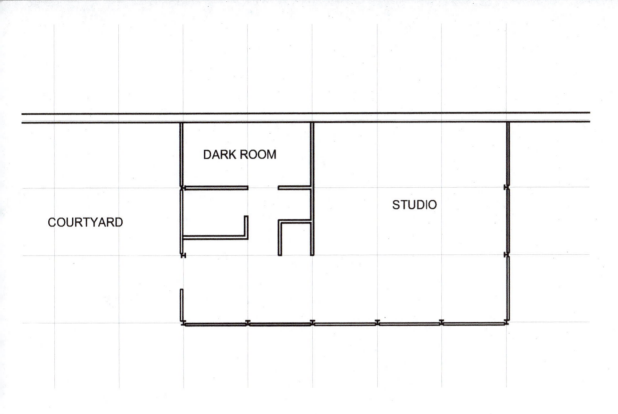

DARK ROOM

STUDIO

COURTYARD

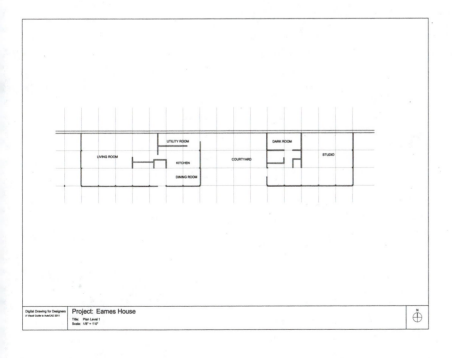

Adding Text to Your Layout

· Set the current layer to **TB-TEXT.**

· Using the **TEXT** command, add the appropriate labels to your layout/ title block to match the drawing to the left.

· Use the text style **ARIAL 1-4** for the project name
Use the text style **ARIAL 1-8** for the remaining text on the layout.

· Save your drawing.

· Congratulations, you have completed the learning exercise for this chapter.

CHAPTER 8
Hatches and
Dashed Lines

The topics discussed in this chapter should be familiar to you from your experience drafting by hand. Hatches are used to indicate material in plan, elevation, section, or detail. Dashed lines are used to indicate an object position relative to the cutting plane. Dashed lines can also be used to indicate special wall assemblies (e.g., fire rated walls).

These two graphic conventions take a considerable amount of time and attention in manual drawing. AutoCAD simplifies the process of adding each to your design drawings.

Drawing Hatch Patterns

Hatch patterns are used in design drawings as graphic shorthand to symbolize specific materials in your drawing. AutoCAD contains a series of predefined hatches that match acceptable industry standards.

3" SS CORNER GUARD

10⅝".

3"

3"

½" MTL REVEAL

You should consider the following when adding hatch patterns to your drawings:

- The scale of your drawing or detail may inform the scale of the hatch pattern.
- Materials are identified with different hatch patterns in plan, section, and elevation.
- Hatches are an additional layer of information you communicate in design drawings. Make sure your hatches do not visually overpower the drawing.
- The **BHATCH** command fills a predrawn area in your drawing with a hatch pattern. If the lines defining the edge of the material are not connected at all endpoints, AutoCAD will not be able to properly identify your desired fill area.

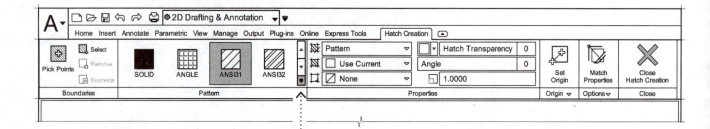

Adding Hatch Patterns

In this example, we will fill a floor slab in the detail with a concrete hatch.

Create the following layers. You can open the layer properties manager by typing the command **LAYER** and pressing **ENTER**.
- **A-HATCH**   Color 8
- Set the current layer to **A-HATCH**.

- **Step 1:** Type the command **BHATCH** and press **ENTER** to open **HATCH CREATION** ribbon.
- **Step 2: CLICK ONCE** the button in the bottom right of the Pattern panel. This expands the Pattern panel.

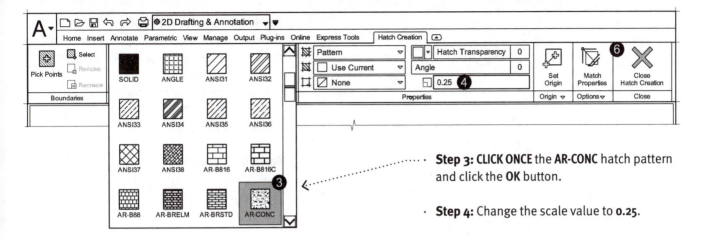

Step 3: CLICK ONCE the **AR-CONC** hatch pattern and click the **OK** button.

Step 4: Change the scale value to **0.25**.

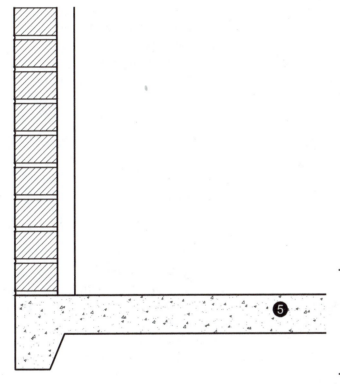

Step 5: As you move the cursor over your drawing, AutoCAD will preview fill each possible boundary area in the detail. **CLICK ONCE** inside the area you want to fill with the Concrete hatch.

TIP: If you are not satisfied with the hatch preview, make any required changes in the **HATCH CREATION** ribbon before you click to fill the hatch area in your drawing.

Step 6: When you are through selecting areas to fill, press the **CLOSE HATCH CREATION** button on the top right of the **HATCH CREATION** ribbon.

HATCH PATTERN

SECTIONS/DETAILS 1 1/2" = 1'-0"

AR-SAND

TWO LAYERS OF 5/8" GWB

AR-SAND
SCALE: .25

AR-CONC

6" CONC SLAB

AR-CONC
SCALE: 0.25

ANSI31

CLAY BRICK & MORTAR

ANSI31
SCALE: 3.0

ANSI32

+ =

PLYWOOD
COMBINE ANSI32 WITH
VERTICAL LINES
ANSI32
SCALE: 4.0

MULTIPLE ARCS

HARDWOOD
(HEAVY TIMBER)

MULTIPLE ARCS
(NO HATCH)

Section/Detail Hatch Patterns
· The following hatch patterns are included with AutoCAD and appropriate for objects drawn in section.
· An appropriate hatch scale is listed for different drawing scales. You may modify these scales to your preference.

Drywall – In Detail
· AR-SAND
· Hatch Scale: 0.3–0.5
  for drawings larger than 1-1/2" = 1'-0"

Concrete – In Detail
· AR-CONC
· Hatch Scale: 0.50–1.0

Brick – In Detail
· ANSI31
· Hatch Scale: 5.0
  for drawings larger than 1-1/2" = 1'-0"

Plywood – In Detail
· The plywood section hatch is created by combining lines and the ANSI32 hatch pattern.
· The lines represent the plies in the wood and run the length of the wood in section.

Hardwood – In Detail
· The hardwood section hatch is created by copying multiple circles and trimming the portion of the circle that exists outside the hardwood.

HATCH PATTERN

ELEVATION/PLAN
1/4" = 1'-0"

AR-SAND

PLASTER WALL

AR-SAND
SCALE: 12

AR-SAND

CONCRETE
FLOOR

AR-SAND
SCALE: 12

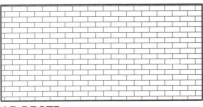

AR-BRSTD

BRICK WALL

AR-BRSTD
SCALE: 1.0

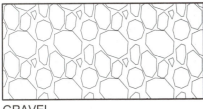

GRAVEL

FIELDSTONE
FLOOR

GRAVEL
SCALE: 24

ANSI37

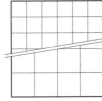

8" TILE FLOOR
ANSI37
SCALE: 64 / ROTATION:45

12" TILE FLOOR
ANSI37
SCALE: 96 / ROTATION:45

Plan/Elevation Hatch Patterns
- The following hatch patterns are included with AutoCAD and appropriate for objects drawn in plan or elevation.
- An appropriate hatch scale is listed for different drawing scales. You may modify these scales to your preference.

Plaster – Plan and Elevation
- AR-SAND
- Hatch Scale: 3.0–12.0
  for 1/16" = 1'-0" to 1/4" = 1'-0"

Concrete – Plan and Elevation
- AR-SAND
- Hatch Scale: 3.0–12.0
  for 1/16" = 1'-0" to 1/4" = 1'-0"

Brick – Elevation
- AR-BRSTD
- Hatch Scale: 1.0

Field Stone – Plan
- GRAVEL
- Hatch Scale: 24.0

8" Tile – Plan
- ANSI37
- Hatch Scale: 64.0 / Rotation: 45

12" Tile – Plan
- ANSI37
- Hatch Scale: 96.0 / Rotation: 45

Line Type

Understanding how to use clear and legible line types will better communicate your design drawings than any combination of AutoCAD commands. You most likely have been introduced to these concepts in a manual drafting studio, conceptual drawing studio, or design studio.

· Drawing dashed lines by hand can be a time consuming process.
· In AutoCAD, you adjust line type by selecting different line types for different kinds of lines.

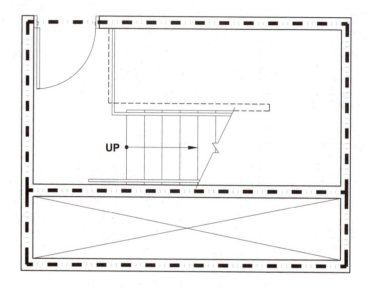

Industry Standard Line Types

· The following line types are included with AutoCAD.

HIDDEN2 (Color 5) _____

· Hidden Line – Used in drawing to indicate objects that are above the cutting plane or hidden beyond objects in the current view.

CENTER2 (Color 5) ____ _ ____ _ ____ _ ____

· Center Line – Used in drawings to indicate the center of an object. It is usually used in combination with dimensions.

PHANTOM2 (Color 5) __ _ _ ____ _ _ ____ _ _ __

· Property Line – The **PHANTOM2** line type is used to indicate property lines in site plans.

· Fire Rating – A variation of the **CENTER2** and **DIVIDE2** line types can be used to indicate wall fire ratings in floor plans. Draw an additional polyline in the center of the indicated wall. Adjust the thickness of the polyline so the line will clearly communicate your desired wall ratings.

CENTER2 (Color 5) ▬▬ ▪ ▬ ▪ ▬▬ ▪ ▬▬

· **CENTER2** can be used for one-hour rated wall assemblies.

DIVIDE2 (Color 5) ▪ ▬ ▪ ▬ ▪ ▬ ▪ ▬

· **DIVIDE2** can be used for two-hour rated wall assemblies.

Line Type Scale

The **LTSCALE** settings helps AutoCAD adjust the size of the dashes to match your drawing scale. These settings tell AutoCAD to use the annotative scale in model space and each viewport (layout views) to adjust dashed lines.

Setting the Ltscale

· Type the command **LTSCALE** and press **ENTER**.
· Type **0.5** and press **ENTER**.

· Type the command **MSLTSCALE** and press **ENTER**.
· Type **1** and press **ENTER**.

· In each of your layouts, type **PSLTSCALE** and press **ENTER**.
· Type **1** and press **ENTER**.

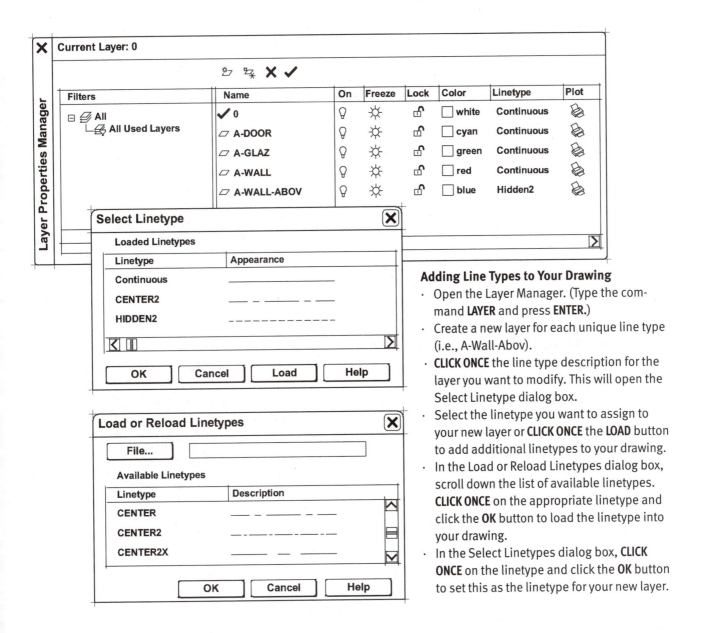

Adding Line Types to Your Drawing

· Open the Layer Manager. (Type the command **LAYER** and press **ENTER**.)
· Create a new layer for each unique line type (i.e., A-Wall-Abov).
· **CLICK ONCE** the line type description for the layer you want to modify. This will open the Select Linetype dialog box.
· Select the linetype you want to assign to your new layer or **CLICK ONCE** the **LOAD** button to add additional linetypes to your drawing.
· In the Load or Reload Linetypes dialog box, scroll down the list of available linetypes. **CLICK ONCE** on the appropriate linetype and click the **OK** button to load the linetype into your drawing.
· In the Select Linetypes dialog box, **CLICK ONCE** on the linetype and click the **OK** button to set this as the linetype for your new layer.

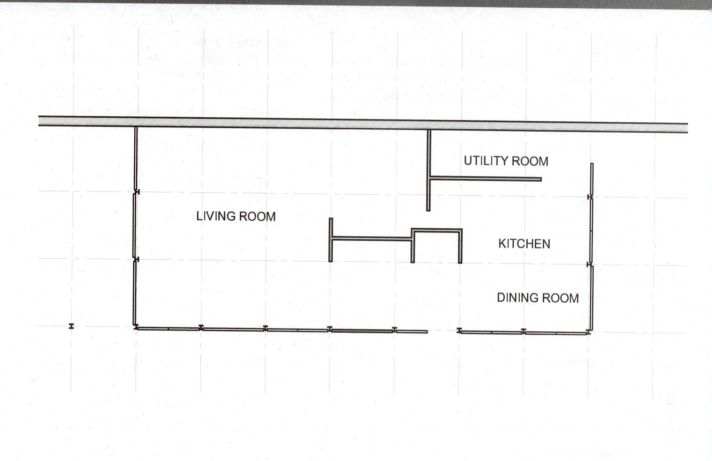

Learning Exercise

In this chapter exercise, you will add visual hierarchy to the wall in your plan through poché. You will use the Hatch command to poché the walls.

Open Your Drawing
· Open AutoCAD.
· Open the drawing you created in the previous chapter: **DDFD-EAMES.DWG**

Hatching Your Walls

Create the following layers:
· **A-WALL-HATCH** Color 9
· Set the current layer to **A-WALL-HATCH**.

· Using the Hatch command, poché the walls (indicated above) with pattern ANSI31 and hatch scale 10.

· Save your drawing.

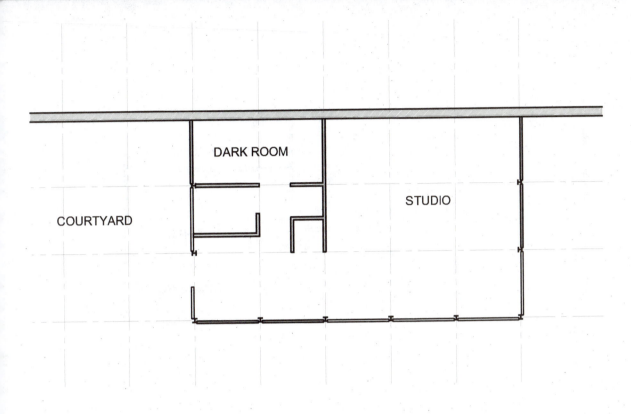

DARK ROOM

COURTYARD

STUDIO

Set the Line Type Scale
· In model space, set the **LTSCALE** to **0.5**
· In model space, set the **MSLTSCALE** to **1**

· In the layout, set the **PSLTSCALE** to **1**

· Set the linetype for layer **S-COL-GRID** to **CENTER2**

· Save your drawing.

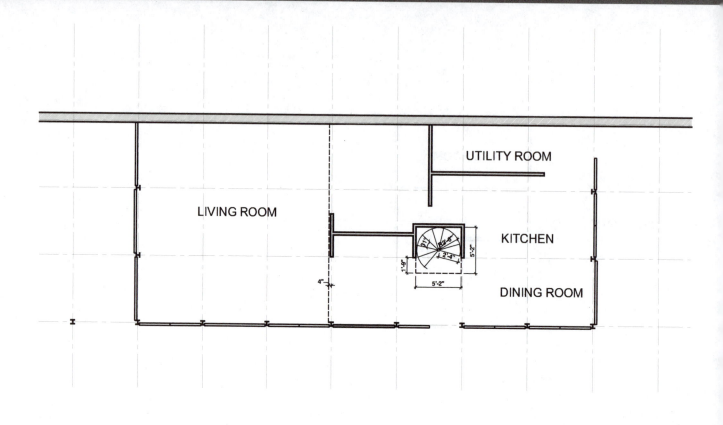

Learning Exercise

In this chapter exercise, you will use dashed and continuous lines to add the stairs to your floor plan.

Open Your Drawing

· Open AutoCAD.
· Open the drawing you created in the previous chapter:
  DDFD-EAMES.DWG

Creating Your Layers

Create the following layers:

· **A-FLOR-ABOV**   Color 6   HIDDEN2
· **A-FLOR-STAIR**   Color 7   Continuous
· Set the current layer to **A-FLOR-ABOV.**

Adding Stairs

· Using the line command and the offset command, draw the stair in the workshop.
· Using the circle command and the offset command, draw the circular stair in the main residence.

· Save your drawing.

Congratulations, you have completed the learning exercise for this chapter.

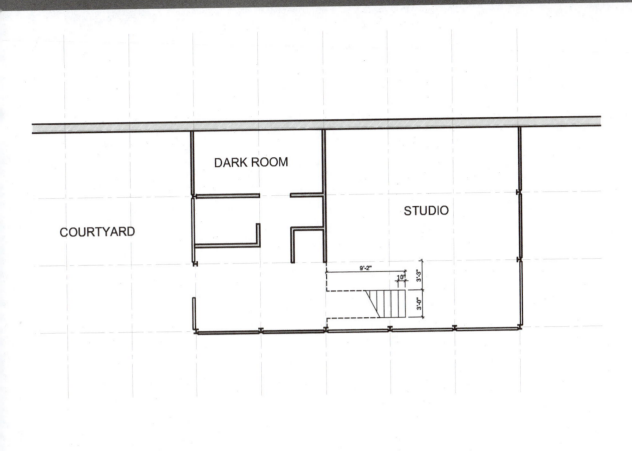

COURTYARD

DARK ROOM

STUDIO

9'-2"

10"

3'-3"

3'-0"

Advanced
Drawing Tools

CHAPTER 9
Stencils and Blocks

One advantage to drawing in AutoCAD is the ability to quickly move drawing symbols (like toilets, doors, and furniture) between drawings. It may take you 10 minutes to draw a chaise lounge in AutoCAD, but you can insert that chair as a block into any other AutoCAD drawing in less than a minute.

Consider the following questions as you work through this chapter:
· How are AutoCAD blocks similar to drawing stencils?
· How do you move AutoCAD blocks between drawings?

Drawing with Stencils

A stencil helps you quickly and accurately add symbols like toilets, doors, and sinks to your drawing. The AutoCAD equivalent to the drawing stencil is the **block** command.

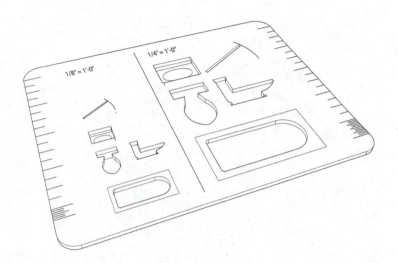

Stencils

· You can purchase stencils with various themes, including kitchen design and bathroom design.
· Stencils are scale specific, so you need different stencils for 1/8" = 1'-0" and 1/4" = 1'-0".

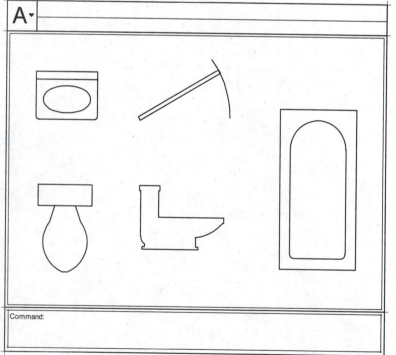

Blocks

· You can make a custom block to use as a symbol in your drawing or you can insert predefined blocks into your drawings.
· Blocks are always drawn at full scale (like everything else in AutoCAD), so a single toilet block can be used in various scaled drawings.
· Blocks can be shared among AutoCAD drawings.
· Blocks group lines together into a single object.

· The drawings in the AutoCAD window to the left are all blocks.

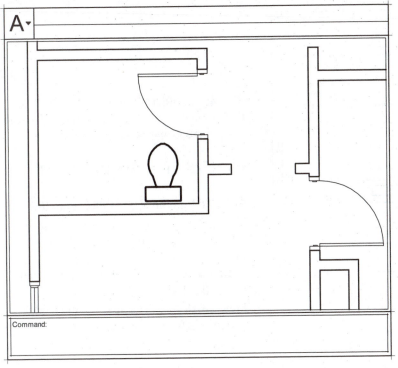

Creating a Block

The following steps will guide you through the process of creating a custom block. In this example, we will make a block of a toilet.

- **Step 1:** Move all the lines you are using to create your block onto Layer 0.

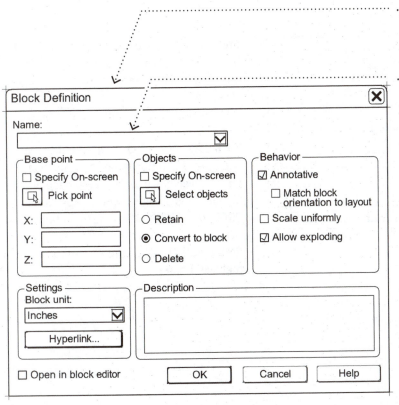

- **Step 2:** Type the command **BLOCK** and press **ENTER**. This will open the Block Definition dialog box.

- **Step 3:** Type the name for your block. Block names can have up to 255 characters. The block name will help you identify this block and other blocks in your drawing. Type the name **TOILET**.

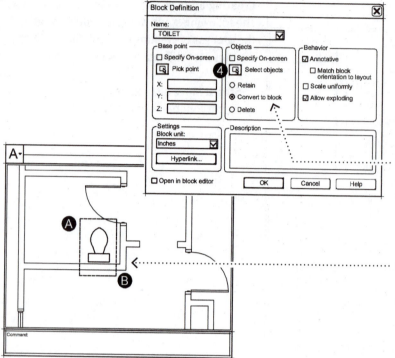

· **Step 4:** The Objects portion of the Block Definition dialog box allows you to select the lines that you want to add to your block.

CLICK ONCE on the **CONVERT TO BLOCK BUTTON.**

· **CLICK ONCE** on the **SELECT OBJECTS BUTTON.** The Block Definition dialog box will disappear, allowing you to select the lines for your block.

· Draw a **WINDOW SELECTION** around the lines that make the toilet.

· Press **ENTER** when you have finished selecting objects for your block.

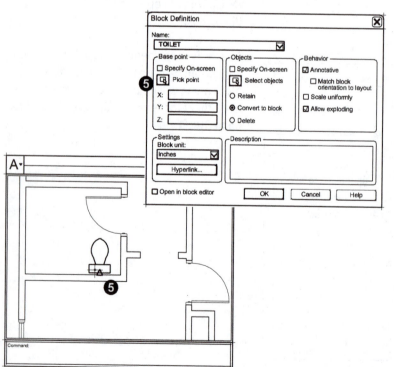

· **Step 5:** The Base Point portion of the Block Definition dialog box allows you to select the base point or reference point for your block. This point will be the reference point when you insert additional copies of this block.

· **CLICK ONCE** on the **PICK POINT BUTTON.**

· The Block Definition dialog box will disappear, allowing you to select the base point for your block. Using object snaps, **CLICK ONCE** on the **MIDPOINT** of the toilet tank.

· **Step 6: CLICK ONCE** on the **OK** button to complete your block.

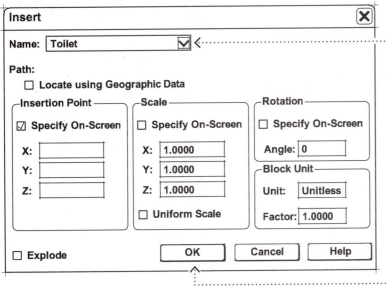

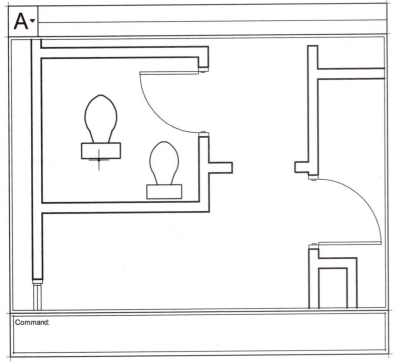

Inserting Blocks into Your Drawing

The following steps will guide you through the process of adding or inserting a block into your drawing. In this example, we insert the toilet block created in the previous section.

- **Step 1:** Type the command **INSERT** and press **ENTER**. This will open the Insert dialog box.

- **Step 2:** The Name drop-down menu lists all the blocks that are currently in your drawing. Select the **TOILET** block from this list.

- **Step 3:** In the Insertion Point portion of the dialog box, **CHECK** the **SPECIFY ON-SCREEN** option.
- In the Scale portion of the dialog box, **UNCHECK** the **SPECIFY ON-SCREEN** option and set the scale values to **1.00**.
- In the Rotation portion of the dialog box, **UNCHECK** the **SPECIFY ON-SCREEN** option and set the rotation value to **0**.

- **Step 4: CLICK ONCE** on the **OK** button to complete your block.

- **Step 5:** After you click the OK button, the Insert dialog box will disappear. The AutoCAD cursor will have the toilet block attached to it.
- **CLICK ONCE** where you want to insert the toilet block. You can modify the position of any block after it is inserted into your drawing.

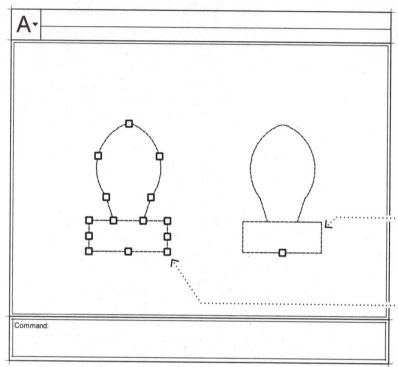

Exploding Blocks

The **EXPLODE** command will convert a block back into its original objects. Once you explode a block, you can no longer make global changes to the block.

· Type the command **EXPLODE** and press **ENTER**.
· **CLICK ONCE** on the block in your drawing.
· Press **ENTER**.

· In this example, the toilet on the right is a block. When you select a block, you will see one grip (which is located at the block's base point).

· In the example, the toilet on the left is an exploded block. When you select an exploded block, you will see grips for each AutoCAD object.

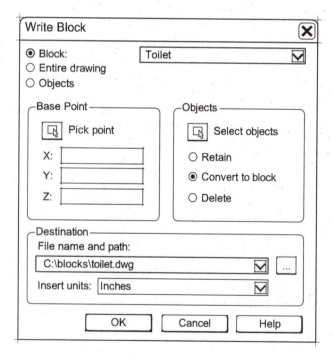

Exporting Blocks

The **WBLOCK** command (short for Write Block) will export any block in your drawing so you can use it in other AutoCAD drawings.

· Type the command **WBLOCK** and press **ENTER**.
· Select **BLOCK** as your source.
· The Block drop-down menu lists all the blocks that are currently in your drawing. Select the **TOILET** block from this list.
· In the Destination portion of the Write Block dialog box, select the place on your computer where you want to save your exported block.
· **CLICK ONCE** on the **OK** button to complete your block export.

· Create a blocks folder on your computer to save all of your blocks for future drawings.

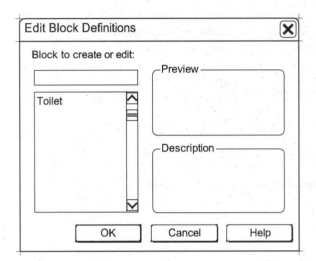

Editing Blocks

One advantage of using blocks in AutoCAD is the ability to make global changes. For example, if you modify a chair block, every version of that block will automatically update in the current drawing.

·   Type the command **BEDIT** (short for block edit) and press **ENTER**. This will open the Edit Block Definition dialog box.
·   Select the block that you want to edit and click **OK**.
·   AutoCAD will open the block in edit mode. You can add, subtract, or modify any line within the block.
·   When you have finished editing the block, type the command **BCLOSE** and press **ENTER**.

·   AutoCAD will prompt you to save changes to the current block. If you click **YES**, all versions of the block will be updated in the current drawing. If you click **NO**, nothing will be updated and all changes will be lost.

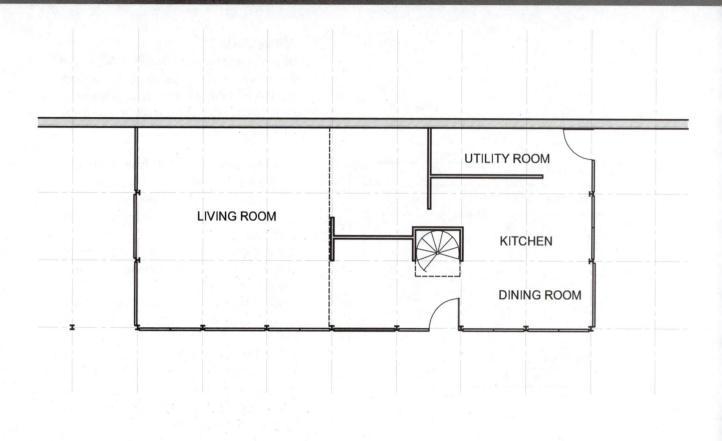

Learning Exercise

In this exercise, you will create a door block and insert it into your floor plan.

Open Your Drawing

· Open AutoCAD.
· Open the drawing you created in the previous chapter:
  DDFD-EAMES.DWG

Creating Your Layers

Create the following layers:

· **A-DOOR**   Color 6
· Set the current layer to **LAYER 0.**

DARK ROOM

COURTYARD

STUDIO

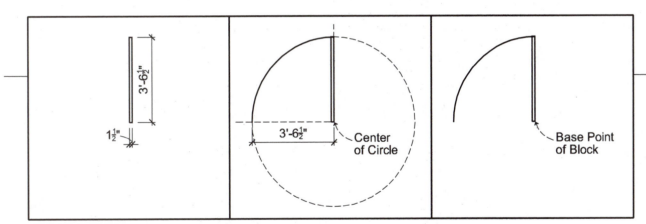

$3'-6\frac{1}{2}"$

$1\frac{1}{2}"$

$3'-6\frac{1}{2}"$ — Center of Circle

— Base Point of Block

Drawing the Door

· Using the line command and the circle command, draw a door with the dimensions above.

· Using the block command, create a block of the door using the insertion point indicated above. Name the block **DOOR**.

NOTE: Before you create your block, make sure the lines for your door are all on **LAYER 0**.

· Save your drawing.

Inserting the Door

· Set the current layer to **A-DOOR**.

· Using the insert command, insert the three doors indicated in the plan above. You can insert one door and copy it to each location or insert the door three separate times.

· Save your drawing.

Congratulations, you have completed the learning exercise for this chapter.

Companion Download
The companion download contains additional AutoCAD drawings that allow you to test your understanding of using blocks in AutoCAD.

Look inside the Learning Exercises folder for these files.

The following websites feature the companion download for this book: www.fairchildbooks.combook.cms?bookid=179 or www.DDFDbook.com/ch9

CHAPTER 10
Advanced Editing Tools

At this point in your AutoCAD education, you know most of the commands and concepts required to create a presentation-quality design drawing. This chapter discusses several different editing tools that will help you complete common editing tasks in a shorter period of time.

Consider the following questions as you work through this chapter:
· How can the concepts and commands in this chapter help me draw more efficiently?
· Many of the commands in this chapter are a combination of multiple commands you already know. What commands would you combine to achieve the same result as the commands discussed in this chapter?

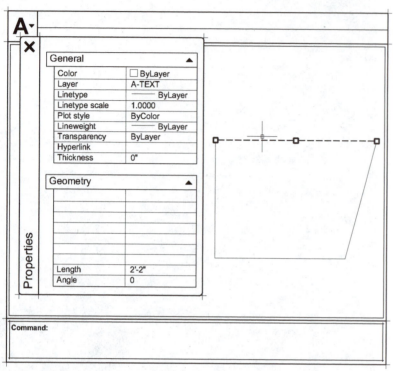

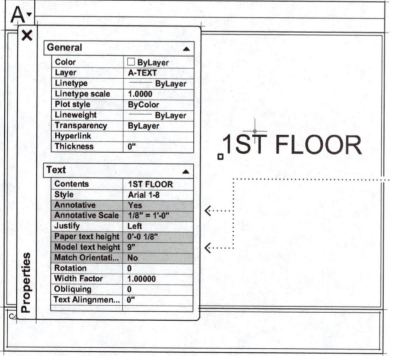

Properties Palette

The **PROPERTIES PALETTE** displays and controls the properties of objects in your drawing.

- Properties displayed include the object's Layer, Color, and Rotation.
- When more than one object is selected, the Properties palette displays only the common properties of the selected objects.
- To open the **PROPERTIES PALETTE**, type **CH** and press **ENTER**.

Line Properties

When you select a line in your drawing, the **PROPERTIES PALETTE** will display information about the line selected.

- The General section in the palette displays the line's Color, Layer, Linetype, Linetype Scale, and Thickness.
- The Layer and Linetype should be set to **BYLAYER**. The Linetype Scale should be set to **1.0**.
- The Geometry section displays the length and angle of the line. This is one way to verify the length of a line in your drawing.

Text Properties

When you select text in your drawing, the **PROPERTIES PALETTE** will display information about the text selected.

- The General section in the palette displays the line's Color, Layer, Linetype, Linetype Scale, and Thickness.
- The Text section of the palette displays the text's Style, Annotative Scale, Justification, Height, Rotation, and Width Factor.
- In this example, several annotative options are visible because **ANNOTATIVE** is set to **YES**.
- Use the properties palette to adjust text style, justification, and rotation.

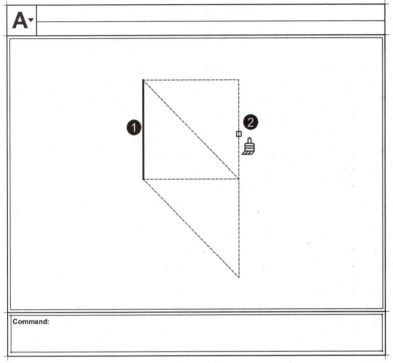

Command:

Match Properties

The Match Properties command allows you to copy the properties of one object to other objects in your drawing.

- Matchprop is a quick way to move a large number of lines to a specific layer.
- Matchprop will copy the following properties for lines, circles, and arcs: Color, Layer, Linetype, Linetype Scale, and Thickness.
- Matchprop will copy the following properties for text: Color, Layer, Linetype, Linetype Scale, Thickness, Style, Justification, Height, Rotation, and Width Factor.

- Type the command **MATCHPROP** and press **ENTER**.
- **Step 1: CLICK ONCE** on the object whose properties you want to copy.
- **Step 2: CLICK ONCE** on the destination objects (the objects to which you want to copy the properties). You can select the destination objects one at a time or with the Crossing window selection.
- Press **ENTER** on the keyboard to end the **MATCHPROP** command.

Distance

The Distance command allows you to verify the length of a line or space within your drawing.

- Type the command **DI** and press **ENTER**.
- **Step 1:** Using the mouse, **OBJECT SNAP** on the first point of your distance inquiry.
- **Step 2:** Using the mouse, **OBJECT SNAP** on the second point of your distance inquiry.

- The distance is reported in the command prompt. Information displayed includes the **DISTANCE**, the angle of the line, the horizontal distance (**DELTA X**), and the vertical distance (**DELTA Y**).
- A horizontal line will have a matching **DISTANCE** and horizontal distance (**DELTA X**). A vertical line will have a matching **DISTANCE** and vertical distance (**DELTA Y**).

Command: DIST Specify first point: Specify second point:
Distance = 2'-2", Angle in XY Plane = 0, Angle from XY Plane = 0
Delta X = 2'-2", Delta Y = 0'-0",   Delta Z = 0'-0"

Command:

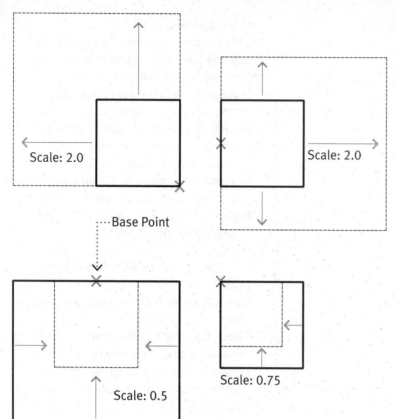

Base Point

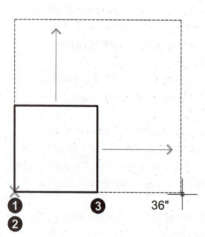

Scale

The Scale command allows you to adjust the size of an object or group of objects in your drawing.

· Type the command **SCALE** and press **ENTER**.
· Using the mouse, select the objects you want to scale. Press **ENTER** when you have finished selecting objects.
· Using the mouse, **SELECT THE BASE POINT** for your scale. The base point is the point from which your objects will grow or shrink.
· Type the **SCALE FACTOR** and press **ENTER**. To make something twice its original size, scale it by **2**. To make something half its original size, scale it by **0.5**.

Scale Reference

The Scale Reference command allows you to adjust the size of an object or group of objects in your drawing based on your desired length for a part of the selected object.

· There are times when you will receive a floor plan that is not drawn at real world scale. Using Scale Reference, you can adjust the scale of an unscaled floor plan so the door openings are 36".

· Type the command **SCALE** and press **ENTER**.
· **Step 1**: Using the mouse, select the objects you want to scale. In this example, you want to select the entire plan. Type **ALL** and press **ENTER**. Press **ENTER** one more time.
· Using the mouse, **SELECT THE BASE POINT** for your scale. The base point is the point from which your objects will grow or shrink.
· Type the letter **R** and press **ENTER**.
· **Steps 2 and 3**: Define the reference length by object snapping to either end of the door-jamb.
· Type the desired length (**36"**) and press **ENTER**.

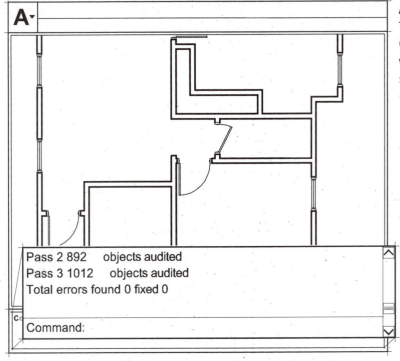

Pass 2 892   objects audited
Pass 3 1012   objects audited
Total errors found 0 fixed 0

Command:

Audit

The **AUDIT** command looks through your Auto-CAD file for errors or problems. The command will take longer to complete on larger files and slower computers.

· Run the Audit command when you first open a drawing received from a consultant or from another designer.
· You can run the Audit command on your own drawings after a file crash.

· Type the command **AUDIT** and press **ENTER**.
· AutoCAD prompts you to fix errors detected. Type the letter **Y** and press **ENTER**.
· You have successfully audited your drawing.

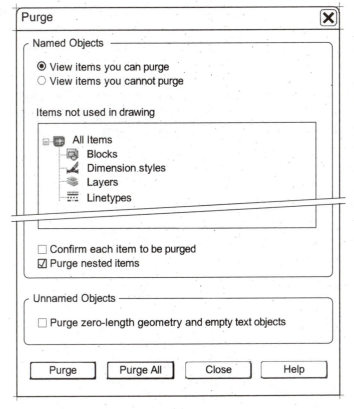

Purge

The **PURGE** command will clean your drawing of items that are taking up space but are no longer being used in your drawing. These items can include blocks, layers, text styles, and dimension styles.

· Type the command **PURGE** and press **ENTER**. AutoCAD will open the Purge dialog box.
· To purge individual items, select them from the "Items not used in drawing" area and **CLICK** the **PURGE** button.
· To purge all unused items in your drawing, place a checkmark in the "Purge nested items" option and **CLICK** the **PURGE ALL** button.
· Click the **CLOSE** button and **SAVE** your drawing.

AutoCAD Express Tools

The AutoCAD Express Tools are a collection of program enhancements that simplify many commands within AutoCAD. When installed, they are integrated into the AutoCAD menus and toolbars. The following pages describe several Express Tools that are commonly used when drawing in AutoCAD.

· Express Tools enhance a wide range of AutoCAD functions, including layer management, dimensioning, drawing, object selection, and object modification.

· Express Tools are included with versions of AutoCAD released after 2004 but may need to be installed separately from AutoCAD. (Check your AutoCAD CD for an Express folder.)

· Express Tools Vols. 1–9, which can be purchased from the AutoCAD store, work with all AutoCAD 2002–, 2000i–, and 2000–based products.

· Express Tools are not compatible with AutoCAD LT.

Flatten (Express Tool)

Although AutoCAD allows you to draw in three dimensions, 99 percent of all design drawings created in AutoCAD are two-dimensional.

· The **FLATTEN** command will adjust the **Z COORDINATE** of all objects in your drawing to **0**. This can be an important first step when you receive drawings from consultants or other designers.

· Type the command **FLATTEN** and press **ENTER**.
· Using the mouse, select the objects you want to flatten. In most cases, you want to flatten the entire drawing. Type **ALL** and press **ENTER**. Press **ENTER** one more time.
· AutoCAD prompts you to remove hidden lines. Type the letter **Y** and press **ENTER**.
· You have successfully flattened all the objects in your drawing.

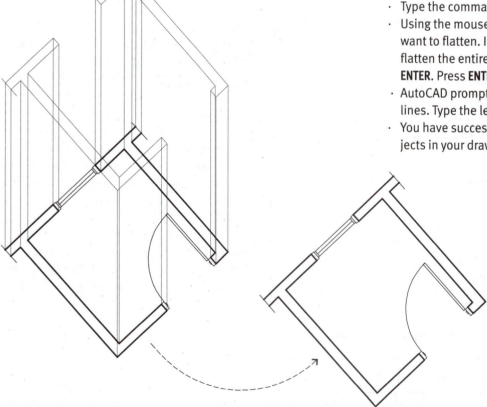

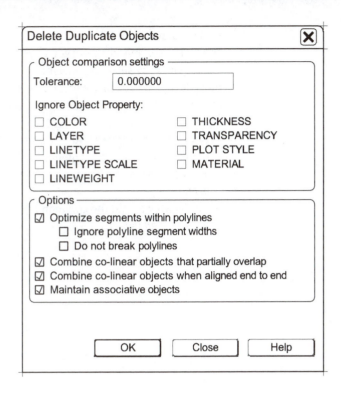

Delete Duplicate Objects (Express Tool)
The **DELETE DUPLICATE OBJECTS** command will remove lines, arcs, and circles that sit exactly on top of one another. In poorly executed Auto-CAD drawings, multiple lines are drawn exactly on top of one another. This can significantly increase drawing editing time.

- Type the command **OVERKILL** and press **ENTER**.
- Using the mouse, select the objects you want to check for duplicates. In most cases, you want to check the entire drawing. Type **ALL** and press **ENTER**. Press **ENTER** one more time.
- The Overkill dialog box will open. Select your desired settings and **CLICK OK**. The standard settings are shown to the left.
- You have successfully cleaned your drawing of duplicate objects.

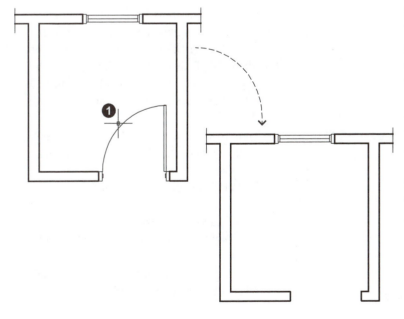

Layer Off (Express Tool)
The **LAYOFF** command allows you to turn off layers by selecting objects. If you select an object on the A-DOOR layer, the A-DOOR layer will be turned off.
- Type the command **LAYOFF** and press **ENTER**.
- Using the mouse, select objects on layers you want to turn off.
- Press **ENTER** to end the command.

Turn On All Layers (Express Tool)
The **LAYON** command turns on all layers.
- Type the command **LAYON** and press **ENTER**. All layers in the current drawing are turned on.

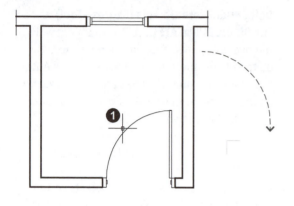

Layer Isolate

The **LAYISO** command allows you to visually isolate layers by selecting specific objects on those layers. If you isolate the A-DOOR layer, all layers will be turned off except the A-DOOR layer.

· Type the command **LAYISO** and press **ENTER**.
· Using the mouse, select objects on layers you want to isolate. You may isolate several layers.
· Press **ENTER** to end the command and isolate the selected layers.

Layer Freeze (Express Tool)

The **LAYFRZ** command allows you to freeze layers by selecting objects. If you select an object on the A-DOOR layer, the A-DOOR layer will be frozen. When a layer is frozen, all objects on that layer are not visible and cannot be modified.

· Type the command **LAYFRZ** and press **ENTER**.
· Using the mouse, select objects on layers you want to freeze.
· Press **ENTER** to end the command.

Thaw All Layers (Express Tool)

The **LAYTHW** command allows you to thaw all layers.

· Type the command **LAYTHW** and press **ENTER**. All layers in the current drawing are thawed.

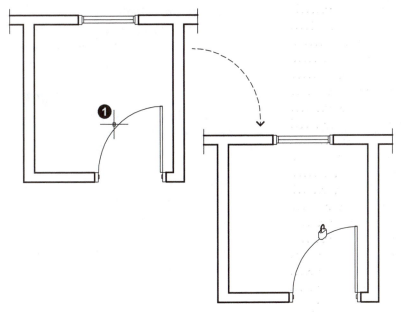

Layer Lock (Express Tool)

The **LAYLCK** command allows you to lock layers by selecting objects. If you select an object on the A-DOOR layer, the A-DOOR layer will be locked. When a layer is locked, all objects on that layer are visible but cannot be modified.

- Type the command **LAYLCK** and press **ENTER**.
- Using the mouse, select an object on the layer you want to lock. The layer is locked and the command ends.

Layer Unlock (Express Tool)

The **LAYULK** command allows you to unlock layers by selecting objects. If you select an object on the A-DOOR layer, the A-DOOR layer will be unlocked.

- Type the command **LAYULK** and press **ENTER**.
- Using the mouse, select an object on the layer you want to unlock. The layer is unlocked and the command ends.

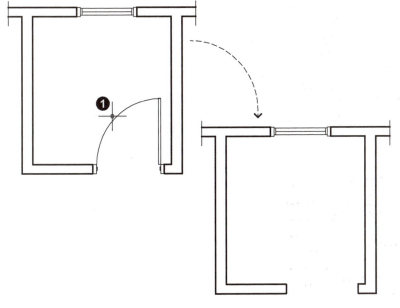

Layer Delete (Express Tool)

The **LAYDEL** command allows you to delete layers (and all objects on those layers) by selecting objects on those layers. If you select an object on the A-DOOR layer, the A-DOOR layer will be deleted (along with all objects on this layer).

- Type the command **LAYDEL** and press **ENTER**.
- Using the mouse, select an object on the layer you want to delete.
- Press **ENTER** when you are finished selecting layers to delete.
- AutoCAD warns, "*You are about to permanently delete layer window from this drawing.*" Type the letter **Y** and press **ENTER** to delete the selected layers.

Layer Merge (Express Tool)

The **LAYMRG** command allows you to merge one or more layers onto another layer in your drawing. You could merge the DOOR layer into the A-DOOR layer.

- Type the command **LAYMRG** and press **ENTER**.
- **STEP 1**: Using the mouse, select an object on the layer(s) you want to merge from.
- Press **ENTER** when you are finished selecting layers.
- **STEP 2**: Using the mouse, select an object on the layer you want to merge to.
- AutoCAD warns, "*You are about to permanently merge layer door into layer a-door.*" Type the letter **Y** and press **ENTER** to merge the selected layers.

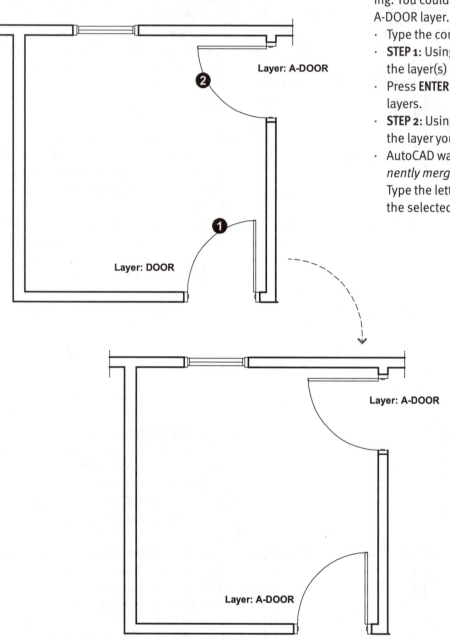

Layer: A-DOOR

Layer: DOOR

Layer: A-DOOR

Layer: A-DOOR

Learning Exercise

In this exercise, you will clean your drawing and become more familiar with the routine maintenance AutoCAD drawings require. Do not forget to save your drawing frequently when cleaning your drawing. AutoCAD has been known to crash while trying to fix a problem. Frequent saves will ensure that you have an up-to-date drawing when AutoCAD does crash.

Open Your Drawing

· Open AutoCAD.
· Open the drawing you created in the previous chapter:
  DDFD-EAMES.DWG

Cleaning Your Drawing

Complete the following commands to clean your drawing and to remove any extra or potentially corrupt information.

· Set the current layer to **0**.
· **UNLOCK** all layers in your drawing.
· Turn **ON** and **THAW** all layers in your drawing.

· Run the **AUDIT** command to check for any file errors in your drawing.
· **SAVE** your drawing.

· Use the **MATCHPROP** command to fix any lines that are on an incorrect layer.
· **SAVE** your drawing.

· Run the **OVERKILL** command to delete any duplicate lines or objects.
· **SAVE** your drawing.

· Run the **PURGE** command to remove unused blocks, layers, and linetypes.
· **SAVE** your drawing.

Congratulations, you have completed the learning exercise for this chapter.

CHAPTER 11
Dimensioning Your Drawing

The previous chapters introduced you to the tools that can help you draw more efficiently in AutoCAD when compared to manual drawing. Dimensioning in AutoCAD can save you more drawing time than any other tool about which you have learned. Dimensioning can also cause many headaches if the drawing is not accurate.

In manual drawings, dimensions are based on an overall understanding of the project design. If two walls scale to a little more than 20'-6" apart in your manual drawing, you will probably write the dimension as 20'-6".

In digital drawings, dimensions are based on the information AutoCAD receives as the drawing is created. Digital drawings are often worked on over several weeks or months by multiple designers. This alone creates an environment where errors can find their way into digital drawings. If two walls scale to a little more than 20'-6" apart in AutoCAD, the computer will give you the precise dimension: 20'-6 5/32".

Consider the following questions as you work through this chapter:
· What are Dimension Styles, and how can they help organize the visual appearance of dimensions in your drawings?
· How does the scale of your drawing affect the process of dimensioning your drawing?
· How do digital drawing errors become obvious when dimensioning a drawing in AutoCAD?

Dimension Your Drawing
AutoCAD simplifies the process of adding dimensions to your drawing.
By selecting and setting up a specific dimension style, you will ensure
that all the dimensions in your drawing are consistent.

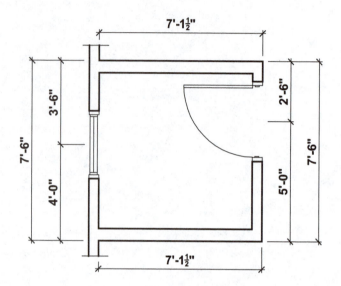

Tick Dimension Style
This dimension style is commonly found in
hand-drafted design drawings.

· The text used in this dimension style is san-
  serif and bold.
· The tick marks clearly identify where the
  dimension starts and stops.
· The extension lines do not touch the lines in
  the drawing.

· See page 158 to set up this dimension style
  in your drawings.

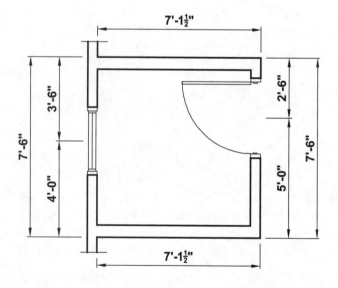

Arrow Dimension Style
This dimension style is a modified version of a
common style in hand-drafted design drawings.

· The text used in this dimension style is san-
  serif and bold.
· The arrows clearly identify where the dimension starts and stops.
· The extension lines do not touch the lines in
  the drawing.

· See page 162 to set up this dimension style
  in your drawings.

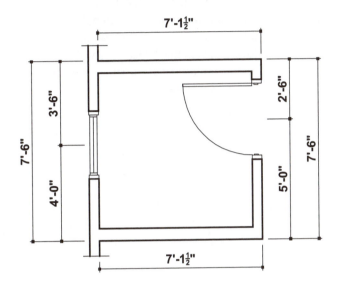

Box Dimension Style

This dimension style is a modernized version unique to AutoCAD design drawings.

- The text used in this dimension style is san-serif and bold.
- The box identifies where the dimension starts and stops.
- The extension lines do not touch the lines in the drawing.

- See page 166 to set up this dimension style in your drawings.

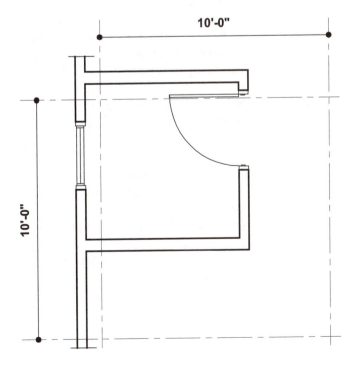

Dot Dimension Style

This dimension style is commonly used to iden-tify distances between column grids.

- The text used in this dimension style is san-serif and bold.
- The dot identifies where the dimension crosses the column grid.
- There are no extension lines.

- See page 170 to set up this dimension style in your drawings.

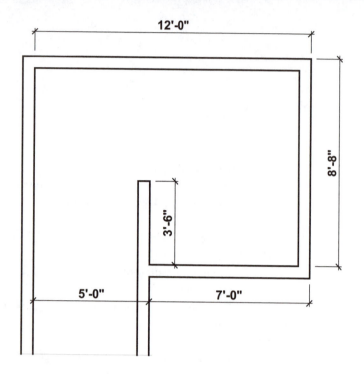

Dimensioning Walls

· In floor plans, wall dimensions are generally completed in a continuous line. line of dimensions is referred to as a dimension string.

· In the example to the left, the horizontal dimension strings locate the right finish face of all walls and the vertical dimension strings locate the top finish face of all walls. When dimensioning walls, attempt to dimension to a consistent side of all walls.

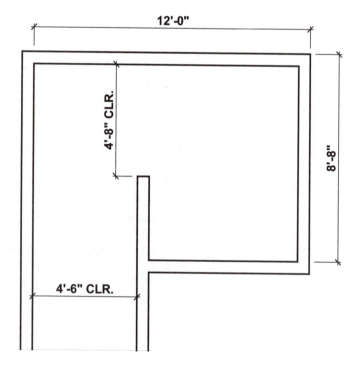

Dimensioning Corridors

· Critical dimensions such as corridor widths are dimensioned to indicate a clear opening dimension. This helps the builder understand your intentions and dimension priorities during construction.

· You can add the word **CLEAR** or the abbreviation **CLR** after any dimension to indicate a clear opening dimension.

Editing Dimension Text

· To edit dimension text type the command **DDEDIT** and press **ENTER**.
· **CLICK ONCE** on the dimension text that you want to edit.
· press **ENTER** when you have finished editing the dimension text.

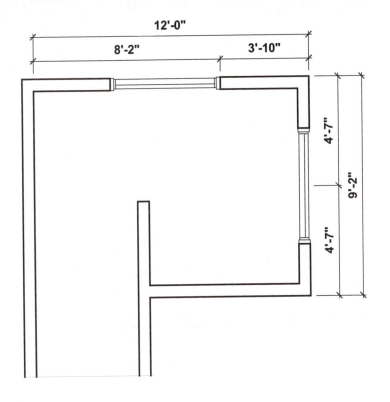

Dimensioning Windows

· Windows are most commonly dimensioned to their centerline.

· The width of a window is rarely dimensioned in floor plans because this information is located in the window schedule.

· Select and use a consistent method to dimension all of the windows in your project.

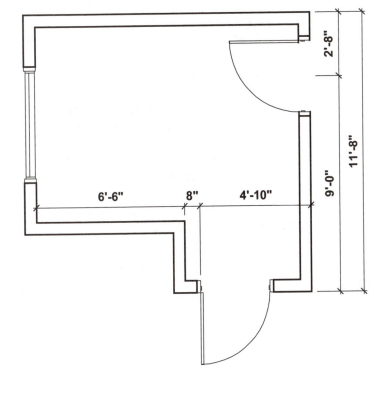

Dimensioning Doors

· Doors are most commonly dimensioned to their centerline or to the hinge side of the door.

· The width of a door is rarely dimensioned in floor plans because this information is located in the door schedule.

· Select and use a consistent method to dimension all of the doors in your project.

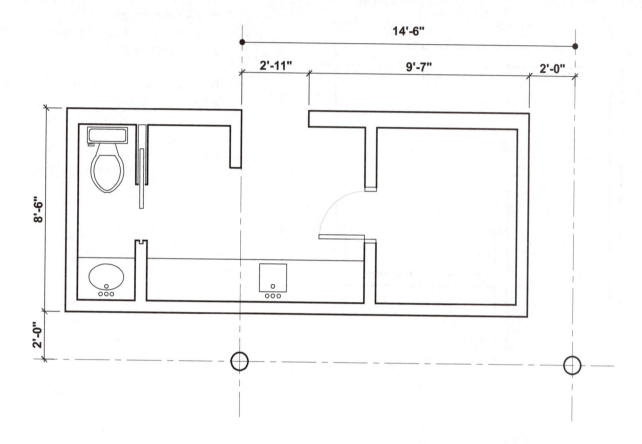

Dimensioning to Structure

· Structural column grids are usually extended beyond the exterior walls and dimensioned outside the building footprint.

· Structural columns are located at the intersection of the structural column grid.

· Structural columns are most commonly dimensioned to the centerline.

· Structural beams are most commonly dimensioned to the top of the beam.

Adding Dimensions to Your Drawing

The Dimension menu contains many dimensioning options. From this menu, you will use **LINEAR**, **ALIGNED**, and **CONTINUE** to complete most dimensioning tasks in AutoCAD.

Horizontal and Vertical Dimensions

Linear dimensions are either horizontal or vertical and are used to dimension most elements in plans, sections, and elevations.

- Type the command **DIMSTYLE** and press **ENTER**.

- Using the mouse, select the **DIM-TICK** dimension style and click the **SET CURRENT** button. (See page 158 to set up the **DIM-TICK** dimenssion style.)
- Click the **CLOSE** button.

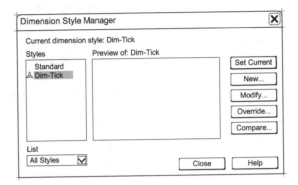

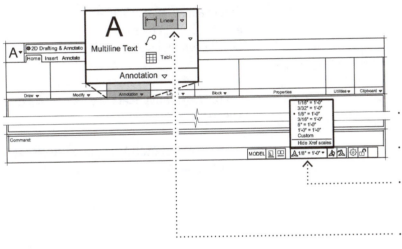

- Create a new layer in your drawing:
  A-DIM   Color 7
- Set the current layer to **A-DIM**.

- Set the **ANNOTATIVE SCALE** of your drawing to **1/8"=1'-0"**.

- From the **ANNOTATION PANEL**, in the **HOME TAB**, select **LINEAR**.

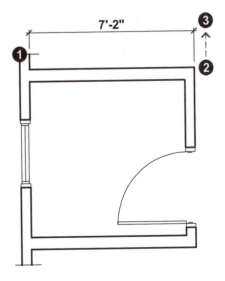

- **Steps 1 and 2**: Using object snaps, precisely select the first and second points of your dimension string.
- **Step 3**: Drag the cursor away from the dimensioned objects to locate or place the dimension string. **CLICK ONCE**.

- If you want to continue your dimension string, select **CONTINUE** from the **DIMENSION MENU**.

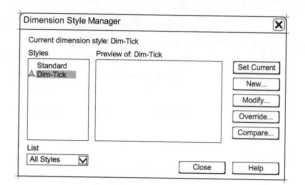

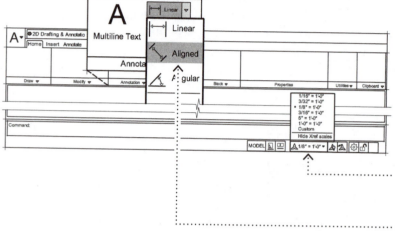

Aligned Dimensions

Aligned dimension strings are always parallel to the object or wall they are dimensioning. This type of dimension string is helpful in dimensioning the length of non-orthogonal (angled) walls.

· Type the command **DIMSTYLE** and press **ENTER**.

· Using the mouse, select the **DIM-TICK** dimension style and click the **SET CURRENT** button. (See page 158 to set up the **DIM-TICK** dimenssion style.)

· Click the **CLOSE** button.

· Create a new layer in your drawing:
  A-DIM   Color 7
· Set the current layer to **A-DIM**.

· Set the **ANNOTATIVE SCALE** of your drawing to **1/8"=1'-0"**.

· From the **ANNOTATION PANEL**, in the **HOME TAB**, select **ALIGNED**.

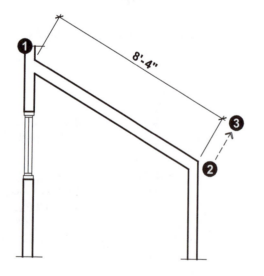

· **Steps 1 and 2:** Using object snaps, precisely select the first and second points of your dimension string.
· **Step 3:** Drag the cursor away from the dimensioned objects to locate or place the dimension string. **CLICK ONCE.**

· If you want to continue your dimension string, select **CONTINUE** from the **DIMENSION MENU.**

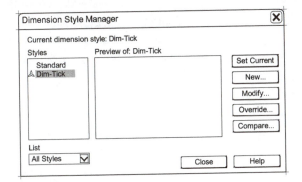

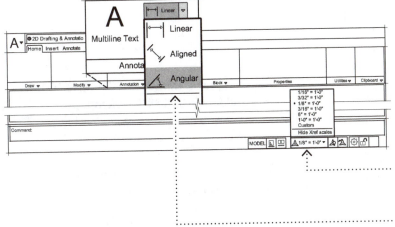

Angular Dimensions

Angular dimension strings display the angle of a wall relative to the horizontal or vertical planes. This type of dimension string is helpful in dimensioning the angle of non-orthogonal (angled) walls.

· Type the command **DIMSTYLE** and press **ENTER**.

· Using the mouse, select the **DIM-TICK** dimension style and click the **SET CURRENT** button. (See page 158 to set up the **DIM-TICK** dimenssion style.)
· Click the **CLOSE** button.

· Create a new layer in your drawing:
  A-DIM   Color 7
· Set the current layer to **A-DIM**.

· Set the **ANNOTATIVE SCALE** of your drawing to **1/8"=1'-0"**.

· From the **ANNOTATION PANEL**, in the **HOME TAB**, select **ANGULAR**.

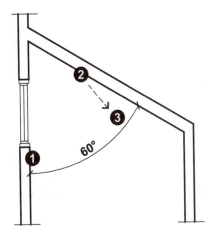

· **Steps 1 and 2**: Select the first line and the second line that define the angle.
· **Step 3**: Drag the cursor away from the dimensioned objects to locate or place the angular dimension string. **CLICK ONCE.**

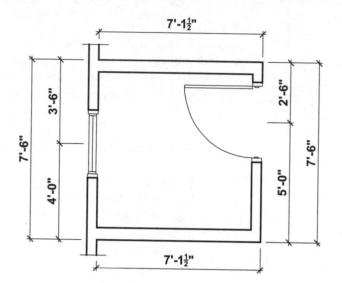

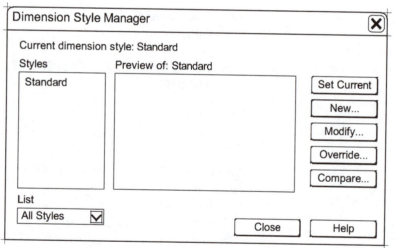

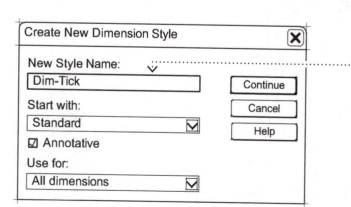

Adding the Tick Dimension Style

The following pages will guide you through the process of setting up a Tick Dimension Style (pictured left).

· Set your drawing's **UNIT LENGTH** to **ARCHITEC-TURAL** and **UNIT PRECISION** to **1/32"**.

· Create a new layer in your drawing:
  A-DIM   Color 7

· Type the command **DIMSTYLE** and press **ENTER**. This will open the Dimension Style Manager.

· Click the **NEW** button to create a new dimension style.

· Type the style name **DIM-TICK** and press the **CONTINUE** button.

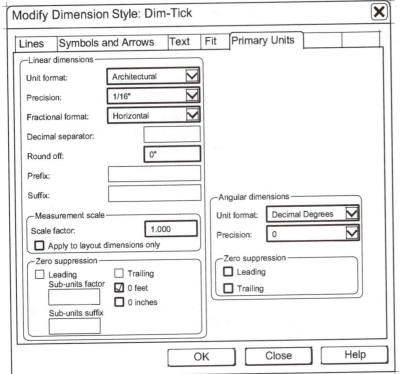

Primary Units Tab

Click once on the Primary Units tab and make the following modifications:

- Set the Unit format to: **ARCHITECTURAL**
- Set the Precision to: **1/16"**
- Set the Fractional format to: **HORIZONTAL**
- Set the Round off to: **0"**

- Set the Measurement scale to: **1.000**
- In the Zero suppression section (linear dimension), **CHECK** the **0 FEET** option.

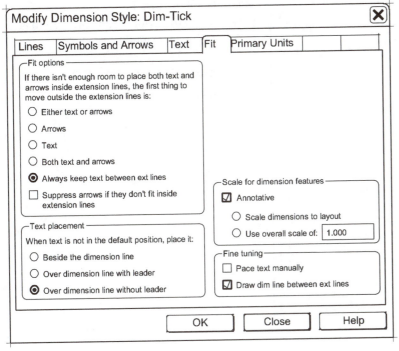

Fit Tab

Click once on the Fit tab and make the following modifications:

- Set Fit options to: **ALWAYS KEEP TEXT BETWEEN EXT LINES**
- Set Text placement to: **OVER DIMENSION LINE WITHOUT LEADER**

- In the Scale for dimension features section, **CHECK** the **ANNOTATIVE** option.

- In the Fine tuning section, **CHECK** the **DRAW DIM LINE BETWEEN EXT LINES** option.

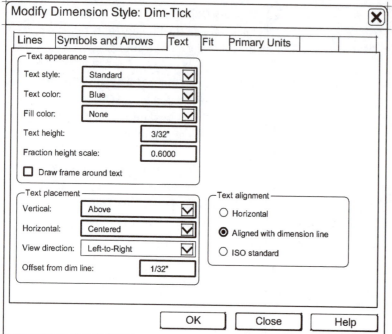

Text Tab

Click once on the Text tab and make the following modifications:

- Set the Text style to: **STANDARD**
- Set the Text color to: **BLUE**
- Set the Fill color to: **NONE**
- For construction documents, set the Text height to: **3/32"**
- For presentation drawings, set the Text height between: **1/8"** and **1/4"**

- Set the Fraction height scale to: **0.6000**
- Set the Vertical text placement to: **ABOVE**
- Set the Horizontal text placement to: **CENTERED**
- Set the Offset from dim line to: **1/32"**
- Set the Text alignment to: **ALIGNED WITH DIMENSION LINE**

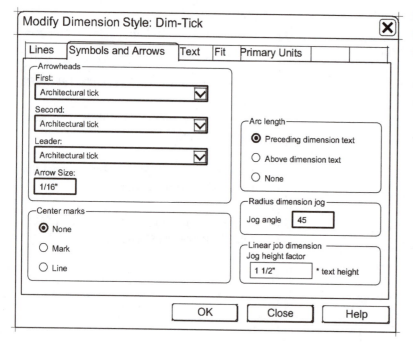

Symbols and Arrows Tab

Click once on the Symbols and Arrows tab and make the following modifications:

- Set all Arrowheads to: **ARCHITECTURAL TICK**
- Set Arrow Size to **1/16"**

- Set Center marks to: **NONE**

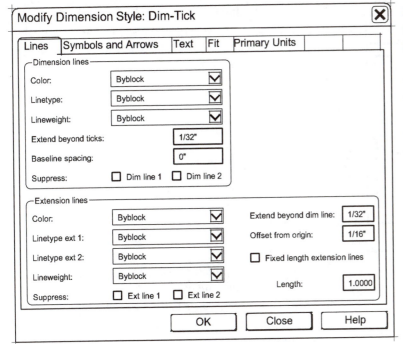

Lines Tab

Click once on the Lines tab and make the following modifications:

- Set Extend beyond ticks to: **1/32"**
- Set Baseline spacing to: **0"**

- Set Extend beyond dim line to: **1/32"**
- Set Offset from origin to: **1/16"**

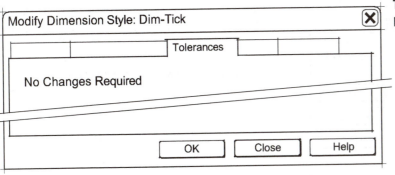

Alternate Units Tab

No modifications are required for this tab.

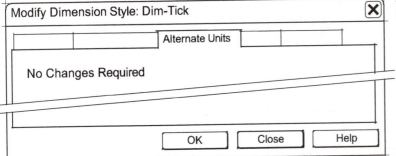

Tolerances Tab

No modifications are required for this tab.

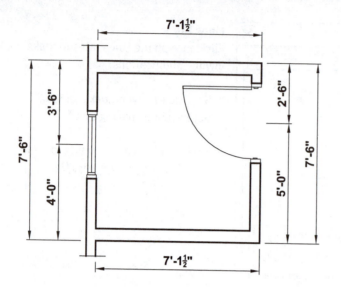

Adding the Arrow Dimension Style
The following pages will guide you through the process of setting up an Arrow Dimension Style (pictured left).

· Set your drawing's **UNIT LENGTH** to **ARCHITECTURAL** and **UNIT PRECISION** to **1/32"**.
· Create a new layer in your drawing:
  A-DIM   Color 7

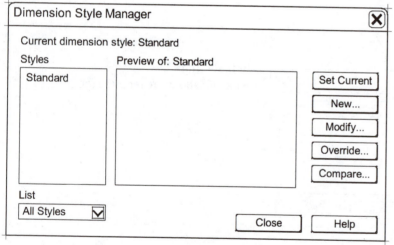

· Type the command **DIMSTYLE** and press **ENTER**. This will open the Dimension Style Manager.
· Click the **NEW** button to create a new dimension style.

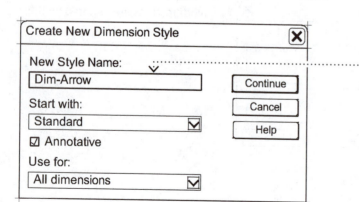

Type the style name **DIM-ARROW** and press the **CONTINUE** button.

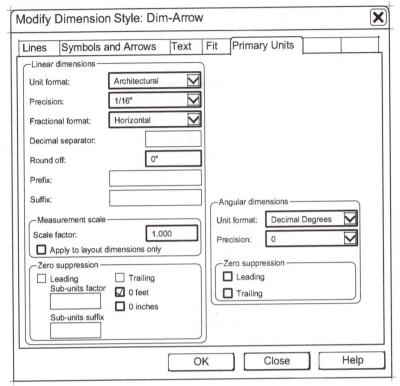

Primary Units Tab

Click once on the Primary Units tab and make the following modifications:

- Set the Unit format to: **ARCHITECTURAL**
- Set the Precision to: **1/16"**
- Set the Fractional format to: **HORIZONTAL**
- Set the Round off to: **0"**

- Set the Measurement scale to: **1.000**
- In the Zero suppression section (linear dimension), check the option: **0 FEET**

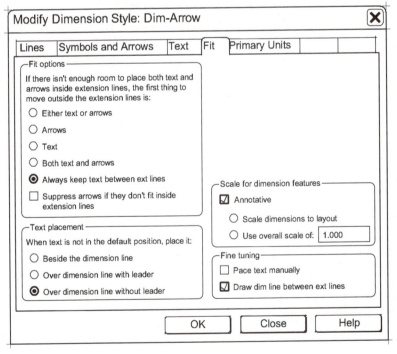

Fit Tab

Click once on the Fit tab and make the following modifications:

- Set Fit options to: **ALWAYS KEEP TEXT BETWEEN EXT LINES**
- Set Text placement to: **OVER DIMENSION LINE WITHOUT LEADER**

- In the Scale for dimension features section, **CHECK** the **ANNOTATIVE** option.

- In the Fine tuning section, **CHECK** the **DRAW DIM LINE BETWEEN EXT LINES** option.

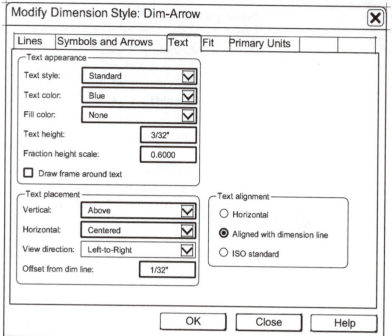

Text Tab

Click once on the Text tab and make the following modifications:

- Set the Text style to: **STANDARD**
- Set the Text color to: **BLUE**
- Set the Fill color to: **NONE**
- For construction documents, set the Text height to: **3/32"**
- For presentation drawings, set the Text height between: **1/8"** and **1/4"**

- Set the Fraction height scale to: **0.6000**
- Set the Vertical text placement to: **ABOVE**
- Set the Horizontal text placement to: **CENTERED**
- Set the Offset from dim line to: **1/32"**
- Set the Text alignment to: **ALIGNED WITH DIMENSION LINE**

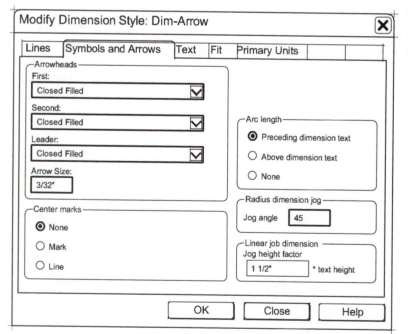

Symbols and Arrows Tab

Click once on the Symbols and Arrows tab and make the following modifications:

- Set all Arrowheads to: **CLOSED FILLED**
- Set Arrow Size to: **3/32"**

- Set Center marks to: **NONE**

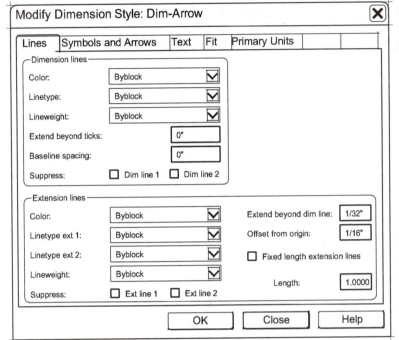

Lines Tab

Click once on the Lines tab and make the following modifications:

· Set Extend beyond ticks to: **0"**
· Set Baseline spacing to: **0"**

· Set Extend beyond dim line to: **1/32"**
· Set Offset from origin to: **1/16"**

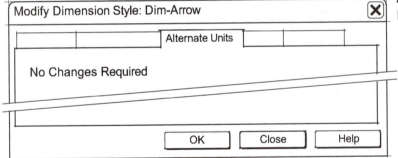

Alternate Units Tab

No modifications are required for this tab.

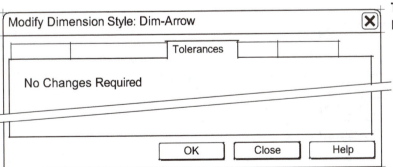

Tolerances Tab

No modifications are required for this tab.

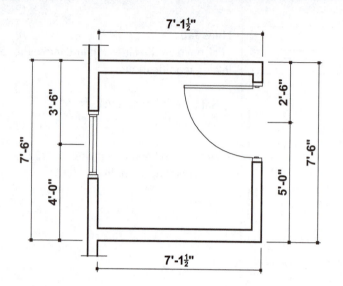

Adding the Box Dimension Style

The following pages will guide you through the process of setting up a Box Dimension Style (pictured left).

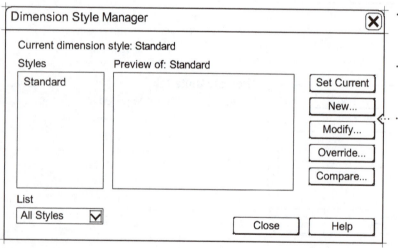

· Set your drawing's **UNIT LENGTH** to **ARCHITECTURAL** and **UNIT PRECISION** to 1/32".
· Create a new layer in your drawing:
  A-DIM   Color 7

· Type the command **DIMSTYLE** and press **ENTER**. This will open the Dimension Style Manager.
· Click the **NEW** button to create a new dimension style.

Type the style name **DIM-BOX** and press the **CONTINUE** button.

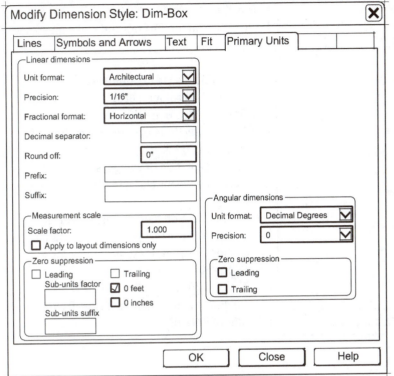

Primary Units Tab

Click once on the Primary Units tab and make the following modifications:

- Set the Unit format to: **ARCHITECTURAL**
- Set the Unit precision to: **1/16"**
- Set the Fractional format to: **HORIZONTAL**
- Set the Round off to: **0"**

- Set the Measurement scale to: **1.000**
- In the Zero suppression section (linear dimension), check the option: **0 FEET**

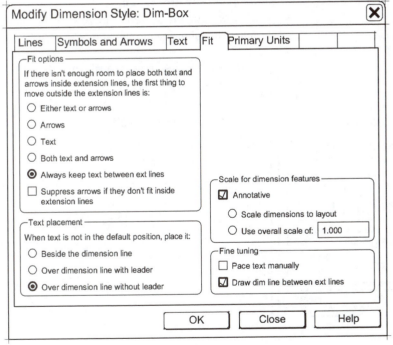

Fit Tab

Click once on the Fit tab and make the following modifications:

- Set Fit options to: **ALWAYS KEEP TEXT BETWEEN EXT LINES**
- Set Text placement to: **OVER DIMENSION LINE WITHOUT LEADER**

- In the Scale for dimension features section, **CHECK** the **ANNOTATIVE** option.

- In the Fine tuning section, **CHECK** the **DRAW DIM LINE BETWEEN EXT LINES** option.

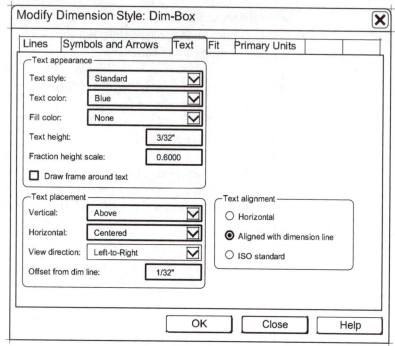

Text Tab

Click once on the Text tab and make the following modifications:

- Set the Text style to: **STANDARD**
- Set the Text color to: **BLUE**
- Set the Fill color to: **NONE**
- For construction documents, set the Text height to: **3/32"**
- For presentation drawings, set the Text height between: **1/8"** and **1/4"**

- Set the Fraction height scale to: **0.6000**
- Set the Vertical text placement to: **ABOVE**
- Set the Horizontal text placement to: **CENTERED**
- Set the Offset from dim line to: **1/32"**
- Set the Text alignment to: **ALIGNED WITH DIMENSION LINE**

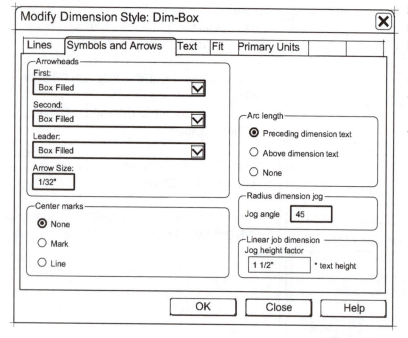

Symbols and Arrows Tab

Click once on the Symbols and Arrows tab and make the following modifications:

- Set all Arrowheads to: **BOX FILLED**
- Set Arrow Size to: **1/32"**

- Set Center marks to: **NONE**

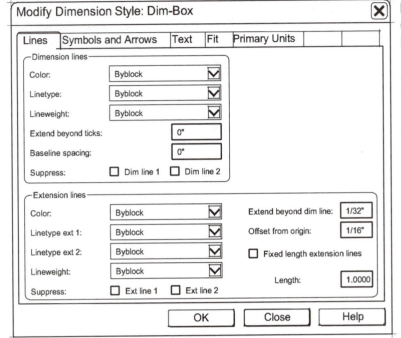

Lines Tab

Click once on the Lines tab and make the following modifications:

· Set Extend beyond ticks to: **0"**
· Set Baseline spacing to: **0"**

· Set Extend beyond dim line to: **1/32"**
· Set Offset from origin to: **1/16"**

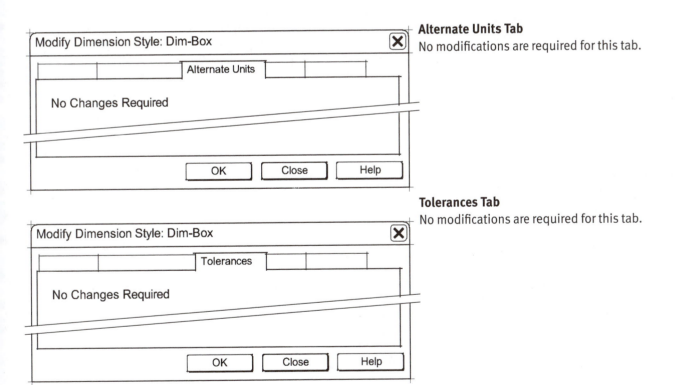

Alternate Units Tab

No modifications are required for this tab.

Tolerances Tab

No modifications are required for this tab.

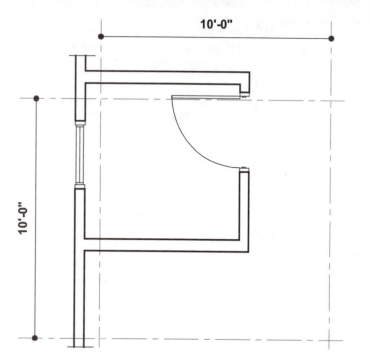

Adding the Dot Dimension Style
The following pages will guide you through the process of setting up a Dot Dimension Style (pictured left).

· Set your drawing's **UNIT LENGTH** to **ARCHITEC-TURAL** and **UNIT PRECISION** to **1/32".**
· Create a new layer in your drawing:
    A-DIM   Color 7

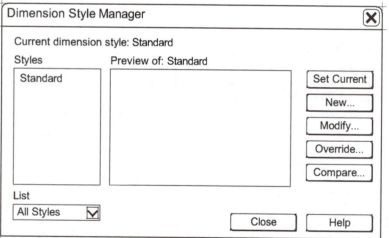

· Type the command **DIMSTYLE** and press **ENTER.** This will open the Dimension Style Manager.
· Click the **NEW** button to create a new dimension style.

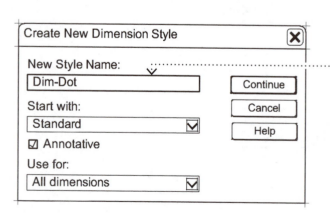

Type the style name **DIM-DOT** and press the **CONTINUE** button.

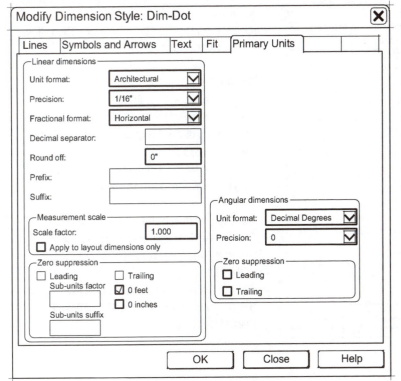

Primary Units Tab

Click once on the Primary Units tab and make the following modifications:

· Set the Unit format to: **ARCHITECTURAL**
· Set the Precision to: **1/16"**
· Set the Fractional format to: **HORIZONTAL**
· Set the Round off to: **0"**

· Set the Measurement scale to: **1.000**
· In the Zero suppression section (linear dimension), check the option: **0 FEET**

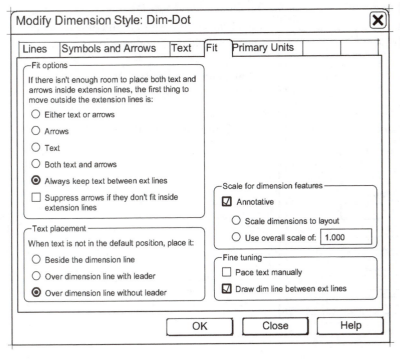

Fit Tab

Click once on the Fit tab and make the following modifications:

· Set the Fit options to: **ALWAYS KEEP TEXT BETWEEN EXT LINES**
· Set the Text placement to: **OVER DIMENSION LINE WITHOUT LEADER**

· Set the Scale for dimension features to match the scale factor for your drawing. In this example, we are dimensioning a 1/4"=1'-0" drawing with a scale factor of 48.

· In the Fine tuning section, check the option to: **DRAW DIM LINE BETWEEN EXT LINES**

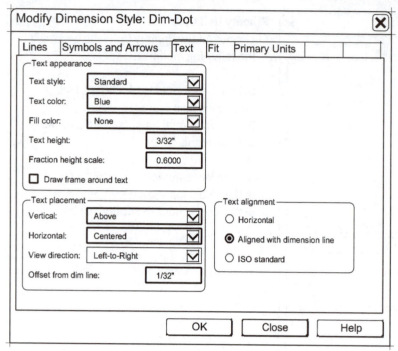

Text Tab

Click once on the Text tab and make the following modifications:

- Set the Text style to: **STANDARD**
- Set the Text color to: **BLUE**
- Set the Fill color to: **NONE**
- For construction documents, set the Text height to: **3/32"**
- For presentation drawings, set the Text height between: **1/8"** and **1/4"**

- Set the Fraction height scale to: **0.6000**
- Set the Vertical text placement to: **ABOVE**
- Set the Horizontal text placement to: **CENTERED**
- Set the Offset from dim line to: **1/32"**
- Set the Text alignment to: **ALIGNED WITH DIMENSION LINE**

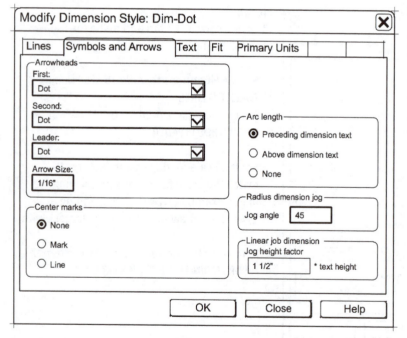

Symbols and Arrows Tab

Click once on the Symbols and Arrows tab and make the following modifications:

- Set all Arrowheads to: **DOT**
- Set Arrow Size to: **1/16"**

- Set Center marks to: **NONE**

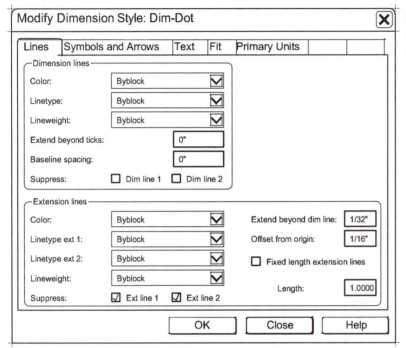

Lines Tab

Click once on the Lines tab and make the following modifications:

- Set Extend beyond ticks to: **0"**
- Set Baseline spacing to: **0"**

- Set Extend beyond dim line to: **1/32"**
- Set Offset from origin to: **1/16"**

- Suppress: **EXT LINE 1**
- Suppress: **EXT LINE 2**

Alternate Units Tab

No modifications are required for this tab.

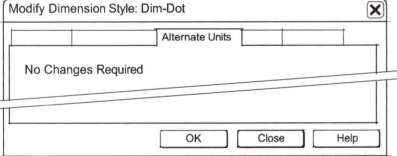

Tolerances Tab

No modifications are required for this tab.

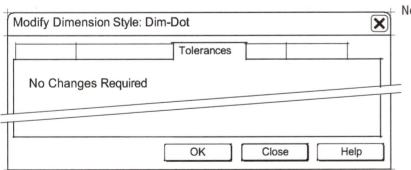

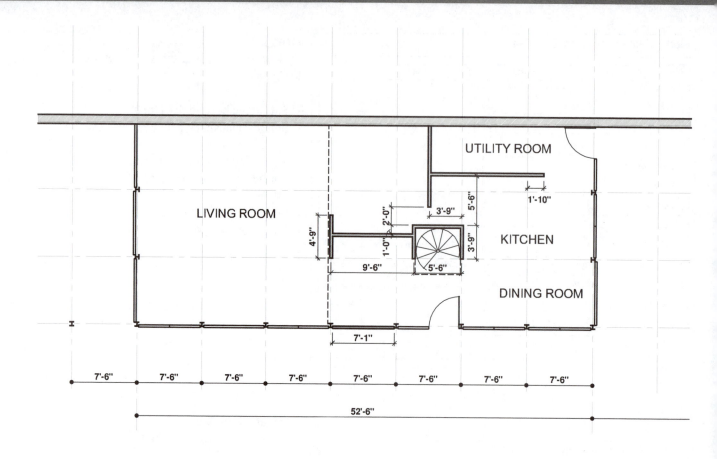

Learning Exercise

In this exercise, you will set up a dimension style and add dimensions to your floor plan.

Open Your Drawing
· Open AutoCAD.
· Open the drawing you created in the previous chapter:
  DDFD-EAMES.DWG

Creating Your Layers

Create the following layers.

· **A-DIM**   Color 7
· Set the current layer to **A-DIM.**

Adding a Dimension Style

· Using the guides in this chapter, create the Tick and Dot dimension style in your drawing.

· Set the current dimension style to: **DIM-TICK.**

· Save your drawing.

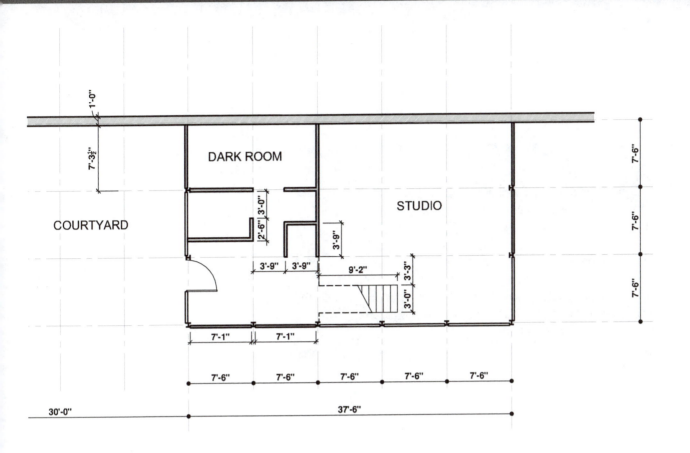

Dimensioning Your Drawing

· In model space, set the annotative scale of your drawing to **1/8"=1'-0"**.

· Using the various dimension commands and dimension styles, add dimensions to your drawing to match the drawing above.

· Save your drawing.

Congratulations, you have completed the learning exercise for this chapter.

Companion Download

The companion download contains additional AutoCAD drawings that allow you to test your understanding of using dimensions in AutoCAD.

Look inside the Learning Exercises folder for these files.

The following websites feature the companion download for this book: www.fairchildbooks.combook.cms?bookid=179 or www.DDFDbook.com/ch11

CHAPTER 12
Text Leaders

As you develop design drawings you will increasingly need to add notes to your drawings. At the same time, you may also find that there is not enough space inside your drawing to include the amount of text required to communicate your design idea.

The Text Leader command in AutoCAD allows you to draw a leader line with an arrow or dot on one end and multiline text on the other end. This method of adding notes to drawings is used primarily in construction drawings.

Notes/Text Leaders

Like dimensions, AutoCAD simplifies the process of adding notes (text leaders) to your drawing. By selecting and setting up a specific dimension style, you will ensure that the notes in your drawing are consistent.

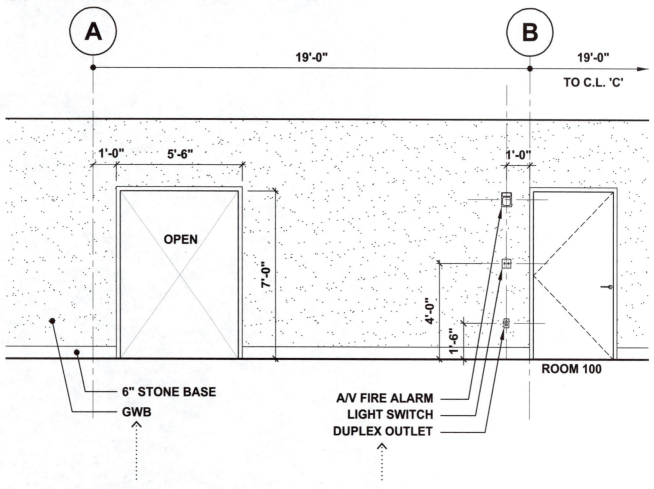

Dot Text Leaders

This dimension leader style is commonly used to note surfaces in plan, section, elevation, and details.

· The text used in this dimension style is sanserif and bold.
· The dot is clearly located on the surface noted.
· The leader lines are parallel to each other and, when possible, cross other lines in the drawing at an angle.

· See page 182 to set up this dimension style in your drawings.

Arrow Text Leaders

This dimension leader style is commonly used to note objects in plan, section, elevation, and details.

· The text used in this dimension style is sanserif and bold.
· The arrow points directly to the object noted.
· The leader lines are parallel to each other and cross other lines in the drawing at an angle.

· See page 180 to set up this dimension style in your drawings.

ADDING TEXT LEADERS

Adding Notes to Your Drawing

The Dimension menu contains several dimensioning options. From this menu, you will use the **MULTILEADER** button to complete most of the note tasks in your AutoCAD drawing.

Text Leader

Leaders always start at the object or surface and continue off the drawing at an angle.

- Type the command **MLEADERSTYLE** and press **ENTER**.

- Using the mouse, select the **LEADER-ARROW** multileader style and click the **SET CURRENT** button. (See page 180 to set up the **LEADER-ARROW** multileader style.)
- Click the **CLOSE** button.

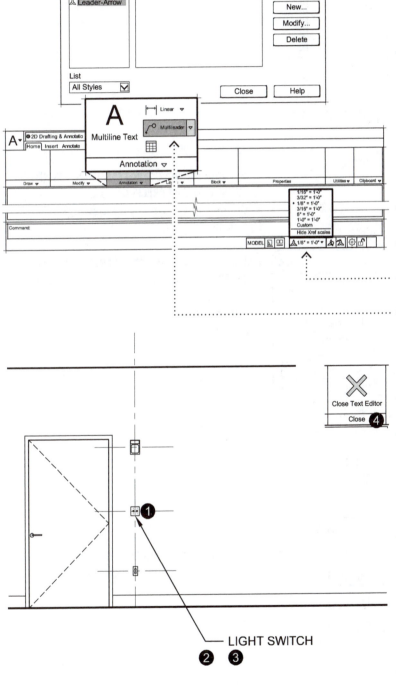

- Create a new layer in your drawing:
  A-NOTE   Color 4
- Set the current layer to **A-NOTE**.

- Set the **ANNOTATIVE SCALE** of your drawing to **1/8"=1'-0"**.
- From the **ANNOTATION PANEL**, in the **HOME TAB**, select **MULTILEADER**.

- **Step 1**: Using object snaps, precisely select the first point of your leader.
- **Step 2**: Drag your cursor away from the object and **CLICK** to locate the end of the angled leader. As you drag the cursor, notice that AutoCAD has locked your line to a 30-degree angle.
- **Step 3**: Type the note for this leader.
- **Step 4**: When you are finished, **CLICK** the **CLOSE TEXT EDITOR** button located on the right side of the ribbon.

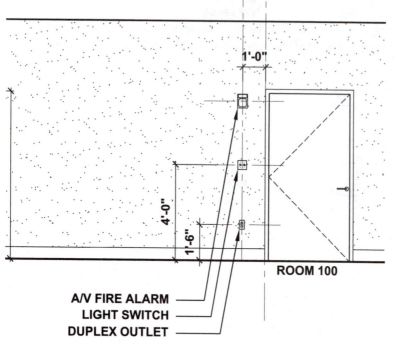

1'-0"

4'-0"

1'-6"

ROOM 100

A/V FIRE ALARM
LIGHT SWITCH
DUPLEX OUTLET

Adding the Arrow Multileader Style
The following pages will guide you through the process of setting up an Arrow Multileader Style (pictured left).

- Set your drawing's **UNIT LENGTH** to **ARCHITEC-TURAL** and **UNIT PRECISION** to **1/32"**.
- Create a new layer in your drawing:
  A-NOTE   Color 5

- Type the command **MLEADERSTYLE** and press **ENTER**. This will open the Multileader Style Manager.
- Click the **NEW** button to create a new multi-leader style.

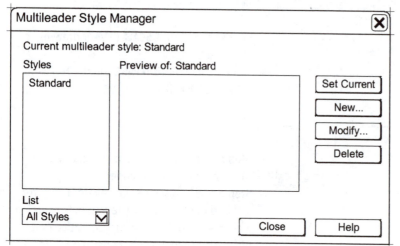

Multileader Style Manager

Current multileader style: Standard

Styles

Standard

Preview of: Standard

Set Current
New...
Modify...
Delete

List

All Styles

Close   Help

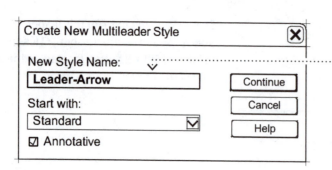

Create New Multileader Style

New Style Name:

Leader-Arrow

Start with:

Standard

☑ Annotative

Continue
Cancel
Help

- Type the style name **ARROW-NOTE-48** and press the **CONTINUE** button.

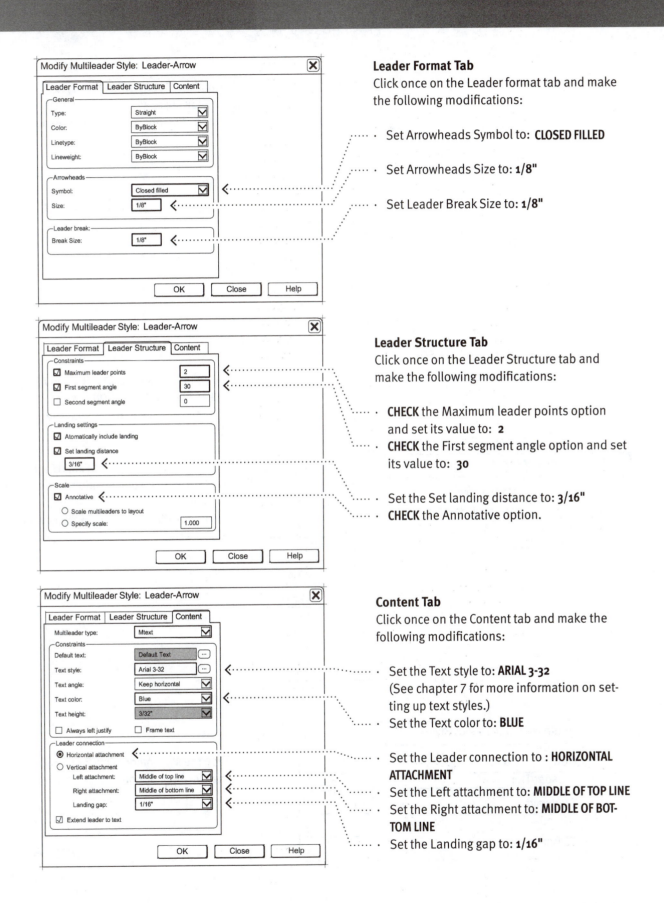

Leader Format Tab

Click once on the Leader format tab and make the following modifications:

· Set Arrowheads Symbol to: **CLOSED FILLED**

· Set Arrowheads Size to: **1/8"**

· Set Leader Break Size to: **1/8"**

Leader Structure Tab

Click once on the Leader Structure tab and make the following modifications:

· **CHECK** the Maximum leader points option and set its value to: **2**
· **CHECK** the First segment angle option and set its value to: **30**

· Set the Set landing distance to: **3/16"**
· **CHECK** the Annotative option.

Content Tab

Click once on the Content tab and make the following modifications:

· Set the Text style to: **ARIAL 3-32** (See chapter 7 for more information on setting up text styles.)
· Set the Text color to: **BLUE**

· Set the Leader connection to : **HORIZONTAL ATTACHMENT**
· Set the Left attachment to: **MIDDLE OF TOP LINE**
· Set the Right attachment to: **MIDDLE OF BOTTOM LINE**
· Set the Landing gap to: **1/16"**

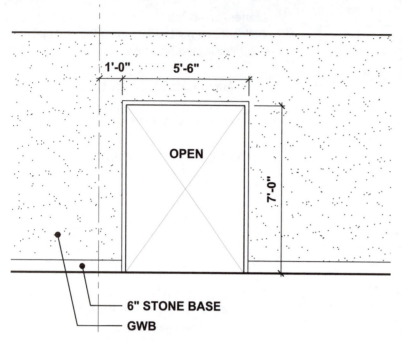

1'-0"   **5'-6"**

OPEN

7'-0"

6" STONE BASE

GWB

Adding the Dot Multileader Style

The following pages will guide you through the process of setting up a Dot Multileader Style.

- Set your drawing's **UNIT LENGTH** to **ARCHITEC-TURAL** and **UNIT PRECISION** to **1/32"**.
- Create a new layer in your drawing:
  A-NOTE   Color 5

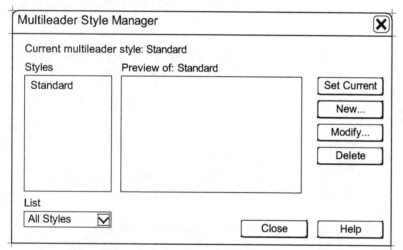

- Type the command **MLEADERSTYLE** and press **ENTER**. This will open the Multileader Style Manager.
- Click the **NEW** button to create a new multileader style.

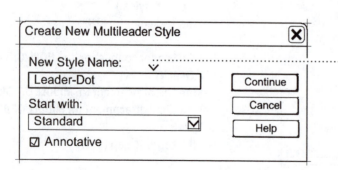

- Type the style name **LEADER-DOT** and press the **CONTINUE** button.

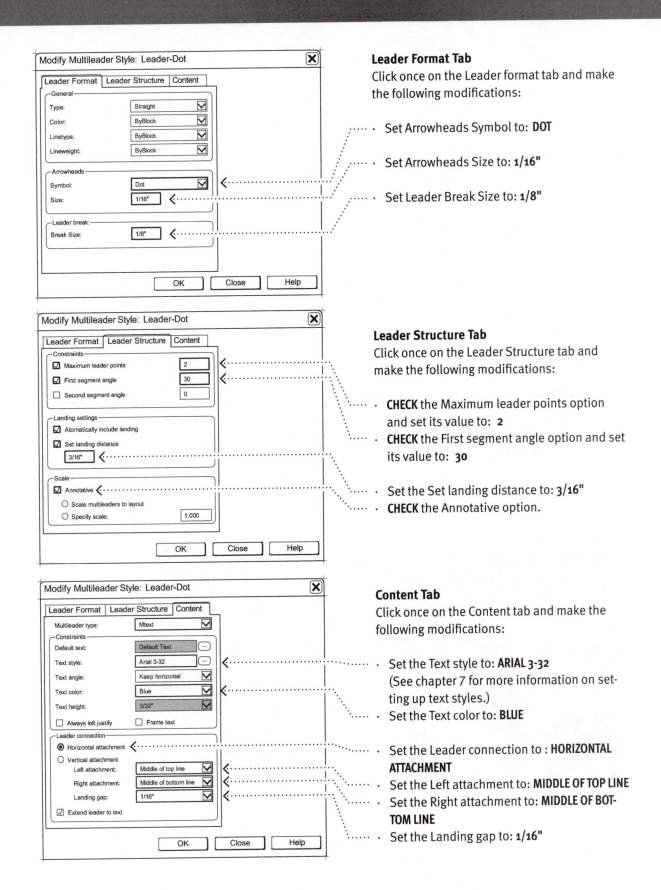

Leader Format Tab

Click once on the Leader format tab and make the following modifications:

· Set Arrowheads Symbol to: **DOT**

· Set Arrowheads Size to: **1/16"**

· Set Leader Break Size to: **1/8"**

Leader Structure Tab

Click once on the Leader Structure tab and make the following modifications:

· **CHECK** the Maximum leader points option and set its value to: **2**

· **CHECK** the First segment angle option and set its value to: **30**

· Set the Set landing distance to: **3/16"**

· **CHECK** the Annotative option.

Content Tab

Click once on the Content tab and make the following modifications:

· Set the Text style to: **ARIAL 3-32** (See chapter 7 for more information on setting up text styles.)

· Set the Text color to: **BLUE**

· Set the Leader connection to : **HORIZONTAL ATTACHMENT**

· Set the Left attachment to: **MIDDLE OF TOP LINE**

· Set the Right attachment to: **MIDDLE OF BOTTOM LINE**

· Set the Landing gap to: **1/16"**

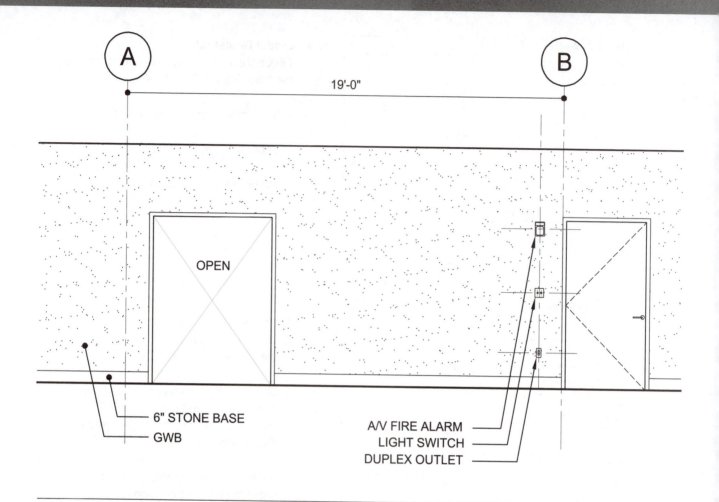

Companion Download

The companion download contains additional AutoCAD drawings that you need for the learning exercise on this page.

The following websites feature the companion download for this book:
www.DDFDbook.com/ch12

Look inside the Learning Exercises folder for the following file:
12_LEADERS_INT_1-4.DWG

Annotating interior elevations: 1/4"=1'-0"

· Open **12_LEADERS_INT_1-4.DWG** from the learning exercises folder in this book's companion download.

· Set the drawing annoataion scale to 1/4"=1'-0".

· Setup both the **LEADER-DOT** and **LEADER-ARROW** multileader styles described in this chapter.

· Add notes to the AutoCAD drawing using the image above as a reference.

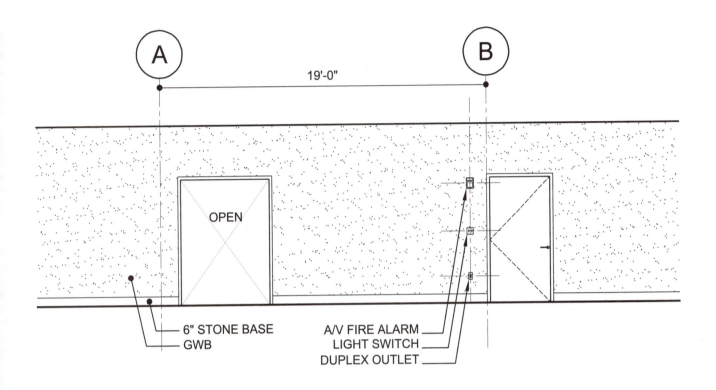

19'-0"

OPEN

6" STONE BASE
GWB

A/V FIRE ALARM
LIGHT SWITCH
DUPLEX OUTLET

Annotating interior elevations: 3/16"=1'-0"
· Open **12_LEADERS_INT_3-16.DWG** from the learning exercises folder in this book's companion download.

· Set the drawing annoataion scale to 3/16"=1'-0".
· Setup both the **LEADER-DOT** and **LEADER-ARROW** multileader styles described in this chapter.
· Add notes to the AutoCAD drawing using the image above as a reference.

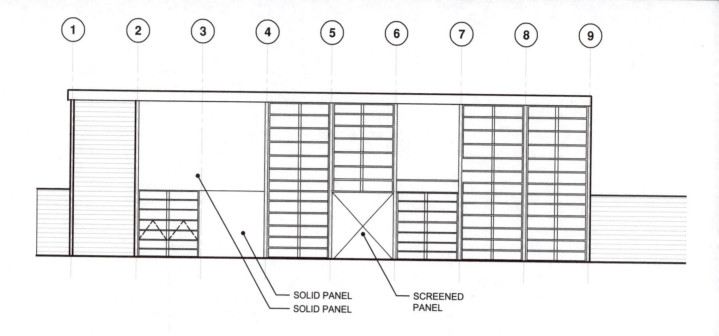

SOLID PANEL
SOLID PANEL
SCREENED PANEL

Companion Download

The companion download contains additional AutoCAD drawings that you need for the learning exercise on this page.

The following websites feature the companion download for this book:
www.DDFDbook.com/ch12

Look inside the Learning Exercises folder for the following file:
12_LEADERS_BLDG.DWG

Annotating building elevations: 1/8"=1'-0"

· Open **12_LEADERS_BLDG.DWG** from the learning exercises folder in this book's companion download.

· Set the drawing annoataion scale to 1/8"=1'-0".
· Setup both the **LEADER-DOT** and **LEADER-ARROW** multileader styles described in this chapter.
· Add notes to the AutoCAD drawing using the image above as a reference.

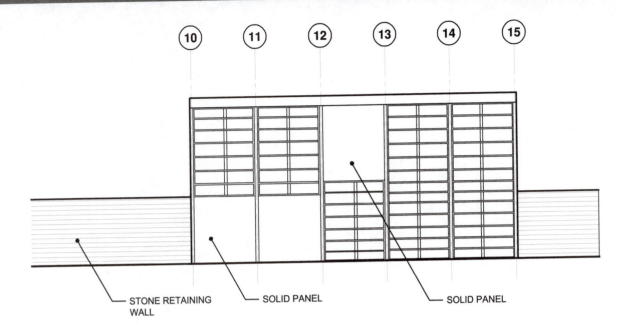

STONE RETAINING
WALL

SOLID PANEL

SOLID PANEL

CHAPTER 13
Drawing Symbols and Attributed Text

In previous chapters you learned the advantages of using blocks to organize repeating elements such as furniture and doors in your drawing. There are also graphic symbols used in design drawings that communicate the relationship between drawings in a presentation or in a set of construction drawings. This second type of symbol contains text that changes to reflect the location of the referenced drawing or a description of the drawing. While the number of sheets in a presentation or construction drawing will vary from 2 to more than 100, the purpose and use of the drawing symbols is always the same: to create a visual link among the drawings.

For example, a small presentation may contain one floor plan, two building sections, and four interior elevations. The building section symbol is used in the floor plan drawing (sheet A1) to identify the location of the first building section cut and the location of the building section in the presentation (drawing 1 on sheet A2). This symbol will also identify the second building section (drawing 2 on sheet A2). The interior elevation symbol is used on the floor plan to identify the walls that are elevated and the location of the interior elevations in the presentation (drawings 1, 2, 3, and 4 on sheet A3). Examples of these symbols are available in the Chapter 13 folder http://www.fairchild-books.com/book.cms?bookId=179.

This chapter explains what these symbols look like, how to create them, and how to use them in your drawings. Most importantly, you will learn how to create blocks with editable text.

Graphic Drawing Symbols

Presentation drawings and construction drawings may contain several sheets. Drawing symbols are used to coordinate or link the drawings within these sheets. In AutoCAD, you will create individual blocks with attributed text for each symbol.

Drawing Name / Detail Name Symbol

· This symbol is used to identify drawings when more than one drawing exists on a printed sheet. For example, if you have three interior elevations on a sheet, then each elevation would have one of these symbols under it identifying it by name and number.

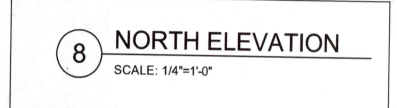

Exterior Elevation Symbol

· This symbol is used on floor plans to identify exterior elevations. The top number refers to the number in the Drawing Name Symbol on the exterior elevation sheet. The bottom number refers to the exterior elevation sheet number. The arrow in this symbol is rotated to point toward the exterior surface that is elevated.

Building Section Symbol

· This symbol is used on floor plans to identify building sections. The top number refers to the building section number on the building section sheet. The bottom number refers to the building section sheet number.
· The arrow is rotated to point in the direction of the cut.
· The section line typically stops short of the exterior wall on either side of the floor plan.

Grid Symbol

· This symbol is used on floor plans to identify the letter or number of the structural grid. The letters I and O are not used because they look too similar to the numbers 1 and 0.

Interior Elevation Symbol

· This symbol is used on floor plans to identify interior elevations. The perimeter numbers refer to the numbers in the Drawing Name Symbol on the interior elevation sheet. The middle number refers to the interior elevation sheet number.
· This symbol is generally located in the middle of a room with the arrows pointing toward the interior surfaces that are elevated.

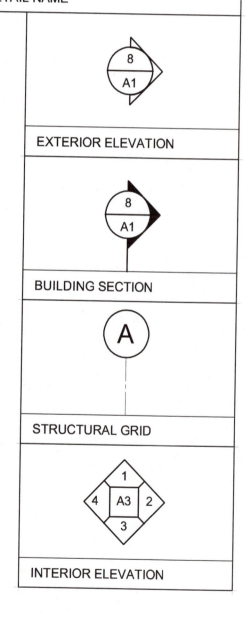

Guidelines for Creating Symbols

The symbols in this chapter will all be saved as blocks for your use in future projects.

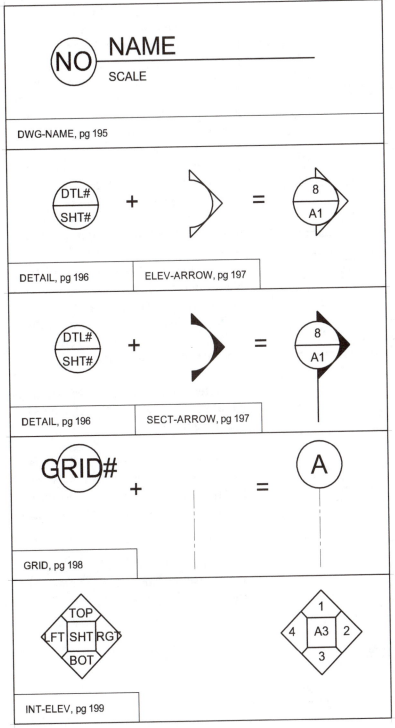

- As shown to the left, some symbols are a combination of multiple blocks.
- Each symbol is listed with its block name and a page number where you can find step-by-step instructions to create the symbol.

The tips below will help you use your symbols in multiple drawings at any scale.

- Know insertion point – the guides on the following pages will identify the desired insertion point. Pay careful attention to these insertion points when creating your blocks.
- Export all your symbols/blocks to a folder on your computer so you can insert them into all of your drawings.
- Draft your symbols at the size you want them to print. When you insert a symbol into a drawing they will atomatically scale based on the annotative scale of your drawing.

Drawing Symbol Lines

- Draw all the lines in your symbols on layer **0**.
- Use **BYLAYER** color for all lines in your symbol.

Adding Symbol Text

- Unless noted otherwise, create text at **3/32"** tall using the same text style you have chosen for your drawing set.
- Place your text on layer **0**.
- Use Attribute Definition (**ATTDEF**) to create text so you can modify the text in your symbols after you convert them to blocks.

Attributed (Editable) Text

AutoCAD allows you to include informational text within a block and later modify it within your drawing. An attribute definition is the template we will use to create the attributed text.

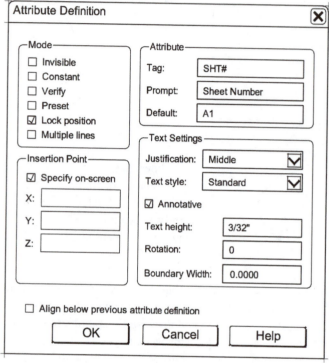

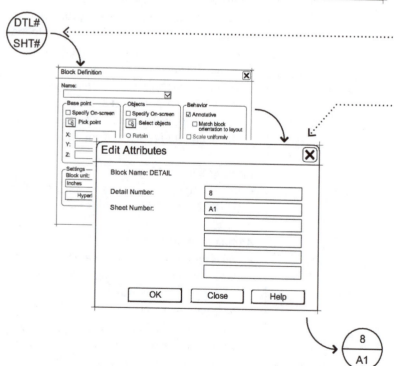

Creating Attributed Text

- Type the command **ATTDEF** and press **ENTER**.
- Create a unique name for the **TAG** value. This attribute cannot be repeated within a single block and cannot contain spaces or special characters.
- The **PROMPT** value is the question AutoCAD will ask you when you edit the attributes for any given block. This value should be descriptive and can contain spaces (e.g., Door Number).
- The **DEFAULT** value sets the initial value for this variable within your block.
- In the Text Settings section, make adjustments as required. Pay close attention to the text **JUSTIFICATION**, **STYLE**, **HEIGHT**, and **ROTATION**.
- Always **CHECK** the **ANNOTATIVE** option for blocks that contain text. Text height for most drawing symbols should be **3/32"**.
- **CLICK** the **OK** button to close the Attribute Definition dialog box and place the attributed text into your drawing.

- Attributed text will display its **TAG** value until it is added to a block (Refer to Chapter 9 for creating a block).

- After you create a block with attributed text, you will be prompted to set the initial values for the attributes in that block. Click the **OK** button after you set the value for each variable.

- Your symbol will be placed in the drawing with the values chosen from the previous step.

Inserting Attributed Blocks

The following steps will guide you through the process of adding or inserting an attributed block into your drawing. This process is the same as the process for inserting a regular block, except AutoCAD will prompt you to set each attribute.

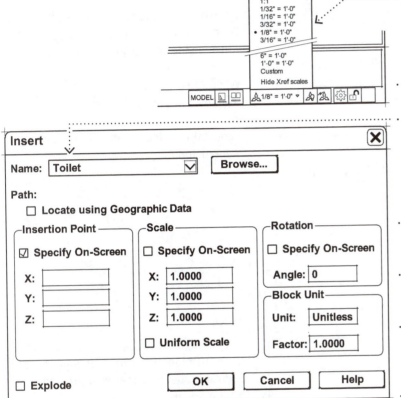

Step 1: Select the proper annotative scale for your drawing.

Step 2: Type the command **INSERT** and press **ENTER**. This will open the Insert dialog box.

Step 3: The Name drop-down box lists all the blocks that are currently in your drawing. Select the block name from this list. You can load additional blocks into your drawing by clicking the browse button.

Step 4: In the Insertion Point section of the insert dialog box, **CHECK** the **SPECIFY ON-SCREEN** option.

- In the Scale section of the insert dialog box, **UNCHECK** the **SPECIFY ON-SCREEN** option and set the **X, Y,** and **Z** scale values to **1.0**.
- In the Rotation section of the insert dialog box, **UNCHECK** the **SPECIFY ON-SCREEN** option and set the angle to **0**.

Step 5: **CLICK ONCE** on the **OK** button to insert your block.

Step 6: After you click the OK button, the Insert dialog box will disappear. The AutoCAD cursor will have the symbol block attached to it.

- **CLICK ONCE** where you want to insert the block. You can modify the position of any block after it is inserted into your drawing.

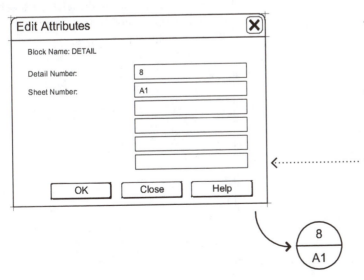

Step 7: After you position the symbol in your drawing, AutoCAD will prompt you to set the values for this symbol. If you do not see the dialog box, look in the command prompt for further instruction.

- Set the values for each variable and **CLICK** on the **OK** button.

Editing Attributed Blocks

You can update attributed text inside an individual block with the Edit Attributes command. This allows you to change the individually set values for each symbol in a single AutoCAD drawing.

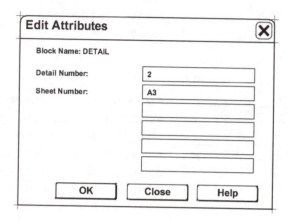

- · Type the command **ATE** and press **ENTER**.
- · **CLICK ONCE** on the block you want to edit. This will open the Edit Attributes dialog box.

- · When you are finished updating the text attributes, **CLICK** the **OK** button.

- · Repeat these steps for each block that you want to update.

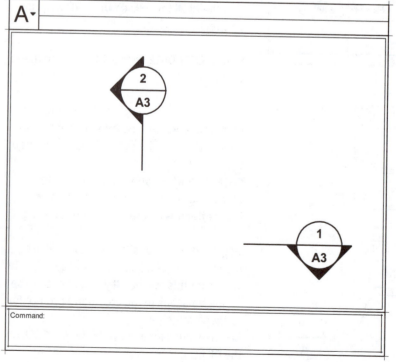

- · Even though the two symbols to the left are the same block, you can individually set the text values because they were created with attributed text.

- · If the two symbols to the left were created with normal AutoCAD text, you could not set the individual text values.

Creating the Drawing Name Symbol

This symbol is used to identify drawings when more than one drawing exists on a printed sheet. For example, if you have three interior elevations on one sheet, each elevation would have this symbol under it to identify the drawing by name and number.

Drawing the Drawing Name Symbol

· In a new AutoCAD drawing, set the current layer to **o** and the units to **ARCHITECTURAL**.
· Draw a circle with a radius of 1/4". Draw a 2-1/2" horizontal line from the right quadrant of the circle.

Add Attributed Text to the Drawing Symbol

You need to add three attributed text definitions to your block. The first is for the drawing number, the second is for the drawing name, and the third is for the scale of the drawing.

· Set the current layer to **o**.
· Type the command **ATTDEF** and press **ENTER**. This will open the Attribute Definition dialog box.

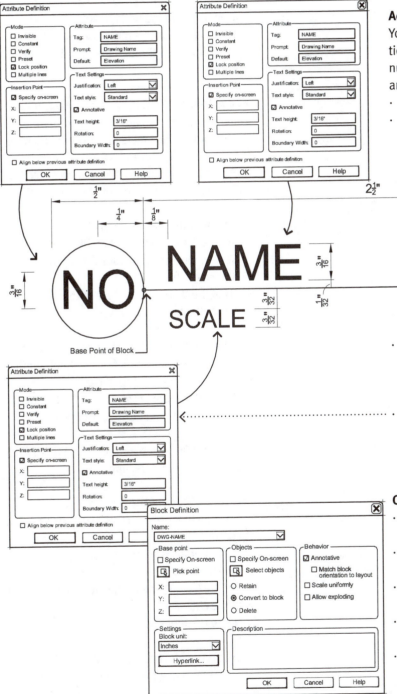

Base Point of Block

· Set the Attribute Tag, Prompt, and Default value for each attributed text definition as indicated. Place each as indicated in the drawing above.
· For example, set the attribute **TAG** to **SCALE**, set the attribute **PROMPT** to **DRAWING SCALE**, and set the attribute **DEFAULT** to **1/4"=1'-0"**.

Creating a Block of the Symbol

· Create a block of the symbol using the **BLOCK** command.
· In the Behavior section, **CHECK** the **ANNOTATIVE** option.
· Set the **BASE POINT** for the block where the circle and horizontal line intersect.
· Name the block **DWG-NAME**.

· Export the block to a symbols folder on your computer using the **WBLOCK** command.

Creating the Detail Symbol

The detail symbol is used in combination with the exterior elevation or section arrow (facing page) on floor plans to identify exterior elevations and building sections. The top number in this symbol matches the drawing number on an elevation, section, or detail sheet. The bottom number in this symbol matches the sheet number for the elevation, section, or detail.

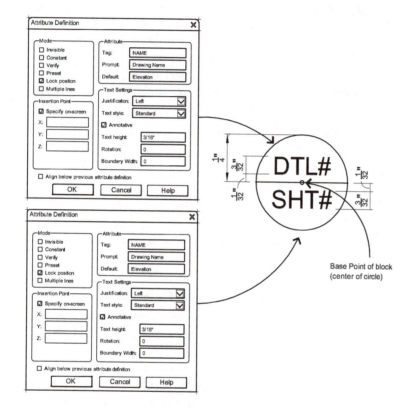

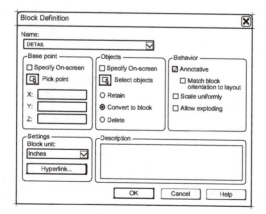

Drawing the Detail Symbol

· In a new AutoCAD drawing, set the current layer to **o** and the units to **ARCHITECTURAL**.
· Draw a circle with a radius of 1/4". Draw a horizontal line through the middle of the circle.

Add Attributed Text to the Detail Symbol

You need to add two attributed text definitions to your block. The first is for the detail number, the second is for the sheet number.

· Type the command **ATTDEF** and press **ENTER**. This will open the Attribute Definition dialog box.
· Set the Attribute Tag to: **DTL#**.
· Set the Attribute Prompt to: **DETAIL NUMBER**.
· Set the remaining attributes to match the drawing to the left.
· **CLICK** the **OK** button and place the text 1/32" above the horizontal line.

· Follow the steps above to create a second attributed text definition for the sheet number.
· Set the Attribute Tag to: **SHT#**.
· Set the Attribute Prompt to: **SHEET NUMBER**.
· Set the remaining attributes to match the drawing to the left.
· **CLICK** the **OK** button and place the text 1/32" below the horizontal line.

Creating a Block of the Symbol

· Create a block of the symbol using the **BLOCK** command.
· In the Behavior section, **CHECK** the **ANNOTATIVE** option.
· Set the Base Point for the block at the center of the circle.
· Name the block **DETAIL**.

· Export the block to a symbols folder on your computer using the **WBLOCK** command.

Creating the Section and Exterior Elevation Arrows

These symbols are used in combination with the detail symbol (facing page) on floor plans to identify exterior elevations and building sections. The arrow in this symbol is rotated to point toward the exterior surface that is elevated or in the direction of the section cut.

Drawing the Exterior Elevation Arrow

· In a new AutoCAD drawing, set the current layer to **o** and the units to **ARCHITECTURAL**.
· Draw a 9/16" square. Rotate it 45 degrees.
· Draw a circle with a radius of 1/4" at the center of this square. Trim the lower half of the circle and square.

Creating a Block of the Symbol

· Create a block of the symbol using the **BLOCK** command.
· In the Behavior section, **CHECK** the **ANNOTATIVE** option.
· Set the Base Point for the block at the center of the arc.
· Name the block **ELEV-ARROW**.
· Export the block to a symbols folder on your computer using the **WBLOCK** command.

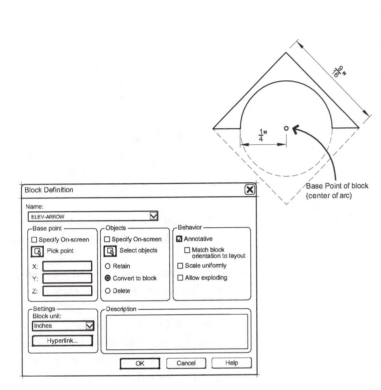

Drawing the Section Arrow

· In a new AutoCAD drawing, set the current layer to **o** and the units to **ARCHITECTURAL**.
· Draw a 9/16" square. Rotate it 45 degrees.
· Draw a circle with a radius of 1/4" at the center of this square. Trim the lower half of the circle and square.
· Fill the arrow with the hatch pattern ANSI31.

Creating a Block of the Symbol

· Create a block of the symbol using the **BLOCK** command.
· In the Behavior section, **CHECK** the **ANNOTATIVE** option.
· Set the Base Point for the block at the center of the arc.
· Name the block **SECT-ARROW**.
· Export the block to a symbols folder on your computer using the **WBLOCK** command.

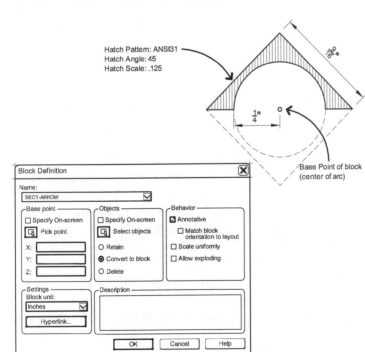

Creating the Grid Symbol

This symbol is used on floor plans to identify the letter or number of the structural grid. The letters I and O are not used because they look too similar to the numbers 1 and 0. The text in this symbol is always horizontal to the page.

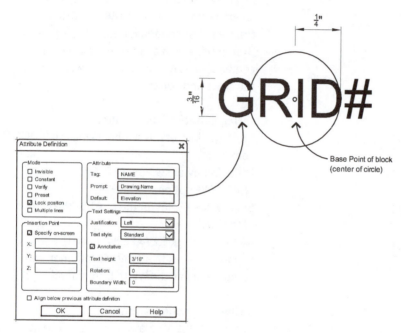

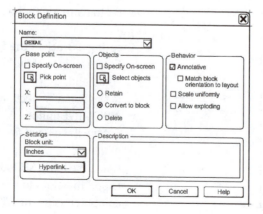

Drawing the Grid Symbol

· In a new AutoCAD drawing, set the current layer to **o** and the units to **ARCHITECTURAL**.
· Draw a circle with a radius of 1/4".

Add Attributed Text to the Grid Symbol

You need to add one attributed text definition to your block.

· Type the command **ATTDEF** and press **ENTER**. This will open the Attribute Definition dialog box.
· Set the Attribute Tag to: **GRID#**
· Set the Attribute Prompt to: **GRID NUMBER**
· Set the remaining attributes to match the drawing to the left.
· **CLICK** the **OK** button and place the text in the middle of the circle.

Creating a Block of the Symbol

· Create a block of the symbol using the **BLOCK** command.
· In the Behavior section, **CHECK** the **ANNOTATIVE** option.
· Set the Base Point for the block at the center of the circle.
· Name the block **GRID**.

· Export the block to a symbols folder on your computer using the **WBLOCK** command.

INTERIOR ELEVATION SYMBOL

Creating the Interior Elevation Symbol

This symbol is used on floor plans to identify interior elevations. The numbers match the Drawing Name Symbol number on the interior elevation sheet. This symbol is generally located in the middle of a room with the arrows pointing toward the interior surfaces that are elevated.

Drawing the Interior Elevation Symbol

· In a new AutoCAD drawing, set the current layer to **0** and the units to **ARCHITECTURAL**.
· Draw a square with sides measuring **5/8"**. Rotate this square 45 degrees.
· Draw a second square with sides measuring **5/16"**.
· Center the small square inside the large rotated square. (Hint: use construction lines to find the center of both squares.)
· Complete the symbol to match the one drawn to the left.

Add Attributed Text to the Grid Symbol

You need to add five attributed text definitions to your block.

· Type the command **ATTDEF** and press **ENTER**. This will open the Attribute Definition dialog box.
· Set the Attribute Tag to: **SHT**
· Set the Attribute Prompt to: **SHEET NUMBER**
· Set the remaining attributes to match the drawing to the left.
· **CLICK** the **OK** button and place the text in the middle of the small sqaure.

· Create four more attributed text definitions for each of the elevations (top, right, left, and bottom).

Creating a Block of the Symbol

· Create a block of the symbol using the **BLOCK** command.
· In the Behavior section, **CHECK** the **ANNOTATIVE** option.
· Set the Base Point for the block at the bottom of the large square.
· Name the block **INT-ELEV**.

· Export the block to a symbols folder on your computer using the **WBLOCK** command.

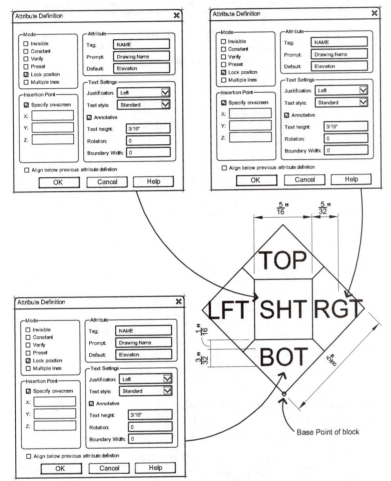

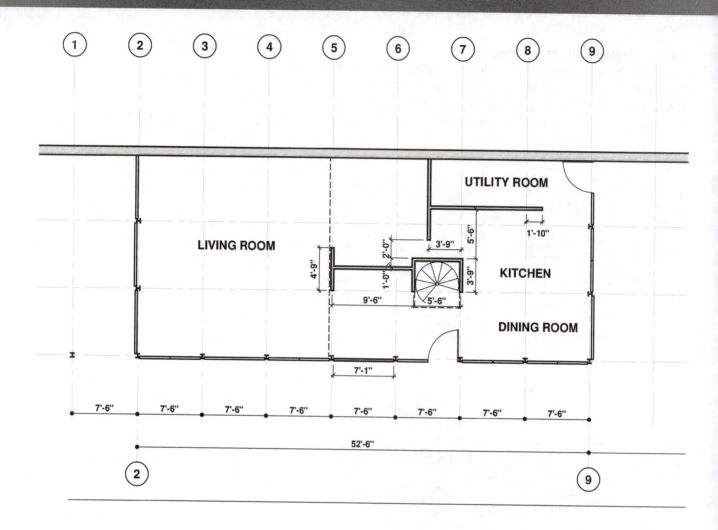

Learning Exercise

In this exercise, you will add grid symbols and a drawing title to your floor plan.

Open Your Drawing

· Open AutoCAD.
· Open the drawing you created in the previous chapter:
  DDFD-EAMES.DWG

Creating Your Layers

Create the following layers:

· **A-SYMBOL**   Color 4
· Set the current layer to **A-SYMBOL.**

Adding the Structural Grid Symbols

· Using the **INSERT** command, add the grid number symbol you created earlier in this chapter to your drawing as indicated above.
· Use the **ATE** command to adjust the value of each symbol.
· Notice that the symbol is used only on grids that intersect a column.

· Save your drawing.

Congratulations, you have completed the learning exercise for this chapter.

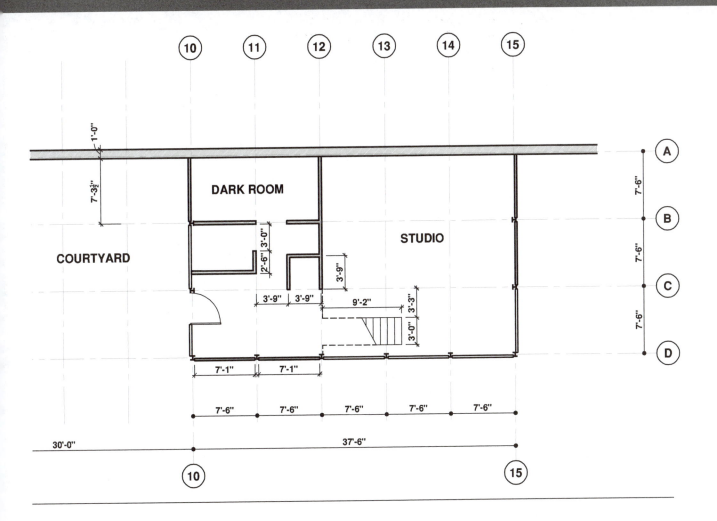

CHAPTER 14

Linking Drawings/ External References

In Chapter 9, you learned how to use blocks to import symbols into an AutoCAD drawing. External References (XREFS) are conceptually very close to blocks. Just like blocks, XREFS allow you to import drawings like a title block into any other AutoCAD drawing with one advantage: external references will automatically import changes made to the original drawing.

In larger design firms, XREFs are primarily used to link title sheets and floor plans. They allow you to quickly and easily update an entire set of drawings.

· If you need to change the issue date for a presentation or a set of construction drawings, you can update the references title sheet and every drawing in the set will automatically update.

· If you change the location of a door in a room or office in the referenced floor plan, then every plan (enlarged, reflected ceiling plan, finish plan, furniture plan, and so on) in the drawing set will automatically update.

Drawing with Overlays

When you draw by hand, you may overlay several sheets of drafting mylar to see the relationship between drawings. This technique is commonly used in reflected ceiling plans so the designer does not have to redraw the floor plan. Overlay both sheets, run it through the blueprint machine, and you have a combined drawing.

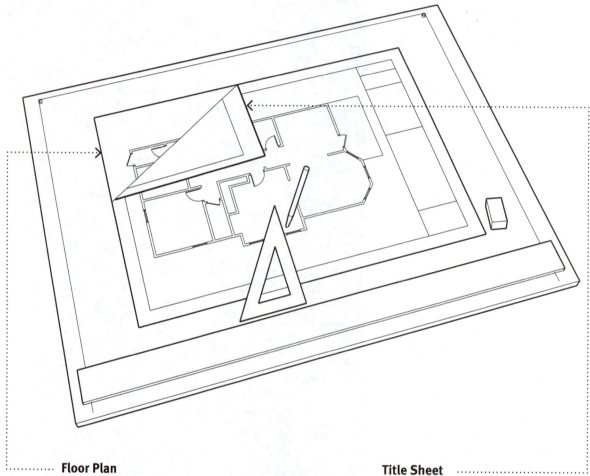

Floor Plan

This drawing usually contains all of the floor plan information that may find its way into the final floor plan, the reflected ceiling plan, and other enlarged floor plans.

· When you update the base plan (e.g., move a wall or a door), all other overlaid drawings are updated.

Title Sheet

This drawing contains the page border and generic project information. It can be overlaid onto every drawing in your presentation or drawing set.

· When you make a change to the title sheet (e.g., change the submission date or project phone number), all other overlaid drawings are updated.

Drawing with XREFS

When you draw in AutoCAD, you can link several drawings to see the relationship between drawings. This technique is commonly used to link title sheets to floor plans, reflected ceiling plans, and elevations. XREFS help the designer quickly update title sheet items (like a presentation date) for every drawing.

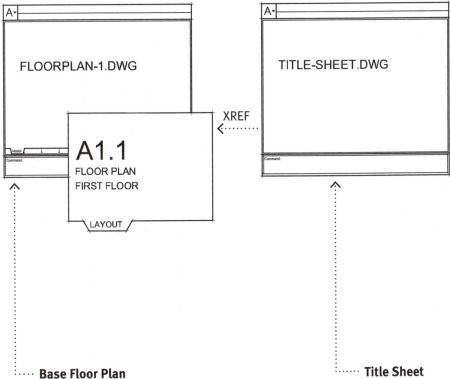

Base Floor Plan

This drawing usually contains all of the floor plan information that may find its way into the final floor plan, the reflected ceiling plan, and other enlarged floor plans.

· In AutoCAD, you can link this base floor plan to Model Space of multiple plans or formatted sheets.
· When you update the base plan (e.g., move a wall or a door), all other drawings that link to the base floor plan are automatically updated.
· You can adjust the layer color and layer visibility in linked drawings.

Title Sheet

This drawing contains the page border and generic project information. It will be linked to every drawing in your presentation or drawing set.

· In AutoCAD, you can link the title sheet to the layout view of every formatted sheet.
· When you update the title sheet (e.g., change the submission date or project phone number), all other drawings that link to the title sheet are automatically updated.

XREF Manager

The XREF Manager displays XREFs in your current drawing. It also allows you to add new XREFs to your drawing or modify XREFs currently attached to your drawings.

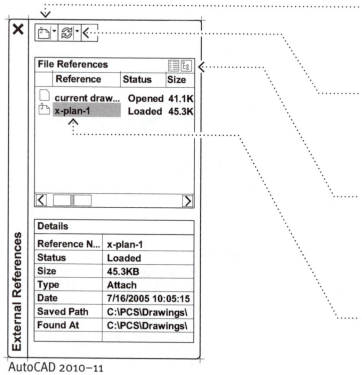

AutoCAD 2010–11

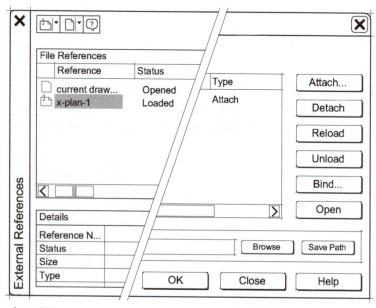

AutoCAD 2007–09   AutoCAD 2006 and earlier

Opening the XREF Manager

· Type the command **XREF** and press **ENTER.**

XREF Manager

· The **ATTACH** button allows you to add an XREFs to your drawing. Click the arrow to the right of this button to attach images and PDFs.

· The **REFRESH** button will refresh an XREF in your current drawing. This can be helpful if you have made changes in a referenced drawing but do not see the changes reflected in the current drawing.

· The **TREE VIEW** and **LIST VIEW** buttons adjust the display methods for the XREF Manager. The **LIST VIEW** (default) shows a list of all XREFs in the current drawing. The **TREE VIEW** shows the relationship between all XREFs and the current drawing.

· **RIGHT CLICK** on a listed XREF to **UNLOAD, RELOAD,** and **BIND** the XREF.

· An unloaded XREF is visibly remove from your drawing. The XREF can be turned back on at any time by selecting reload.

· Binding will insert one or more XREFs into the current drawing as a block. This will break the link between the referenced drawing and the current drawing.

Earlier XREF Managers

Prior to AutoCAD 2010, there were serveral changes to the XREF manager.

· AutoCAD 2007–09 includes an XREF manager similar in appearance and operation to AutoCAD 2010–11.

· AutoCAD 2006 and earlier includes a XREF manager with XREF options listed as buttons down the right side of the dialog box.

Adding an XREF to Your Drawing

To complete the following exercise you will need a title sheet drawing and a plan or elevation drawing.

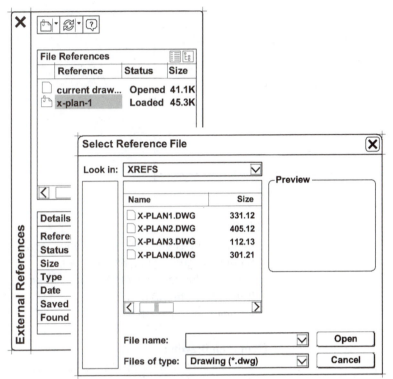

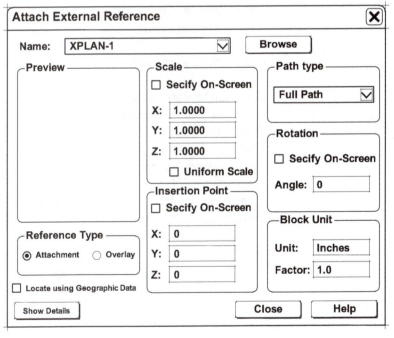

· **Step 1:** Open the plan or elevation drawing in AutoCAD and switch to a layout view (Paper Space).
· **Step 2:** Set the current layer to **0**.
· **Step 3:** Type the command **XREF** and press **ENTER.**
· **Step 4: CLICK ONCE** on the **ATTACH** button. This will open a File dialog box.

· **Step 5:** Locate your title block file on your computer in the file dialog box and click the **OPEN** button.

· **Step 6:** Set the Reference Type to: **ATTACHMENT**
· **Step 7:** Set the Path Type to: **FULL PATH**
· **Step 8:** Set the X, Y, and Z coordinates of Insertion Point to: **0**
· **Step 9: CLICK ONCE** on the **OK** button.

· The title sheet will be attached to the layout view of your elevation or plan drawing.
· Modify the size or scale of the viewport in this layout.
· Adjust the page layout for this view to match your title sheet.

· Save your drawing.

XREF Strategies for Individual Designers

If you have one or two designers working on a project, you can use the following XREF strategy to set up your plans. This strategy minimizes the number of drawings required to complete a drawing set. (Two AutoCAD drawings are created to plot four different floor plans.)

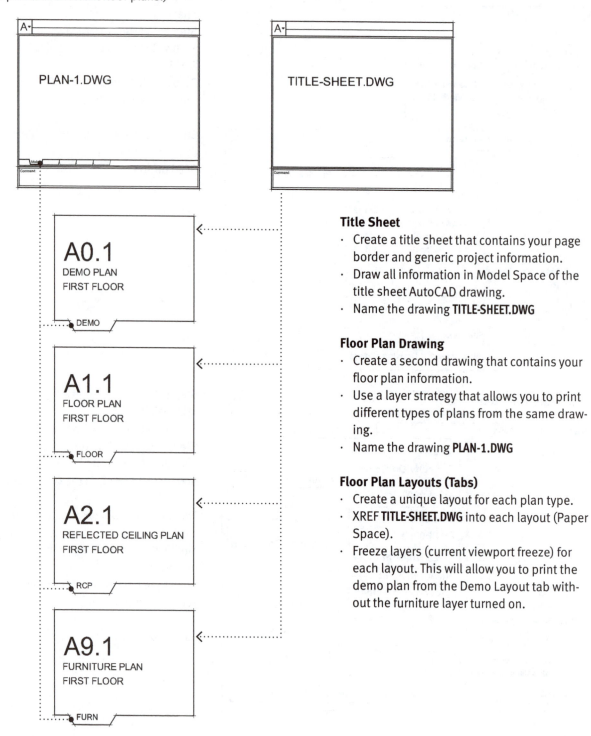

Title Sheet

· Create a title sheet that contains your page border and generic project information.
· Draw all information in Model Space of the title sheet AutoCAD drawing.
· Name the drawing **TITLE-SHEET.DWG**

Floor Plan Drawing

· Create a second drawing that contains your floor plan information.
· Use a layer strategy that allows you to print different types of plans from the same drawing.
· Name the drawing **PLAN-1.DWG**

Floor Plan Layouts (Tabs)

· Create a unique layout for each plan type.
· XREF **TITLE-SHEET.DWG** into each layout (Paper Space).
· Freeze layers (current viewport freeze) for each layout. This will allow you to print the demo plan from the Demo Layout tab without the furniture layer turned on.

XREF Strategies for Multiple Designers

If you have multiple designers working on a project, you can use the following XREF strategy to set up your plans. This strategy maximizes the number of drawings that can be edited by different designers. (Six AutoCAD drawings are created to plot four different floor plans.)

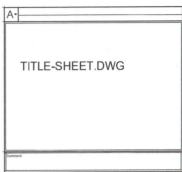

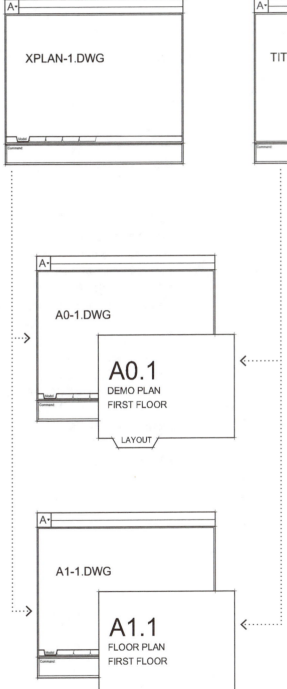

Title Sheet

· Create a title sheet that contains your page border and generic project information.
· Draw all information in Model Space of the title sheet AutoCAD drawing.
· Name the drawing **TITLE-SHEET.DWG**

Base Floor Plan Drawing

· Create a second drawing that contains your base floor plan information.
· Minimize sheet-specific text and dimensions. This information will be placed in the formatted sheet drawings.
· Name the drawing **XPLAN-1.DWG**

Formatted Sheets

· Create a unique drawing for each plan type.
· XREF **XPLAN-1.DWG** into Model Space.
· XREF **TITLE-SHEET.DWG** into Paper Space.
· Add additional information in Model Space such as room names, dimensions, notes, and door tags.
· Name the drawing similar to its sheet number. Therefore, sheet A1.1 would be named **A1-1.DWG**.

ELEVATION XREFs/INDIVIDUAL DESIGNERS

Elevation XREF Strategies for Individual Designers

If you have one or two designers working on a project, you can use the
following XREF strategy to set up your elevation. This strategy minimizes the number of drawings required to complete a drawing set. (Two
AutoCAD drawings are created to plot four different elevation sheets.)

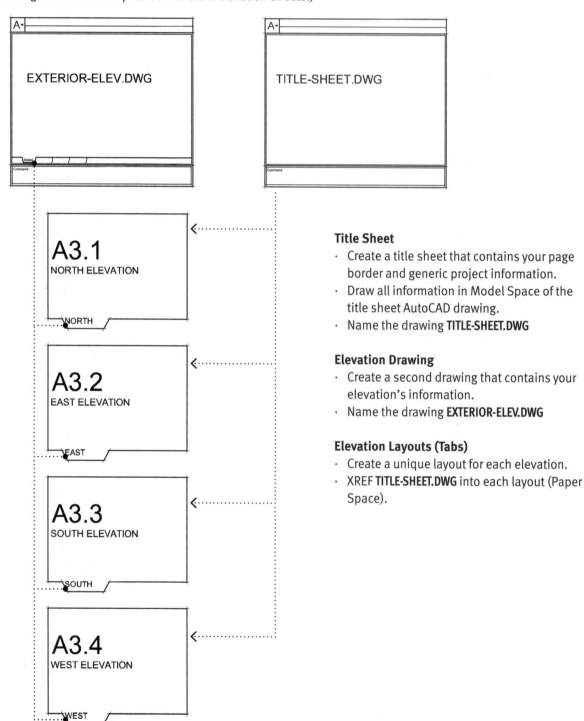

Title Sheet

· Create a title sheet that contains your page
  border and generic project information.
· Draw all information in Model Space of the
  title sheet AutoCAD drawing.
· Name the drawing **TITLE-SHEET.DWG**

Elevation Drawing

· Create a second drawing that contains your
  elevation's information.
· Name the drawing **EXTERIOR-ELEV.DWG**

Elevation Layouts (Tabs)

· Create a unique layout for each elevation.
· XREF **TITLE-SHEET.DWG** into each layout (Paper
  Space).

Elevation XREF Strategies for Multiple Designers

If you have multiple designers working on a project, you can use the following XREF strategy to set up your elevations. This strategy maximizes the number of drawings that can be edited by different designers. (Six AutoCAD drawings are created to plot four different elevations).

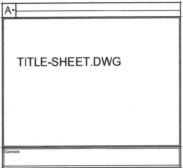

Title Sheet

· Create a title sheet that contains your page border and generic project information.
· Draw all information in Model Space of the title sheet AutoCAD drawing.
· Name the drawing **TITLE-SHEET.DWG**

Base Elevation Drawing

· Create a second drawing that contains your base elevation information.
· Minimize sheet-specific text and dimensions. This information will be placed in the formatted sheet drawings.
· Name the drawing **XELEV.DWG**

Formatted Sheets

· Create a unique drawing for each plan type.
· XREF **XELEV.DWG** into Model Space.
· XREF **TITLE-SHEET.DWG** into Paper Space.
· Add additional information in Model Space such as room names, dimensions, notes, and door tags.
· Name the drawing similar to its sheet number. Therefore, sheet A3.1 would be named **A3-1.DWG**.

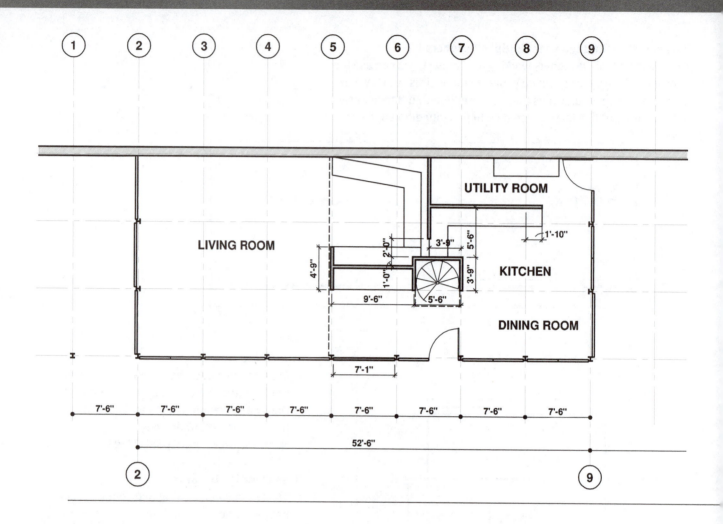

Learning Exercise

In this exercise, you will complete your floor plan by adding the casework and a graphic scale.

Open Your Drawing

· Open AutoCAD.
· Open the drawing you created in the previous chapter:
  DDFD-EAMES.DWG

Creating Your Layers

Create the following layers:

· **A-CASE**   Color 5
· Set the current layer to **A-CASE.**

Adding the Casework

· Cabinets are drawn on their own layer and are typically 24" deep. Add the cabinets to your drawing to match those in the drawing above.

· Save your drawing.

Congratulations, you have completed the learning exercise for this chapter.

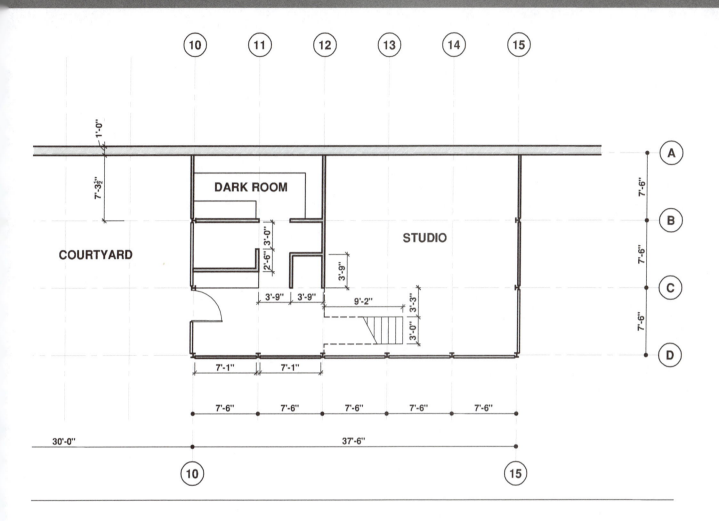

CHAPTER 15
AutoCAD WS

AutoCAD WS is Autodesk's mobile solution for AutoCAD. This mobile AutoCAD application allows users to view and modify AutoCAD DWG files in locations that were previously unavailable to most computer users. If you have a touch screen smart phone, or tablet, there is a good chance you can review, edit, and share DWG files knowing that updates are automatically synced to your AutoCAD WS online account. AutoCAD WS is a free app and is currently available for Android and Apple iOS devices, including smart phones, tablets, iPhones, and iPads. AutoCAD WS is also available on any modern web browser.

This chapter introduces you to the AutoCAD WS platform, including both the mobile and web app. This introduction includes step-by-step instructions on uploading drawings to your AutoCAD WS account.

The remaining portion of the chapter explores the AutoCAD WS mobile app, including instruction on viewing, modifying, and sharing DWG files through the "touch" interface.

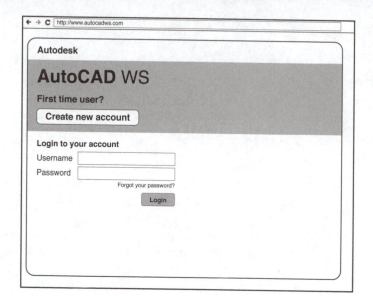

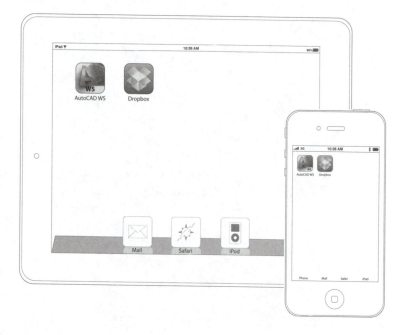

Introducing AutoCAD WS

AutoCAD WS is Autodesk's mobile solution for AutoCAD. The mobile application is free and is currently available for Android and Apple iOS devices, including smart phones and tablets. You can also access AutoCAD WS from any web browser.

- AutoCAD WS is compatible with any DWG file.
- Upload DWG files from AutoCAD 2012, through a web browser, or through the mobile application on an iOS or Android device.
- With AutoCAD WS, you can share drawings with multiple people even if they don't own a copy of AutoCAD.
- AutoCAD WS allows real time collaboration with multiple people on the same AutoCAD drawing.
- AutoCAD WS files can be downloaded to any computer and opened for editing in Auto-CAD.

Access the latest AutoCAD WS news and additional resources at www.DDFDbook.com/autocadws

Companion Download

The companion download contains additional AutoCAD drawings that you need for the learning in this chapter.

The following website features the companion download for this book: www.DDFDbook.com/ch15

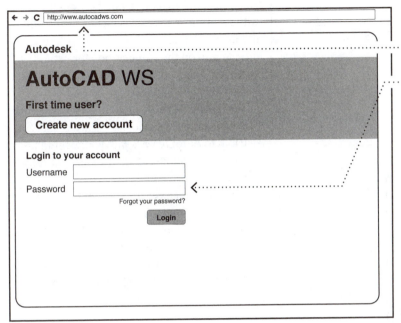

AutoCAD WS Web App

The AutoCAD WS web app allows you to view, edit, and manage your DWG files.

- Visit www.autocadws.com in your web browser.
- **LOGIN** to AutoCAD WS with your username (your e-mail address) and your AutoCAD WS password.
- If you already have an Autodesk account (which you may have created to download the student version of AutoCAD), use this existing account with AutoCAD WS.
- If you do not have an Autodesk account, **CLICK** the **CREATE NEW ACCOUNT** button.

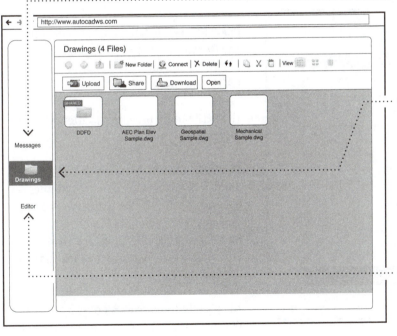

There are three main sections in the AutoCAD WS web app: Message, Drawings, and Editor.

- **MESSAGES** is the default section after login. The Messages section includes a list of recently updated drawings, AutoCAD WS news, and a log of your AutoCAD WS activity.

- The **DRAWINGS** section shows the DWG files and folders in your AutoCAD WS account. From this section you can create folders and manage your DWG files. Use the Drawings section to upload, download, share, and duplicate DWG files.
- If this is your first time using AutoCAD WS, this section will contain sample drawings provided by Autodesk.

- The **EDITOR** section allows you to view, edit, and share DWG files.

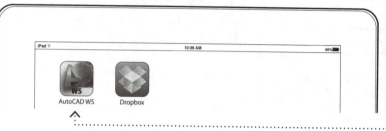

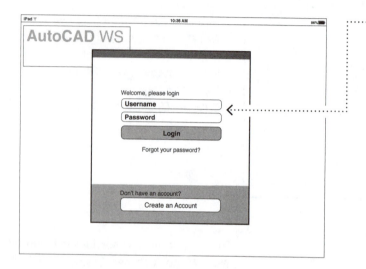

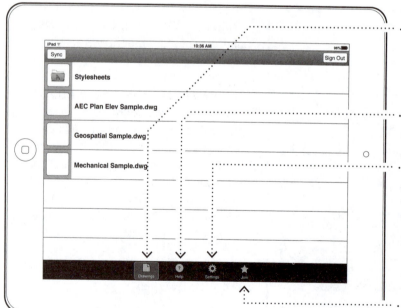

AutoCAD WS for iOS

The AutoCAD WS mobile app is compatible with all Apple iOS devices including the iPhone, iPad, and iPod touch. Download the free mobile app on the iTunes App Store at www.DDFDbook.com/autocadws

· **TAP** the **AUTOCAD WS** icon to launch AutoCAD WS on your iOS device.

· **LOGIN** to AutoCAD WS with your username (your e-mail address) and your AutoCAD WS password.

· If you already have an Autodesk account (which you may have created to download the student version of AutoCAD), use this existing account with AutoCAD WS.

· If you do not have an Autodesk account, **CLICK** the **CREATE NEW ACCOUNT** button.

· There are four main screens in AutoCAD WS app for iOS: Drawings, Help, Settings, and Join.

· **DRAWINGS** is the default screen after login. The Drawings screen allows you to browse DWG files and folders stored in your Auto-CAD WS account.

· The **HELP** button provides a variety of support topics.

· The **SETTINGS** button allows you to set the amount of space available for DWG files on your device. This allows you to work on your drawings even when you do not have an Internet connection. If you receive memory error messages, increase the local storage limit to 500MB.

· The **JOIN** button provides links to AutoCAD WS social media. This button also includes a link to provide AutoCAD WS feedback.

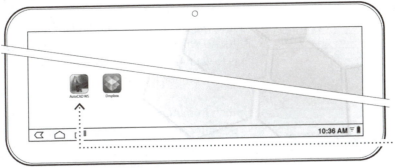

AutoCAD WS for Android

The AutoCAD WS mobile app is compatible with all Android devices, including smart phones and tablets. You must be running Android 2.1 or higher to install this app. Download the free mobile app from the Android Market www.DDFDbook.com/autocadws

- **TAP** the **AUTOCAD WS** icon to launch AutoCAD WS on your Android device.
- **LOGIN** to AutoCAD WS with your username (your e-mail address) and your AutoCAD WS password.
- If you already have an Autodesk account (which you may have created to download the student version of AutoCAD), use this existing account with AutoCAD WS.
- If you do not have an Autodesk account, **CLICK** the **CREATE NEW ACCOUNT** button.

- There are four main screens in AutoCAD WS app for Android: Drawings, Help, Settings, and Join.

- **DRAWINGS** is the default screen after login. The Drawings screen allows you to browse DWG files and folders stored in your AutoCAD WS account.

- The **HELP** button provides a variety of support topics.

- The **SETTINGS** button allows you to set the amount of space available for DWG files on your device. This allows you to work on your drawings even when you do not have an Internet connection. If you receive memory error messages, increase the local storage limit to 500MB.

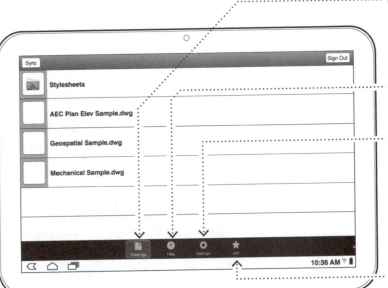

- The **JOIN** button provides links to AutoCAD WS social media. This button also includes a link to provide AutoCAD WS feedback.

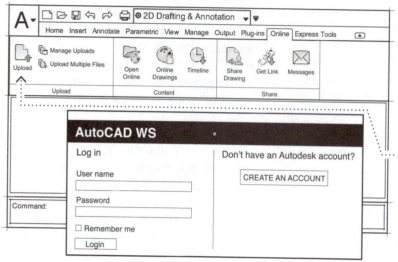

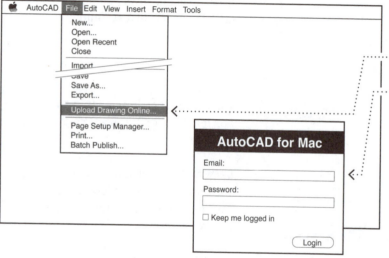

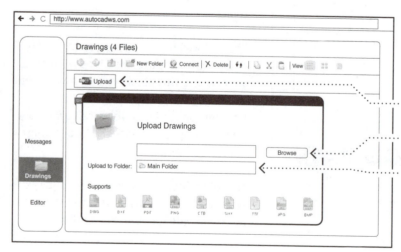

Uploading Drawings

Before you can view or edit DWG files on an AutoCAD WS app, you must upload these drawings to your AutoCAD WS account. There are several methods to upload your DWG files.

Upload from AutoCAD 2012

- On your computer, **OPEN** the DWG file in AutoCAD 2012.
- From the **ONLINE** toolbar **CLICK** the **UPLOAD** icon.
- At the login prompt, **TYPE** your e-mail address and AutoCAD WS password. **CLICK** the **LOGIN** button.
- Once your drawing is uploaded, you can access it on any AutoCAD WS app.

Upload from AutoCAD for Mac

- On your computer, **OPEN** the DWG file in AutoCAD for Mac.
- From the **FILE** menu select **UPLOAD DRAWING ONLINE...**
- At the login prompt, **TYPE** your e-mail address and AutoCAD WS password. **CLICK** the **LOGIN** button.
- Once your drawing is uploaded, you can access it on any AutoCAD WS app.

Upload from AutoCAD 2010 & 2011

- Upload drawings directly from AutoCAD 2010 and AutoCAD 2011 using the AutoCAD WS plug-in. Download the plug-in at www.DDFDbook.com/autocadws

Upload with the AutoCAD WS Web App

- **LOGIN** to the AutoCAD WS web app and **CLICK** the **DRAWINGS** link on the left side of the web app.
- **CLICK** the **UPLOAD** button in the tool bar to open the Upload Drawings dialog box.
- **BROWSE** for the DWG file on your computer hard drive.
- **SELECT** the AutoCAD WS folder for your uploaded drawing.
- The web app will automatically upload your drawing.

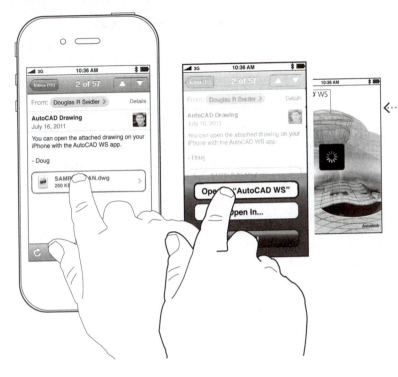

Upload from AutoCAD WS Mobile

Drawings uploaded through AutoCAD and the AutoCAD WS web app automatically sync with your AutoCAD WS mobile app.

- DWG files sent as e-mail attachments or located on websites can be opened with the AutoCAD WS mobile app. Once opened, these files are automatically saved to your AutoCAD WS account.
- DWG files stored with online storage services can be opened through the service's smart phone app or website. Once opened, these files are automatically saved to your Auto-CAD WS account.

Connect to Service

AutoCAD WS will also connect to online storage solutions allowing you to store your drawings anywhere you choose. These services host your file in the cloud and allow you to sync changes between multiple devices.

- DWG files on storage services are available on your personal computer, the AutoCAD WS web app, and the AutoCAD WS mobile app.
- Supported storage services include Buzz-saw, Box.net, Dropbox, MobileMe, Egnyte, and SharePoint.

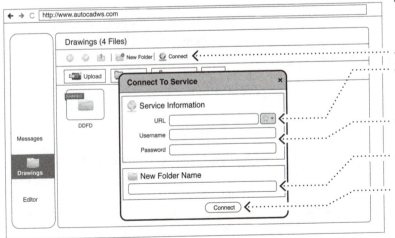

- **LOGIN** to the AutoCAD WS web app and **CLICK** the **DRAWINGS** link on the left side of the web app.
- **CLICK** the **CONNECT** button in the tool bar.
- **SELECT** your storage service or type the storage services WebDAV address in the URL box.
- **TYPE** your username and password for the storage service.
- **TYPE** the name of the folder that will link to documents stored on this service.
- **CLICK** the **CONNECT** button.

- The newly connected storage service will appear as a folder in your AutoCAD WS account. Double click on this folder to see files that are hosted with this storage service.

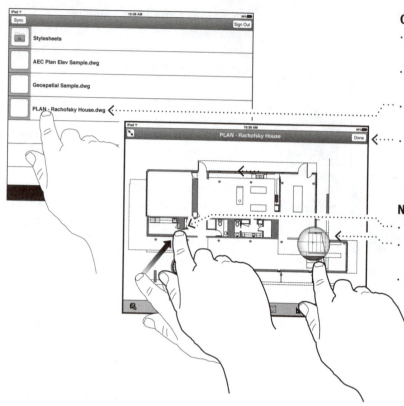

Opening Drawings: Mobile App

· **TAP** the **DRAWINGS** button to view the DWG files in your AutoCAD WS account.
· **TAP** the **SYNC** button to update the drawing list.
· **TAP** on any **DWG FILE** to open it for viewing and editing in the drawing editor.
· In the drawing editor, **TAP** the **DONE** button to close the drawing and automatically save all unsaved changes.

Navigating Drawings: Mobile App

· **TAP** and **DRAG** to pan around your drawing.
· **TAP** and **HOLD** to magnify a portion of your drawing.
· **PINCH** to zoom in and out of your drawing.

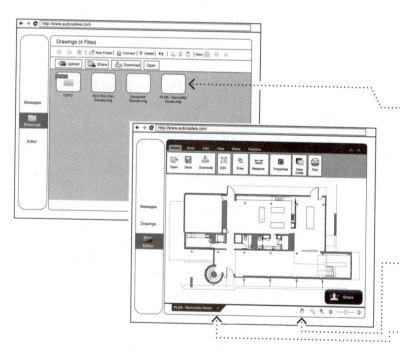

Opening Drawings: Web App

· **CLICK** the **DRAWINGS** link on the left side of the web app to view the DWG files in your AutoCAD WS account.
· **DOUBLE CLICK** on any **DWG FILE** to open it for viewing and editing in the drawing editor.

Navigating Drawings: Web App

· Use the **PAN** button to pan around your drawing.
· Use the **SCROLL WHEEL** on your mouse to zoom in and out of your drawing.
· **CLICK** the **X** on the drawing tab to close the drawing and automatically save all unsaved changes.

Mobile App Command Ribbon

The mobile app's drawing editor contains a command ribbon at the bottom of the screen that reveals a series of toolbars.

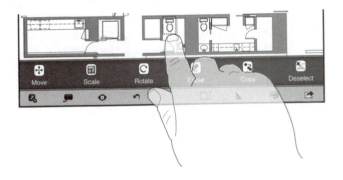

- **TAP** the **DRAW TOOLS** button to reveal the draw circle, line, polyline, and rectangle command buttons. This toolbar also contains buttons for the measure and text commands.

- **TAP** the **MARKUP TOOLS** button to reveal the rectangle markup, revision cloud, text boxes, and paint brush commands. These tools are used to provide feedback for the current drawing.

- **TAP** the **MULTI SELECT** button to toggle between rectangular object selection (TAP and DRAG) and individual object selection (TAP).

- **TAP** the **FULL SCREEN** button to hide the toolbars and menu bar. TAP on the top left of your screen to exit full screen mode.

- **TAP** on any object in your drawing to activate the **EDIT** toolbar. This toolbar includes the Move, Scale, Rotate, and Erase commands.

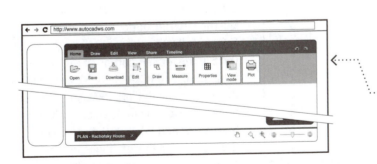

Web App Command Ribbon

- The web app drawing editor contains a command ribbon at the top of the screen. The interface is similar to AutoCAD 2012.
- The ribbon is divided into the following tabs: Home, Draw, Edit, View, Share, and Timeline.

Drawing Tools: Mobile App

The draw toolbar in AutoCAD WS mobile contains a limited set of drawing commands.

· Everything added to drawings in AutoCAD WS mobile is placed on the **AutoCAD WS Annotations** layer. There is currently no way to manage layers in the mobile app.

· **OPEN** the drawing titled **CH15 DRAWING TOOLS.dwg** to follow the instruction in this section of the textbook.

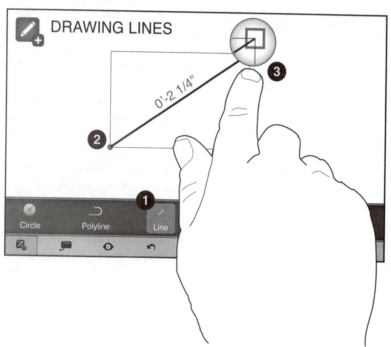

Drawing Lines

Following the example to the left, draw a line from one corner of the rectangle to the opposite corner in the sample drawing.

· **Step 1:** TAP the **DRAW TOOLS** button and then TAP the **LINE** button.

· **Step 2:** TAP and **HOLD** to specify the first point of the line. Use the automatic ENDPOINT SNAP to start the line on the rectangle's bottom left corner.

· **Step 3:** To specify the second point of the line, **TAP** and **HOLD** close to the top right corner of the rectangle. **DRAG** towards the corner until you see the **ENDPOINT SNAP** icon.

· Notice that when you TAP and DRAG, Auto-CAD WS shows you the length of the line.

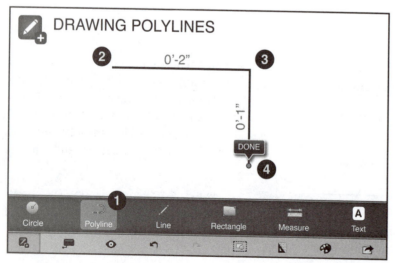

Drawing Polylines

· **Step 1:** TAP the **DRAW TOOLS** button and then TAP the **POLYLINE** button.

· **Step 2:** Following the example to the left, **TAP ONCE** in the top left portion of the screen.

· **Step 3:** TAP and **HOLD** on the screen following the diagram on the left. **DRAG** your finger to draw a horizontal line segment **2"** in length.

· **Step 4:** TAP and **HOLD** on the screen following the diagram on the left. **DRAG** your finger to draw a vertical line segment **1"** in length.

· **Step 5:** TAP the **DONE** button to end the **POLYLINE** command.

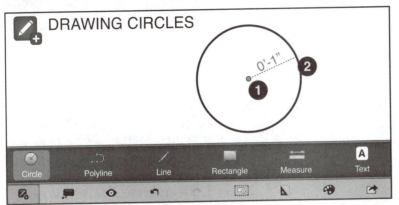

Drawing Circles

The **CIRCLE** command draws a circle with the center point and radius of the circle.

- **TAP** the **DRAW TOOLS** button and then **TAP** the **CIRCLE** button.
- **Step 1: TAP ONCE** to locate the center point of the circle.
- **Step 2: TAP** and **DRAG** to set the radius of the circle.

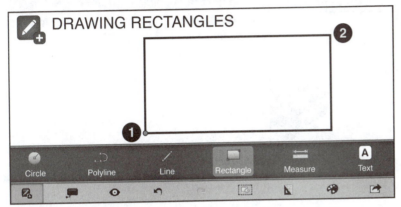

Drawing Rectangles

The **RECTANGLE** command draws a rectangle by locating the rectangle's two opposite corners.

- **TAP** the **DRAW TOOLS** button and then **TAP** the **RECTANGLE** button.
- **Step 1: TAP ONCE** to locate the first corner of the rectangle.
- **Step 2: TAP** and **DRAG** to identify the opposite corner of the rectangle.

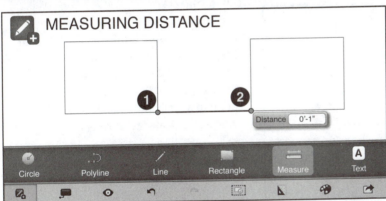

Measuring Distances

The **MEASURE** command shows the distance between objects in the drawing.

- **TAP** the **DRAW TOOLS** button and then **TAP** the **MEASURE** button.
- **Step 1: TAP ONCE** to locate the first point of the measure.
- **Step 2: TAP** and **DRAG** to identify the second point of the measure. **TAP ONCE** on the touch screen to close the **MEASURE** tool.

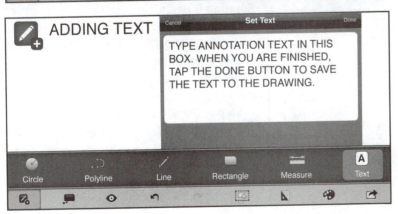

Adding Text

- **TAP** the **DRAW TOOLS** button and then **TAP** the **TEXT** button.
- **TAP ONCE** to locate the text position in the drawing.
- **TYPE** the text in the Set Text dialog box. **TAP** the **DONE** button to save the text to the drawing.
- To edit text in the drawing, **TAP** once on the text object and **TAP** the **EDIT TEXT** button. Text objects added in earlier versions of AutoCAD may not be editable in AutoCAD WS.

Edit Tools: Mobile App

Similar to the draw toolbar, the edit toolbar contains a limited set of editing tools to modify an AutoCAD drawing.

· **OPEN** the drawing titled **CH15 EDIT TOOLS.dwg** to follow the instruction in this section of the textbook.

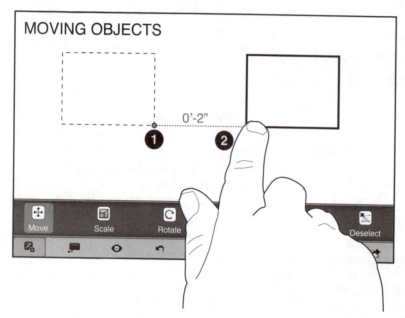

Moving Objects
· **TAP ONCE** on the object you want to move.
· In the **EDIT TOOLBAR, TAP** the **MOVE** button.
· **Step 1:** Following the example to the left, **TAP** the lower right corner of the rectangle.
· **Step 2: TAP** and **DRAG** to the right direction on the screen. **DRAG** until you see the desired move distance. In this example, the move distance is **2"**.

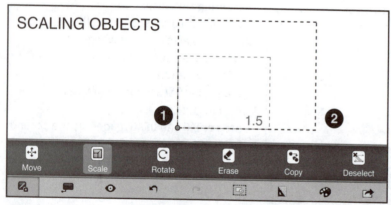

Scaling Objects
· **TAP ONCE** on the object you want to scale.
· In the **EDIT TOOLBAR, TAP** the **SCALE** button.
· **Step 1:** Following the example to the left, **TAP ONCE** to indicate the base point for the scale.
· **Step 2: TAP** and **DRAG** away from the base point to specify the scale factor. In this example, the scale factor is **1.5**.

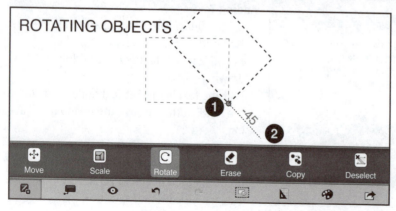

Rotating Objects
· **TAP ONCE** on the object you want to rotate.
· In the **EDIT TOOLBAR, TAP** the **ROTATE** button.
· **Step 1:** Following the example to the left, **TAP ONCE** to indicate the base point for the rotate.
· **Step 2: TAP** and **DRAG** to specify the rotation angle. As you **DRAG** your finger on the touch screen, AutoCAD WS indicates the whole degree rotation and will automatically snap on 90 degree increments.

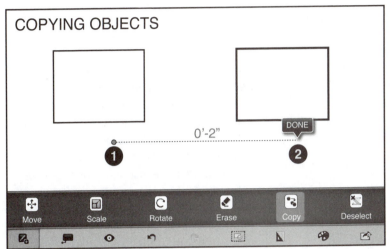

Copying Objects

- **TAP ONCE** on the object that you want to copy.
- In the **EDIT TOOLBAR, TAP** the **COPY** button.
- **Step 1:** Following the example to the left, **TAP** the lower right corner of the rectangle.
- **Step 2: TAP** and **DRAG** to the right direction on the screen. **DRAG** until you see the desired move distance. In this example, the desired distance is **2"**.
- **TAP ONCE** on the **DONE** button to end the copy command.

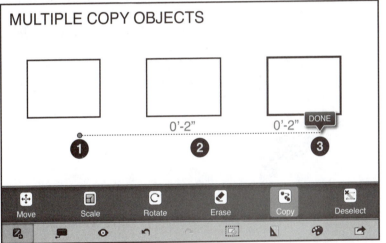

Multiple Copy Objects

- **TAP ONCE** on the object you want to copy.
- In the **EDIT TOOLBAR, TAP** the **COPY** button.
- **Step 1:** Following the example to the left, **TAP** the lower right corner of the square.
- **Step 2: TAP** and **DRAG** to the right direction on the screen. **DRAG** until you see the desired copy distance from the original square. In this example, the desired distance is **2"**.
- **Step 3: TAP** and **DRAG** to the right direction on the screen. **DRAG** until you see the desired copy distance from the newly copied square. In this example, the desired distance is **2"**.
- **TAP ONCE** on the **DONE** button to end the multiple copy command.

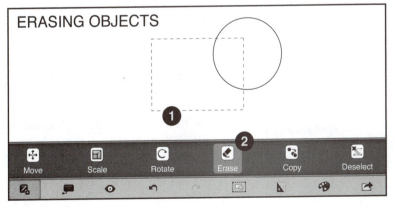

Erasing Objects

† **Step 1: TAP ONCE** on the object you want to erase.
† **Step 2:** In the **EDIT TOOLBAR, TAP** the **ERASE** button.

Markup Tools: Mobile App

The markup toolbar in AutoCAD WS mobile contains several tools to leave comments in an AutoCAD drawing.

- Markups added to drawings in AutoCAD WS mobile are placed on the **AutoCAD WS Annotations** layer.
- **OPEN** the drawing titled **CH15 MARKUP TOOLS.dwg** to follow the instruction in this section of the textbook.

Rectangular & Text Markups

- The **RECTANGLE MARKUP** and **TEXT MARKUP** tools are similar to the **RECTANGLE** and **TEXT** tools in the **DRAW TOOLBAR**.
- Refer to the Drawing Tools section of this chapter for more instruction on these two tools.

Adding Revision Cloud Markups

- The **REVISION CLOUD** markup tool draws a cloud by tracing the location of the cloud on the touch screen. Use this tool to identify and comment on a portion of the drawing.
- **TAP** the **MARKUP TOOLS** button and then **TAP** the **CLOUD** button.
- Use the **REVISION CLOUD** markup tool to draw a revision cloud following the diagram on the left.

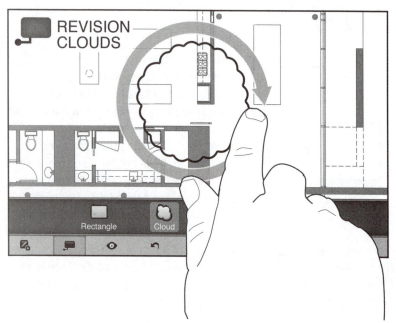

Sketching in AutoCAD WS Mobile

- The **BRUSH** markup tool allows you to freehand sketch over an AutoCAD drawing.
- **TAP** the **MARKUP TOOLS** button and then **TAP** the **BRUSH** button.
- **ADJUST** the thickness of the brush in the **BRUSH TOOLBAR**.
- **TAP** and **DRAG** to sketch over the AutoCAD drawing. Add a door swing to the floor plan to match the example on the left.
- **TAP** the **DONE** button in the **BRUSH TOOLBAR** to end the **BRUSH** command.

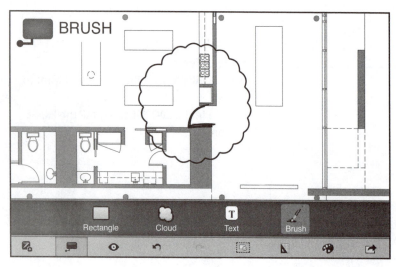

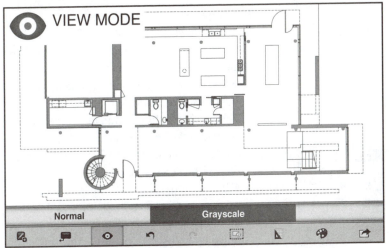

View Mode

· TAP the VIEW MODE button to reveal view options.
· In NORMAL VIEW lines and objects are rendered with their individual colors on a black background.
· In GRAYSCALE VIEW lines are rendered in shades of gray on a white background.

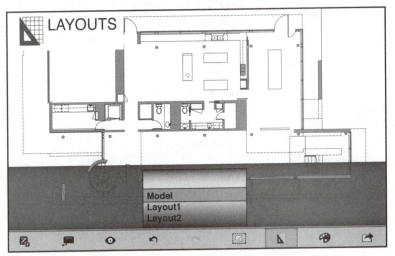

Layouts

· TAP the LAYOUTS button to reveal layouts saved in the current drawing.
· TAP the name of a layout to switch layouts in the open drawing.
· TAP the LAYOUT button to return to edit mode.

Undo / Redo

· In AutoCAD 2012 and AutoCAD for Mac, the UNDO and REDO commands are only available for commands performed since the drawing was last opened.
· In AutoCAD WS, UNDO and REDO history extends back to when the drawing was uploaded to AutoCAD WS.

· This means UNDO is available for edits made to drawing on a previous day and edits on a different device.
· When the UNDO button is TAPPED on one device, the command is automatically synced with open drawings on other devices.

Sharing Drawings: Mobile App

Sharing drawings in AutoCAD WS gives an individual view or edit access to the most current version of the AutoCAD drawing.

· **OPEN** the drawing on your mobile device and **TAP** the **SHARE DRAWING** button.

· **TAP** the plus button to add individuals from your address book. You can also type email addresses directly in the TO: section of the Share Drawing window.

· **ALLOW EDIT** toggles how individuals will access your drawing. In the **ON** position, individuals can make changes to the shared drawing. In the **OFF** position, individuals can only view the current version of the shared drawing.

· **ALLOW DOWNLOAD** toggles whether an individual can download a copy of the AutoCAD drawing. Drawings can be downloaded in DWG and DXF formats.

· **TYPE** a message to be sent with your shared drawing announcement. **TAP** the **SHARE** button to share the drawing.

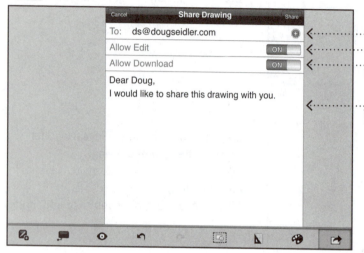

SHARING

Sharing Drawings and Folders: Web App

In addition to the mobile sharing features, the AutoCAD WS web app allows you to share folders. Any DWG file that is moved into a shared folder is automatically shared based on the folder's share settings.

· **LOGIN** to the AutoCAD WS web app and **CLICK** the **DRAWINGS** link on the left side of the web app.

· **CLICK ONCE** on the drawing or folder that you would like to share.

· **CLICK ONCE** on the **SHARE** button in the toolbar. This opens the Share Files dialog box.

· **CLICK** the **TO** button to add individuals from your AutoCAD WS address book. You can also type email addresses directly in the TO: section of the Share Drawing dialog box.

· **CLICK** the **SET PERMISSIONS** button to indicate if this individual can **DOWNLOAD** and/or **EDIT** the shared file.

· **TYPE** a message to be sent with your shared drawing announcement. **CLICK** the **SHARE** button to share the file or folder.

INDEX

QUICK REFERENCE GUIDE

Drawing Commands
Line   12, 13, 14, 15
RECtangle   17
Dashed lines   118

Ortho (F8)   4, 14
Units   5, 22
Running Object Snaps (F3)   21

Circle   16
Arc   18

LAyer Properties Manager   56

Viewport (VP)   96–98

Text   103–109

Hatch (BH)   113–117

Insert Block   131
Polyline (PL)   38–39

Viewing and navigating your drawing
Pan (mouse scroll wheel)   8
Zoom (mouse scroll wheel)   9
Zoom Extents (Z ENTER, E ENTER)   9

Cleaning your drawing
PUrge   141
Audit   141

Editing your drawing
Erase   13
Undo   23

COpy   29
Move   28
MIrror   31
ROtate   30

TRim   40
EXtend   41
Fillet   43
Offset   42

BReak   46
EXplode   46

MAtch properties   139
CHange properties   138

SCale   140
Stretch   32

Dimensioning your drawing
DIstance   139

Dimensions   150–170
Text leaders   178

BASIC METRIC CONVERSION TABLE

DISTANCES	
ENGLISH	**METRIC**
1 inch	2.54 centimeters
1 foot	0.3048 meter / 30.38 centimeters
1 yard	0.9144 meter
METRIC	**ENGLISH**
1 centimeter	0.3937 inch
1 meter	3.280 feet
WEIGHTS	
ENGLISH	**METRIC**
1 ounce	28.35 grams
1 pound	0.45 kilogram
METRIC	**ENGLISH**
1 gram	0.035 ounce
1 kilogram	2.2 pounds